# KAKADU SUNSET

Annie Seaton

Porter Sisters: 1

## Porter Sisters Series

1. *Kakadu Sunset*
2. *Daintree*
3. *Diamond Sky*
4. *Hidden Valley*
5. *Larapinta*
6. *Kakadu Dawn*

Copyright © 2015 Annie Seaton

All rights reserved. This book or any portion thereof may not be reproduced or used in any manner whatsoever without the express written permission of the publisher, except for the use of brief quotations in a book review.

*To my husband, Ian . . . and to the beautiful family we created together. I am blessed.*

*Chapter 1*

*Thursday*
*Arnhem Highway, Northern Territory*

The three oversized trucks in front of Ellie Porter's small red sedan were loaded with pipes and earthmoving equipment, and they'd slowed her trip home along the Arnhem Highway from Darwin airport. After spending two weeks with her mother and sister in Queensland, she was itching to get back to her job at Makowa Lodge, the five-star tourist resort on the South Alligator River, but the construction vehicles had been hogging the road for the last twenty kilometres.

She let out a sigh of relief when the truck in front slowed and indicated it was turning. But a tinge of concern tugged at her when she realised where they were; the truck and the two ahead of it had turned in at the eastern gate of the old mango farm.

Ellie hadn't been back there for years – not since Mum sold it – and would normally have just driven straight past. But today, curiosity won out. She drove another three kilometres until she reached the front gate of the property, then pulled off the highway, parking on the rutted road that led up to the old house.

From here, the place looked abandoned; the grass was long, and the curtains were drawn. The old timber sign proclaiming it was the 'Porter Farm' still hung crookedly from the eaves above the front step. She and Dru had made it the first winter after Emma left for medical school. They'd almost caught the packing shed on fire while trying to give it a charred edge with Dad's blowtorch. She remembered how the wood had glowed orange, and one of the mango cartons on the bench where they'd been working had burst into flame. Dru had laughed as she'd run for a bucket of water from the dam and then doused the small fire. Ellie hadn't heard Dru's husky laugh for a long time. Too long.

She got out of the car, walked over to the fence and rested her arms on the weathered rail. Across the dam was the graceful old homestead where she'd grown up. Once graceful, anyway – 'old' was the operative word these days. From this distance, the posts on the wide front porch were crooked and yellow, and the verandah was sagging. It was a wonder the whole place hadn't toppled down the hill. At least the front fence was still standing. The tropical weather took a toll on anything man-made, but the fence looked remarkably good after – how long was it – eight years?

One hot summer afternoon, she and her sisters had arrived home to find her dad repairing the wire in this fence, working with his friend Bill Jarragah. Emma and Dru had run straight from the school bus, brandishing the latest Dolly magazine to show Mum, but Ellie turned her nose up at such girlish pursuits; she was the tomboy of the family and preferred to spend her afternoons helping Dad and Bill on the farm.

'Our people come from the land and it nurtures us on our journey until we return to it.' Bill had leaned against the fence post, the half-stub of a roll-your-own hanging from his mouth as he strained the wire. 'We must respect it.' He'd looked sharply at Peter, and Ellie's father had dropped his eyes before he picked up a lump of dirt and then let the dry soil run through his calloused fingers.

'Sometimes we have to compromise, Bill. Respect is a fine thing, but a man has to provide for his family.'

'Peter, good seasons and bad.' He'd paused, and Ellie had waited for the rolling cadence of his words to continue. 'The creation ancestors taught us how to live with the land. You whitefellas have to learn patience. The land will renew, but while we wait, we have to care for it. What scars the land scars our spirits too. You remember that.'

Dad had grunted and reached for the wire strainer. 'I'm still thinking.'

The noise of a car door slamming at the top of the hill pulled her from her thoughts. An engine roared to life, and as Ellie watched, a black Jeep backed out from the far side of the homestead and accelerated down the hill, a cloud of red dust billowing behind it. She caught a glimpse of a man in a baseball cap as the vehicle roared past her, kicking up a spray of gravel.

She wondered who the driver was. Mum had sold the farm to a man named Panos Sordina after Dad died, but as far as she knew, he'd never actually lived there. Sordina was another friend of her dad's, and they all figured he'd bought the place as a favour, or out of pity. Last she'd heard, he'd moved back to Darwin and got elected to parliament. Maybe he'd sold the place. Maybe another dreamer like her father had bought it; a man determined to make his fortune from an orchard that could be neglected most of the year. After all, trees grew by themselves while a man was drinking with his mates in the local watering hole, didn't they?

With a final throaty roar, the Jeep disappeared around a bend, and Ellie walked back to her car, taking a last look at the paddocks. The half-dead mango trees at the edge of the dam cast wavering shadows across the water, as insubstantial as her father's dreams. The late afternoon breeze kicked up small waves on the water, making blue plastic drums slap against the rotten wood of the short piers at the end of the jetty where she and her teenage sisters had once lain in the hot tropical sun working on their tans.

She could almost smell the coconut oil they had plastered on their bodies as they lay dreaming of lives far away from the withered trees and the ramshackle house. After Dad's death, Dru and Emma couldn't wait to get away, but the Territory was in Ellie's blood, and she'd made her life here.

The locals loved to complain about the arid heat of the dry season and the pressing humidity of the long wet each year, but Ellie wouldn't have it any other way. When she was away, she felt incomplete, as though part of her had been left behind. It was more than being away from the childhood memories. Her connection with the land was spiritual; she'd shared her father's love for the land and their farm. But in the end, it was the land that had taken his life. Patience was not enough. The three girls had grown up eating mango pie, frozen mango, mango chutney . . . the products of a crop not good enough to go to market. For a couple of summers, Emma and Dru had even manned a fruit stall on the highway with the spotted fruit. But there had never been enough money. In the last six months of Dad's life, Ellie had watched her father's joy in the farm evaporate like the morning mists that hung over the river at the back of the farm. Even all these years later, she remembered the exhaustion in his face, the leaden despair that had eventually driven him to the pub night after night.

Five searing dry seasons had passed since Mum had

found Dad's body hanging in the packing shed. His suicide had come as such a shock – a fundamental line between the before and after of their lives. And now the farm was someone else's responsibility. Funny, she'd forgiven Dad for dying before she'd forgiven Mum for selling up so soon after.

If Ellie could ever afford it, she would buy the farm back and establish the best damn mango plantation in the Territory in her father's memory.

She shrugged and kicked at the fine red dirt with the toe of her boot before she turned back to her car. Time to grow up, maybe.

But the trucks she'd followed up the highway left an uneasy niggle sitting in her stomach. She let out a little sigh as she opened the car door. She could never afford to buy the place back, but at least she had a great job, even if helicopter pilots here in Kakadu didn't earn enough to invest in old dreams.

The hot leather burned the back of her legs as she slid onto the seat. She had just pulled back onto the road when the theme song from Black Hawk Down filled the small car. She grinned at the custom ringtone.

Jock flashed on the screen. She reached for her phone and tapped hands-free.

'Hey, boss. Long time no speak.'

'Ellie? Where are you?' He was barking, a sure sign of stress.

'Just heading back to base.'

'How far out? I need a pilot.'

Ellie glanced down at her watch. For a fleeting second, she thought about reminding him she was still on leave, but the anticipation of going up made her change her mind. 'I'm just down the highway from Jabiru. I could be at Makowa in an hour or so.' If she drove at the same speed as the new owner of a hundred dead mango trees. 'What's up?'

'We've got a group of tourists missing. Stupid fools set out on a walk just on dark last night and they haven't come back.'

'No park choppers available?' Ellie frowned. The lodge choppers weren't usually called in to help this early in the tourist season.

'The National Park choppers are all down at the southern end of the park, so they've asked us if we can get our bird up before dark. They expected the ground rangers would pick them up quickly because they're not in one of the remote areas and they haven't been missing for long.'

'And the ground rangers didn't find them?'

'Not a sign.'

Ellie thought of the wide expanses of the park. When she did her tourist commentary on the scenic flights for the lodge, visitors often found it hard to believe that the park was almost half the size of Switzerland.

'It's not like I can see into a croc's belly from the air,' she pointed out with a little shiver. 'But you never can tell in this place.'

'We're hoping they stayed up in the rocks away from the river. Three adults and a child.' Her boss didn't sound very hopeful. 'The rangers have been out since noon, and now they want our chopper up before dark. Can you make it? You're my only pilot today.'

Ellie was speeding along the road now, heading for the

Kakadu Highway turn-off. Purpose filled her; she was back doing what she loved. 'Where's Mike?'

'His ex-wife tracked him down and he's done a runner. I've hired a new guy, but he doesn't know his way around yet.'

'Can he spot for me?'

'Yeah, I called him in a few minutes ago. I've asked him to check over the chopper for you since he's doubling up as engineer for us.'

'Great. Two pairs of eyes will be good. Log me a search grid and fax it through to the hangar. I'll get there as quick as I can.' She glanced at the turnoff to Ubirr as her car flew past the intersection. Funny to think she'd be up in the air in this same spot within the hour. Ever since Paul Hogan had stood there in Crocodile Dundee, Ubirr Rock had become a tourist icon.

'Thanks, Ellie. Appreciate it.' The phone crackled, and Jock's voice faded in and out as she headed away from the high phone tower behind the Jabiru township. 'It's good to have you back, kid.'

'Ditto.' She turned south onto the Kakadu Highway, opening the window to let the breeze in. For a moment, she let the wind blow her hair back, knowing she was grinning like a fool. Family time was good, but this was what she lived for.

Up in the air, where the world was clear and true. And all hers.

\*\*\*

Kane McLaren drained the last of the avgas into the small Robinson R44 helicopter. He stepped back and placed the empty drum beside the pump and pulled a rag from the back pocket of his jeans, before wiping his hands.

Even though it was late July – winter down under – the heat rose off the tarmac in waves, sending sweat trickling down his bare chest. He'd pulled his shirt off as soon as he'd opened the hangar and the temperature had hit him. Even with the doors open, the air hung thick and humid and motionless.

After the disaster of his last tour, he'd taken the job at Makowa in a bid to lose himself in one of the last untamed areas of Australia for a while. How long he stayed here depended on his mum, and how ill she was. Despite her emails, he'd had a feeling that the prognosis was more serious than she'd let on. Today's visit had confirmed that. Something was seriously wrong. And what the hell was she doing living out here by herself anyway? He'd deal with that later. He was about to start the pre-flight checks when footsteps pounded on the concrete floor behind him.

'Hey.'

Kane put the rag down and turned. Cargo shorts, heavy lace-up boots and a khaki shirt didn't hide the curves of the hot little package standing in front of him. His mood lifted a fraction. He wiped a sweaty hand on his jeans leg before taking her outstretched hand.

'I'm Ellie Porter. You're the new pilot?'

Her grip was firm. 'Kane McLaren. I'm the engineer.'

'Jock told me he'd hired a new pilot.' Her eyebrow was crooked above a steady gaze.

'I am a pilot, but I only signed on here to do the maintenance work.'

She pulled her hand out of his and gave him a smile.

'Okay, you can sort that out with him later. Let's just get this bird up in the air. Is she ready?'

'You're the pilot?' She looked way too young to be in control of a chopper. Her dark hair was pulled back into a braid and she looked like she was barely out of school.

The look she shot him reminded him of the only woman in his unit; Hawk they'd called her – she'd had night vision to rival a superhero.

Ellie didn't respond to his question, so Kane followed her around the back of the chopper. She opened the door on the left and pulled herself up into the cockpit in one lithe, practiced movement. Nice legs. She was short, but her thighs were muscled and slim.

She buckled herself in and pushed the wiring light test switches one by one. He gave a mental shrug and turned towards the back of the chopper to check the fuel tanks for leaks.

'Are we right to go?' Her voice followed him as he went through his routine. 'Are you done with the clutch check? Blades okay?'

'All good so far, but she's not ready to go up yet.' He ran his hands down each side of the tail rotor.

'Why not? Is there something wrong?'

'No. It's all fine. But I always do three checks on my birds before they leave the ground.' He made it a statement, not an excuse.

'We only do one here.' She gestured to the vacant seat beside her as he came back around the front of the R44 and closed the cowl doors over the tanks. 'Climb in.'

'Not yet.' Kane wasn't used to explaining himself and

he didn't intend to start now. He was in charge of the safety routine, and that was that. And besides, he wasn't going up with her. He reached into his pocket for a piece of gum.

'In case you haven't noticed, we're in a hurry. Did Jock tell you why we're going up?' Her voice had an edge now, a husky tone that perversely made it even more attractive.

'Yeah, I know about the search. I'll only be another five minutes. Two and a half minutes each pass around.' Kane blinked as the perspiration ran into his eyes. 'One down, two to go.' Heat or not, a chill was running through his body.

He checked the rotor blades and skids again as Ellie's impatience hung in the air like a heavy cloud. By the time he'd finished his final check, her fingers were drumming on the instrument panel and her mouth was set in a tight line.

Kane strode back around to the side of the cockpit and slapped his hand on the roof. 'You're right to go.'

'What are you talking about? I need you too.' She levelled a steady gaze at him, and he saw that her eyes were pale blue, contrasting with her tanned face. 'Get in.'

'No, babe. I've got stuff to do down here.'

'Look, mister, I don't know where you're from or what you're used to, but we all work together here. I need a spotter for this search and Jock said you were it, so haul your arse into that seat so we can get out of here. An extra pair of eyes could mean the difference between life and death.'

'Sorry. Not in my contract.' He'd made it quite clear when he was hired that he wouldn't be flying.

'We've got four people missing out there in the park and one of them is a young child. There's only one hour of daylight left at most.' She turned away from him and ran a final instrument check. 'The crocs will be on the move as it gets darker. Want that on your conscience?'

*Shit.* Kane paused with one hand on the door and popped another wad of gum into his mouth.

Her eyes were fixed on his, and he could see the worry in them. Going up with her was the only choice he had. No matter how hard it was going to be.

'Let me get my shirt.' He ran over and snatched it from the chair inside the hangar.

'Hurry up. You've . . . we've . . . wasted enough time as it is.

Just get in the seat, please.'

Kane slipped his shirt on but left it unbuttoned. He ducked his head as she depressed the engine starter button until it fired, and then reached over to push the fuel cut-off. Before she could roll on the throttle, he bit down on the side of his cheek and swung himself into the front seat beside her. He grunted an acknowledgement as she passed him a headset.

'Good to go?' Her voice came through clearly, and Kane nodded gruffly.

He stared ahead as the chopper lifted off the short runway and tipped forward as it gathered speed. The forgotten rush of being airborne filled him, and he kept his eyes open, focusing on where he was. The land below was a contrast of lush green forest and patches of scrubby trees on red dirt, interspersed with a network of narrow channels where silver water glinted in the late afternoon sunlight.

Five minutes later, they were swooping over a wide river. She pulled a piece of paper from her shirt pocket and passed it to him as her voice filled his ears.

'Talk me through the grid. Start at Cahill's Crossing.'

With her attention fixed on guiding the helicopter along the search grid, it was a few minutes before Ellie ventured a glance in the direction of the man who was reading the coordinates to her in a flat monotone.

She dipped the chopper low, keeping her eyes fixed on the river and the floodplains below, looking for a flash of colour or movement in the brown and green landscape. The scenic flights she took up most days covered the most popular parts of the national park, and in the four years she'd been working as a pilot for Makowa Lodge, she'd flown over much of it. But Kakadu was such a huge area; there were still gorges and valleys and river flats she had yet to explore from the air.

Luckily, the area plotted in today's search was very familiar. Cahill's Crossing was on the flight path for the scenic route, the twenty-minute whistle-stop tour that most of the tourists chose. Ellie also knew it from the ground; she and Dad had often fished for barramundi at the crossing when she was growing up.

They were low enough to see several huge crocodiles basking on the sand in the late afternoon sun. She swallowed, hoping the missing tourists had been smart enough to stay away from the water.

A gust of wind buffeted the helicopter as she glanced across at her offsider. His gaze was fixed on the ground, but it was his utter stillness that caught Ellie's attention.

Strong hands clutched the piece of paper she'd picked up at the office in the hangar. The edges were crumpled in his grip, and his knuckles were white.

She lifted her gaze to his deeply tanned face and saw

perspiration beaded on his forehead, even though it was cooler up in the air with the breeze from the rotors coming in the air vents on the doors. Not to mention the fact that his shirt was unbuttoned.

It was hard to ignore the glimpse of muscled arms and tight abs when she looked across to his side of the chopper. It was a long time since she'd been up close and personal with a body like that.

Maybe never, if she was strictly honest about it. Suddenly, he pointed. 'Over there.'

Ellie jumped as the deep voice intruded on her thoughts. His dark eyes met hers for a second as he swivelled in his seat and leaned across her, indicating a large stand of sandstone rocks a couple of kilometres to the east of the crossing. His bare arm and chest pressed against her shoulder, and she leaned back a little, keeping a firm grip on the cyclic. His eyesight must be acute; she had already scanned that side of the river and seen nothing out of the ordinary.

She peered across to where he was pointing. Sure enough, two figures were hunched together in the lengthening shadows beneath the rock.

'Good pick-up.' Credit given where credit due.

She swooped down as low as she could go so they knew they'd been spotted.

'Shit, there's only two down there. They must have split up.' She flicked on the radio and waited for her boss to respond. 'Jock, we've spotted a couple of them.'

'Roger that.' The Scottish burr was muffled by the noise of the fresh air rushing in despite her headset. 'Location?'

'We're closer to Ubirr Rock than Cahill's Crossing.'

She looked back to Kane. 'Coordinates?'

As he read them to her, she relayed them to Jock. 'Thanks, I'll let them know at the park base. Well done.'

Kane's dark eyes held her gaze for a moment, and then he looked down again as he shoved the paper into his pocket. 'We're going to have to go down. Look.'

Ellie tipped the bird and leaned to the side, using one hand to hold back some hair which had come adrift from her braid. On the ground, a tall man was waving his arms frantically and gesturing to the rocks.

'Damn it, looks like there's a problem.' Ellie stared down at the scene playing out beneath them as Jock's voice came through her headphones as he relayed their position to the National Park rangers on the ground. 'The others must be there out of sight.'

'There's a search crew three kilometres west of Ubirr Rock.' Jock's voice came through clear. 'They were searching closer to where the vehicle was found. They'll be able to get to them in half hour or so. Thanks, Ellie, great work. Head back to base now.'

'Negative, Jock. Looks like someone's hurt. We're going down to check it out.'

'Watch out for those crosswinds. The wind's picked up over the last couple of hours.'

'Will do.' She noticed Kane brace himself as she lowered the front of the bird and dropped them fifty feet in one swift drop. A gust buffeted the machine and she glanced at his white-knuckled fingers gripping the edge of his seat. She looked up and caught his eyes. He was watching her closely as she gripped the single T-bar cyclic between them. For a split second, he lifted his hand from his seat as though he wanted to take control, but he dropped it again as she held the bird in a hover. The wind buffeted them from side to side, but she held the bird steady. 'Don't worry. She's a reliable machine. Most accidents are usually caused by pilot error.' Ellie kept her eyes on him a moment, then dropped the front down and prepared to land on a large flat patch of sand between the tourists and the river.

'R44s are hard to hold in a hover pattern.' His voice held a tinge of new respect.

'You don't say?' She lifted one hand briefly and patted his leg. Kane's thigh muscles were taut beneath her hand. 'No need to worry, babe. This here is child's play. Wait till you see how hard it is up in the real gorges of the park.'

The bird dropped as a strong gust of wind tipped it end to end. 'Hang on. I'm taking us down.'

By the time she put the chopper down on the river flat, the trepidation that had been roiling in Kane's stomach was replaced with a grudging respect. Despite the difficult crosswind between rock pillars, Ellie had handled the bird as well – almost as well – as he would have.

'Get the first aid kit. It's in the –'

'I know where it is.' Kane cut her off tersely as she swung out and ducked beneath the rotors. Just because she knew her stuff didn't mean he'd let her boss him around.

Ellie was obviously slow on the pick-up because she kept firing instructions. 'Tie down the front blade while I see what's happened here.'

'Yes, ma'am,' he muttered as she ran across the sand to meet the tall guy standing in the shadow of the rocks. This close, he saw that he had his arms around a small child, so it looked like the kid was okay. A second man was seated on a large boulder with his back to them.

Kane kept an eye on them as he quickly secured the rotor blade. He gave the tie-down strap a final tug, retrieved the first-aid kit from under the back seat, and ran across to the rocks where Ellie was crouched down in the shade beside a young woman. The guy was cradling her head in his lap and it appeared she was unconscious.

'What is it?' He caught a glimpse of blood soaked into the dirt and an all-too-familiar nausea hit him as he put the kit on the ground. He swallowed hard as his gut clenched, and cold sweat prickled his skin as it ran down the back of his neck. He dug into his jeans pocket for a fresh piece of gum.

'Looks like a compound fracture.' Ellie's voice was low as her fingers pressed into the woman's foot. The blood had soaked into the loose dirt, leaving only a stain of colour behind – as if the ground itself was thirsty.

Kane's vision suddenly blurred and the scene in front of him tilted for a second. He was in the air again, and red sand hills were the only variation in the expanse of desert below. The dull thuds of improvised explosive devices covered the sound of Ellie's voice.

They got louder, and Kane gagged, touching the rock beside him, grounding himself, remembering where he was.

Kakadu. Northern Territory. Australia. He repeated the words in his mind like a mantra. Kakadu. Northern Territory. Australia.

'Mummy!'

The shrill cry of the child pulled his eyes away from the

patch of blood in the dirt; he'd managed to keep his cool, and his lunch – just.

The kid cried out, one little arm locked around his father's neck, the other reaching towards the woman on the ground. Even to a small child, it was clear that she was in trouble.

'Give me a sterile dressing, and then get on the radio and tell Jock to make sure there's someone still on duty at the medical centre at Jabiru,' Ellie said. She glanced up at the father. 'I think it would be better if you moved your little boy away, sir.'

The man looked at her for a moment before he nodded and led the boy across the sand to sit beside the helicopter. Kane stayed where he was.

'You're not going to try to move her, are you?'

'Of course not. The ground crew will take her in.' Ellie's voice was terse. 'We really need to make sure there's someone at the medical centre when she comes in.' She glanced down at a large watch on her tanned arm. 'They often close up at five o'clock and it's not far off that now. I hope the ground crew aren't too far away. She's lost a lot of blood.'

Kane knew that. Even from a standing position, he could see the huge stain on the ground. Shit, even with his eyes closed he could still see it. He was sure he'd see it in his dreams too.

Moving slower than he knew he should, he snapped open the first-aid kit and reached for a dressing. His limbs would not respond to his brain.

'What else do you need?' He brushed one hand through his cropped hair, trying to ignore the metallic smell of blood that was rising into the hot air. His stomach flipped, and he bit back the nausea. He shoved the dressing at her, his movement rougher than he'd intended.

She looked up at him curiously, but Kane held her gaze, forcing his expression to stay impassive and his hands to stay steady. This was not the time to give in to the shit the psychologist had told him about. He swallowed and straightened up.

'Call in . . . please,' she repeated but her voice was softer this time. 'And get that kid up in the chopper until the ground crew arrives. Every croc within a mile will have smelled the blood by now.'

Kane nodded and walked away. Fast.

Maybe he'd made a mistake, taking on this job. He'd been under the impression that these helicopters were for showing tourists the sights. If there was going to be blood, perhaps he should reconsider.

Just my luck to get a medical evacuation.

He knew better than to rely on luck. It hadn't followed him anywhere before and it sure looked like things hadn't changed. But Kane knew he wouldn't reconsider the job. The next few months were going to be tough enough. His mother was sick . . . maybe dying. He'd go stir crazy if he didn't have a job to keep him occupied while she had her treatment.

There was a squawk from the radio, and Kane started talking, working on autopilot as he spoke to the National Park base.

He was beginning to get the feeling that this role at Makowa was very different to what he'd expected. After the events of the past year, he'd promised himself he'd stay on the ground. He'd do the best job he could as an engineer, but no one would ever rely on his judgement in the air again. No one would be at risk from his decisions. But if they were expecting him to help out in search and rescues . . .

By the time Kane signed off with base, the kid was sitting in the back of the chopper with his father. He could have returned to help work on the woman. He didn't, though.

After reassuring the guy that the medical crew were close, he leaned against the bird, watching Ellie as she deftly bandaged the wound. The metal was hot against his back and he could feel the heat of the sand through his boots. Ellie would have done great over there, in the desert.

Shit. Just forget about it.

Kane turned away. Who am I kidding?

\*\*\*

Ellie and Kane followed the rescue vehicle from the air until it negotiated the last rocky outcrop and turned onto the track that led back to the highway. It wasn't far from there to Jabiru, and Kane had confirmed that a team was waiting for the patient at the medical centre. The young mother had regained consciousness before they'd taken off, and one of the paramedics in the ground crew had given her a morphine injection. They'd done well but Kane's reactions had left Ellie wondering. She'd had to ask him three times to put the call in to the medical centre. He'd frozen at the sight of the blood.

For a tough guy – and he was strong, she knew that instinctively – his confidence was shadowed by something unspoken. He hadn't said a word to her since she put the bird in the air. She pushed the worry away; all types passed through the Territory. Most people had baggage, but it had nothing to do with her. There was no point giving into the curiosity.

'We've got about ten minutes left till sunset. Would you like a quick scenic tour?' She turned to him and he turned his head slowly to meet her gaze. 'It's by far the best time of day to see the park. If you're going to fly in Kakadu, it's much easier to see the fight paths from up here. Get your bearings from the air.'

'No need. I won't be flying here again.'

Ellie shrugged as Kane turned away to look out the side of the helicopter. She'd tried, but that was enough. Whatever his problem was, he could get over it himself.

He wasn't the first male to doubt her skill and he wouldn't be the last, but she was done with trying to crack this tough nut. Chauvinist pig. If he didn't want to fly, that was Jock's problem. But he sure wouldn't last long up here if he wasn't prepared to give a little. This was just the first of the emergencies for the tourist season.

As she turned the helicopter towards Makowa Lodge, lush green river flats were gradually replaced by scrubby trees on red dirt. The route she always followed took them over the rim of the park, and then across the fence that divided the old family farm from the National Park. Today she was curious to see where those trucks had gone this afternoon.

In the paddock below, row after row of dead and shrivelled mango trees formed a geometric pattern. Ellie touched her fingers self-consciously to her lips and whispered, 'Hey Dad,' as she always did when she flew over their old home. The ache of unshed tears settled behind her eyes when she looked ahead at the towering cumulonimbus clouds to the north where the South Alligator River drained into Van Diemen's Gulf.

One afternoon when she was a small child, she and Dad had lain on their backs on the soft grass and looked up at the sky. He'd told her that when he was an old man in heaven, he would be lying up in those fluffy clouds looking down on her and her sisters. She'd never forgotten it, and now those towering pillars of white cloud brought her undone whenever she saw them.

He'd never made it past middle age, let alone become an old man.

A flash of movement from the ground caught her eye and Ellie leaned forward, surprised to see a cleared patch on the southern edge of the property. Heavy machinery was working in the paddock where her father had once planted his new hybrid variety of mangoes. Instead of neat rows of trees, a gaping red hole scarred the ground and a couple of huge yellow earthmoving machines were moving back and forward near the river. As well as the three oversized trucks she'd followed, half a dozen work utes were parked along the edge of the road.

'What the hell?' Ellie muttered. She took her eyes off the controls for a second and craned over her shoulder, looking back as the farm disappeared from sight. She glanced across at Kane, but his head was back against the headrest and his eyes were closed. She dipped the helicopter and turned in a sweeping arc to cross the back of the farm, lower this time. Now what she saw below her filled her with a deep sense of unease. It looked like major earthworks.

What the hell is going on down there?

If something was happening right on the park boundary, surely there would have been something about it in the news. Unless something had happened while she was away.

She'd give Panos a call as soon as she got back to the lodge.

And she'd chase up Bill Jarragah as well.

She glanced across at Kane again. His eyes were still shut, and there were tight lines around his mouth. Ellie took a deep breath; suddenly she felt the mother of a headache coming on. She'd worry about what she'd seen later when she had time to think. The township of Jabiru appeared below, and she took a wide turn to the north to avoid the telecommunications towers. As she banked towards Makowa Lodge, the Ranger mine spread out below them.

'What's that water?' Ellie jumped as Kane's voice intruded on her thoughts. For the first time, he was showing some interest in what was below.

'That's one of the tailing dams at Ranger – the uranium mine.' She turned the bird further to the east and dropped lower. 'Look at this.'

Kane let out a low whistle as the barren landscape appeared below them. A huge circular hole cut a swathe over three kilometres wide through the greenery.

'Ugly, isn't it? It's been there since I was a kid.'

'How come they're allowed to mine here? I thought Kakadu was a World Heritage site?'

'It is. There have been so many close calls since it opened, but the authorities won't shut it down. There's just too much money involved.'

Kane grunted.

'And it's not just uranium. Do you know there are applications to mine for oil and gas on more than a million square kilometres up here in the Territory?' She'd learned all this from her mother over at Em's place. 'And seabed mining too.'

'I don't know much about it.' Kane nodded briefly and looked away, obviously losing interest. 'I've been . . . away.'

Seeing Ranger from the air made Ellie all the more determined to find out what was happening at the back of the old farm. One blight on this beautiful landscape was enough.

Once they were safely down on the ground beside the hangar, she shut everything down, and Kane eased himself stiffly from the helicopter. As he began the post-flight checks, Ellie noticed that he was favouring his right leg and had a slight limp. He was different to the usual light-hearted jocks who arrived to fly the choppers here.

Military? Of course. There was a feeling of the services about him. She could imagine him in a uniform. It was just something about him, something that didn't go with the bare chest, the gum chewing and the casual attitude he was trying so hard to put across.

'Can you finish up here while I do the paperwork?' she asked.

'No problem, babe.'

Ellie strode across the hangar but paused before she went into the office. 'Kane? Do me a favour. My name's Ellie. Nix the "babe".'

She turned without waiting for his answer, but she could feel his gaze on her back as she closed the door.

# Chapter 2

*Thursday*
*Darwin*

'We've got a problem,' Panos Sordina said into the phone as he swung his chair around and looked out over Darwin Harbour. It was the beginning of the busy winter season and tourists were milling through the park on the foreshore beneath him. He waited a moment for a response, but none came. 'Hello? Are you there?'

'I am.' The voice was icy.

'I just had a call from the guys on the ground. One of the yellow Makowa Lodge helicopters was snooping over the property this afternoon.'

'So? Probably some tourists up for a scenic flight.' Fairweather's voice was disinterested, but Panos knew better than to underestimate the man at the other end of the phone.

'The chopper came down low over the drill site. Twice. You know that Peter Porter's daughter Ellie is a pilot there? And on top of that, my bloody stepson has turned up unannounced.'

'Why would he go to the property?'

Panos immediately regretted his slip and rushed on. 'Kane was an officer in the fucking Army. He's not stupid. All he'd need to do is take one look at what's happening down the back and it could all go to shit.' Panos wiped his shaking hand down the leg of his trousers. The blasted air conditioner in the building must be playing up again. It was the middle of bloody winter and he was drenched in sweat. 'We don't have a licence to be drilling yet.'

'You didn't answer my question. Why would your stepson go there? How does he even know the place exists?'

'His mother is living there.' Cold silence.

'My wife. I . . . I had to –' Panos' words ran together as he stumbled on. 'Money is a bit short again. Some bad bets. I had to sell . . . I sold the house in Darwin and I had to move her somewhere.'

'I'm not happy, Panos. And you know what that means?'

Panos swallowed. He well knew.

Meeting Russell Fairweather at the Darwin races six years ago had seemed like an amazing opportunity; to get out of the gambling hole he'd found himself in – and maybe even get ahead. At first it had been like a 'get out of gaol free' card. His debts had suddenly evaporated, and Fairweather's money and influence had opened doors for him that he had never dreamed about. But getting involved with him had turned into the biggest mistake of his life. If he had known that accepting a 'loan' would have brought him to the hell he lived in today, he would have dealt with the men who had threatened him.

He had soon learned that Fairweather considered himself beyond the law, if there was money to be made.

'So what should I do?'

'Pull yourself together to start with. The drilling continues. In two weeks the government committees will have voted on the boundary change and the licence, and everything will be legal anyway. And then your farm will include a section of the river and a few hundred more acres. If your stepson becomes a problem in the meantime, I'll deal with him. The same goes for Ellie Porter.'

Cool as a cucumber, that's what Fairweather was. But it was all right for him. His name wasn't on any of the documents. Even though Fairweather was behind the whole deal, there was nothing to indicate that he had any involvement.

'But I don't want any more mistakes. Are you listening to me, Panos?' The voice was ice cold. 'This project is worth millions, and I won't have it jeopardised by any more of your fuck-ups. Understood?'

'Yes, I –'

Fairweather cut him off. 'Enough. Where are you calling from?'

Goosebumps rose on Panos' arms. 'My office phone. Look, I –'

'When will you ever learn?'

Sweat trickled down his neck onto his collar, and he lifted his hand to undo the top button of his business shirt and loosen his tie.

'I sometimes wonder how you attained such a position of responsibility.'

Panos gulped but didn't reply. If it hadn't been for Fairweather's payoffs and generous 'donations', he would never have been elected to Parliament in the first place.

'Since you have called me from your office, I want you to sit at your desk and make some calls. Pull out the phone book and ring fifty of your constituents and tell them what a wonderful representative you are.'

'I'm sorry, but –'

'Bury this call, Panos. Fifty. Now. And don't ring me from this number again. You have a phone. Use it.'

'Yes. I will. All right.' Panos pulled the handkerchief from his pocket and wiped his brow. 'Now. Right now.'

The call ended and Panos turned to the window and stared at the view in front of him. Was it too late to back out? Maybe he could resign. Just walk off the place. That might work. But where would he go? It would have to be the farm. That was where the problem had started, and now it had come full circle. He'd been a fool. A greedy fool. And now Fairweather had him by the balls.

The phone rang again before he could make his first call. 'Yes?'

'Panos, there's an Ellie Porter on the line for you. Shall I put her through? She said it was important.'

Panos covered his eyes with his free hand and took a deep breath. He swallowed the bile that burned in his throat. 'Take her number please, Ellen. I'll call her back in a while.'

***

The driver sitting in the silver Mercedes in the short stay car park at Darwin Airport turned the key in the ignition. The rumble of the powerful engine muted the sound of the traffic on the Stuart Highway as they turned south onto the busy road. In the back seat, Russell Fairweather slipped his gold iPhone into the inside pocket of his jacket.

'Where to?' Mick flicked him a glance in the rear-vision mirror.

Russell stared through the window, thinking; Panos' call had blackened his mood. 'Take me to Parliament House.'

Without a word, Mick took a right at the next set of traffic lights and turned back towards the city. The traffic was heavy as they drove along the beaches east of the CBD. Five minutes later, he turned onto Mitchell Drive heading for State Square. 'Take the car back to the apartment and wait for me to call. Organise one of the others to drive me around for the rest of the week. I need you down at Kakadu to deal with some issues.'

Mick gave him a cool nod, his eyes cold and empty. He was a tall, good-looking man, with short-cropped blond hair. Mick had worked for him for several years now and was tasked with handling the 'small' problems that occasionally plagued his business dealings. Russell didn't know whether Mick's cool disregard for human life came from his military experiences, or whether he had genuine psychopathic tendencies, but he had proved a loyal employee, and followed orders without asking questions. Personality wasn't a prerequisite.

When they pulled up, Russell climbed out of the car and strode across to the square to Parliament House without a backward glance.

As he entered the main door, his mood was eased somewhat by the deferential nods and greetings directed his way. Once the changes were approved, it wouldn't matter what that meddling Porter bitch saw. The mine was going to be lucrative for the Territory, and that was the card he would continue to play with this idealistic man. If he was difficult to persuade, then less subtle means of persuasion may be necessary.

David Johnson, Chief Minister of the Northern Territory was waiting in the foyer. As soon as he saw Fairweather cross the marble floor, he excused himself from the group of men he was talking to. They shook hands and then headed for the elevator.

'Russell, an unexpected pleasure.'

They emerged from the lift at the rooftop bar, which was beginning to fill with politicians and staffers as the day drew to a close.

'What will you have to drink?' Johnson nodded to a couple of men as they pushed their way through the crowd.

'Glenfiddich. No ice.' Curious glances were being directed their way.

When their drinks arrived, Russell lifted his glass and observed the honourable member. Johnson's usually impeccable white shirt was creased, and his tie was slightly askew. His hair was tousled and his six o'clock shadow gave him an unkempt look. In contrast, Fairweather shaved twice a day. The whisky warmed his throat and he leaned back into his chair. He brushed his hand down the immaculate crease in his Armani trousers.

'So, Russell, what was so urgent that you had to meet with me tonight?' Johnson said, putting his glass on the table.

'I wanted to bring you up to date on stock market trends.' Johnson looked at him curiously.

'My contacts in Asia are predicting some changes in the market over the next few weeks.'

'Yes, I'm aware that the stock market is moving in response to the situation in China.'

'It's not my place to tell you what to do, David, but I'm sure you can see that it's important to get this exploration licence through as a matter of urgency.'

'I don't see the connection.' Johnson sipped his drink and frowned over the rim of the glass before he shook his head.

'And the more discussions I have, the less inclined I am to support this project.'

'That would be a grave mistake. You grew up at Ranger so you know how beneficial mining is for the Territory. It needs your support.' Fairweather stared at him, jaw set and a pulse ticking in his cheek. 'And I've given you a lot of support over the years – financial support.'

'Please don't treat me like a fool, Russell. Your generous support of the party gives you no more say than anyone else. I am considering my decision very carefully and I won't rush it. You have been most generous in sharing your market knowledge and I am grateful for that.' Johnson put his glass down and folded his arms. 'I remain to be convinced that the impact on the environment will be balanced by economic gain. Coal seam mining is controversial and may not be the right direction for the Territory.'

Russell leaned forward and lowered his voice. 'No.'

'I beg your pardon?' Johnson held his gaze steadily. 'No, what?'

'David, I believe you recently signed off on a seabed mining contract. Are you aware that was with one of my subsidiary companies? I've heard you have been trying to reverse that approval. Not a good look for the Chief Minister to make such an error of judgement. There are whispers that you were bribed. I would hate for the media to hear about that.'

'That's a lie.'

'The media would love it.' Russell sat back and watched the perspiration bead on the Chief Minister's forehead.

'Leak what you want.' Johnson's gaze was openly hostile now. 'It will be just another accusation in the torrent of negativity against the party lately.'

'I have more than a passing interest in this approval, David.' Russell stared at him and disgust at Johnson's ethical stance snaked through him. 'The Chinese economy and the fall in the US dollar are losing this project – losing the Territory – a million dollars every day. The preliminary tests have indicated a massive seam of coal. The fracking must begin.'

'Or losing you money?' Johnson's gaze was openly hostile now. 'You assured me you had no pecuniary interest in this project.'

Anger rose in Russell's throat and he narrowed his eyes. He was unused to people challenging him and he held his temper. 'A naive assumption, David. But of course, no one would ever find any association between me and the project, so don't waste your time looking.'

'In hindsight, I'm not surprised.' Johnson's laugh was bitter. 'But your gain or loss – or any threats you make against me – are irrelevant to my decision. Of course I can see the economic benefits, but we're talking about coal seam gas mining at the edge of a World Heritage-listed national park. There's a lot more investigation to be done before I – or the committees – will make a decision either way. One thing you may be certain of is that I will act appropriately and ethically.'

'David, David.' Fairweather shook his head and Johnson's eyes narrowed at his tone. 'It's rather late for you to start playing the environmental card. Do you think I care about the opinions of a bunch of do-gooders beneath the sway of some rabid greenies?' He put his glass down on the polished wooden table with a sharp click. 'There are just two things you have to do.'

'Two things?'

'You will ensure that the boundary change is approved next week. And then it will be an easier matter for the drilling licence to be granted.' Russell let a satisfied smile cross his face. The licence was merely a formality; drilling had already commenced but Johnson didn't need to know that. One of the benefits of drilling in the wilderness; there was no one to snoop – or there hadn't been until that Porter woman had flown over the site.

He continued. 'It will be easy for you with your charismatic leadership, Chief Minister. I believe there are several other committee members working towards a suitable outcome too. Trust me, I will do whatever is necessary. I want this finalised in two weeks.'

'Are you threatening me?'

'Not yet. I am merely protecting your career. And trust me David, I will do whatever it takes to get what I want.'

'Not yet? You need to be careful with what you're saying, Russell.' Johnson leaned forward, his mouth set in a straight line. Fairweather finished the last swallow of his whisky, allowing himself a moment to appreciate its smoky burn. The man clearly needed a reminder of precisely where he stood in the scheme of things.

In short: under his foot.

He pulled out his iPhone and sent a text to Mick to send a driver. He'd heard enough.

'I'm afraid that I have another appointment this evening. It's been lovely to see you, David. Do give my best to Gina, won't you? She's almost due to have another child. I hear? And your other children, of course.'

Johnson's eyes widened and followed Russell as he stood. 'Do you know that I've been reading the most terrible things about childhood accidents in the papers recently? I do hope you look after yours very well, David.'

Johnson put his glass down and stood up. The sudden pallor of his face told Russell that his meaning had been understood. 'Thank you for the drink, David.' He looked over his shoulder as he walked away. 'You have two weeks. Don't let me down.'

# Chapter 3

*Thursday*
*Makowa Lodge, Kakadu National Park*

The tiki torches along the edge of the garden flickered in the early evening breeze and a whiff of sandalwood oil drifted across to Ellie as she walked through the lodge grounds. She made her way past the pool and glanced down at her watch. After half a day spent travelling, and then the emergency call out, she'd not felt much like coming out. The lingering worries about her mother clung to her like a sticky cobweb. Ellie tried to push the thoughts away, but it was impossible after the call she'd just taken from Panos Sordina.

He'd been friendly. Way too friendly.

'Sold up? No, in fact Susan and I are moving back there for my retirement. She's already living there.' The hearty laugh and the booming voice had seemed overdone to Ellie.

'And you're doing some work there?' Dead silence.

'Why would you think that?'

'I saw a couple of trucks turn off there this afternoon.'

'Oh yes. Ah, I'm putting another dam in. I'm going to get the farm back up and running.'

She didn't believe a word. That was no new dam she'd seen from the air. 'So it's nothing to do with exploration? Didn't look like a dam when I flew over there.'

His bluff and blustering response filled her with even more unease.

'Exploration? A ridiculous idea, wherever did you hear that?'

'I've just got back from seeing Mum in the Daintree. Before I left she gave me some papers that suggested the South Alligator area is being explored for coal seam gas.'

'Absolute rot. Fairy stories. One of those silly alliance groups stirring up trouble, I'd say.'

'What she gave me to read made me think her fairy stories are not so silly after all, Panos.' She'd flicked through the folder in her room and been surprised to see several photos of Panos with another man in a suit. There were newspaper clippings as well.

'Look, all sorts of misinformation gets published on social media these days.' He let out an exaggerated sigh. 'One of the difficult things a man in my position has to deal with. Say hello to your mum for me, Ellie. And tell her not to worry herself.'

'I will. Thank you.'

Ellie disconnected. It was obvious that he was lying but she wasn't going to mention it to anyone else yet, especially Mum. Until she checked it out more, anyway. She'd search the back issues of the local paper and ask Bill Jarragah if he'd heard anything.

For now, a quiet drink with her colleagues would take her mind off it. She crossed the lawn to the courtyard where the tables spilled onto the grass facing the west, overlooking the water and positioned to get the best view of the setting sun.

The sunset river cruise would have docked down at the wharf and the bar would soon fill as the tourists arrived for their pre-dinner drinks, ready to relax and compare their crocodile photos. Every afternoon at Makowa Lodge in the winter season was the same; the crowd with their cameras, vying for the best position as the sun set. The smoke from the burn-off of the savannah woodlands generated a spectacular show as it fired the sky to a molten gold. Photographing crocodiles was forgotten for a short while as the cameras pointed to the west.

'Ellie! Over here.' A group of her workmates, all wearing the signature Makowa Lodge khaki shirt, were sitting in the corner of the bar area. Ellie grinned as Heather Jarragah uncrossed her long legs and stood up. 'Welcome home! We weren't expecting you back at work till tomorrow.'

At the sight of her best friend's large brown eyes and dark hair, she felt herself relax. The two had known each other since primary school – introduced by Dad and Bill – and Heather's family had welcomed Ellie into the Aboriginal community at Black Jungle Springs as though she had been one of their own. 'Hey, Heather.' Ellie looped her arm through Heather's. 'You're right. I wasn't rostered on, but I got a call from Jock to take the chopper up when I was on the way back from

Darwin. Missing tourists. So what happened to Mike?'

'He was out on a job a couple of weeks ago when his ex-missus turned up after his blood.' Heather flashed a big smile. 'And she sure got it. Before he landed his bird, she trashed his room and then carried all his gear to the back of the compound. He didn't realise the smoke enhancing the sunset his passengers were snapping was from a fire burning everything he owned.'

'Serves him right,' Ellie said without a drop of sympathy. 'He was a sleaze from the first day he got here.'

'Come on, Els, that's a bit harsh.'

'Harsh! He deserves everything he gets. Remember that line he used to use on the female tourists? Hankering for an "authentic" Aussie experience?'

'Yeah. Still, you gotta admit, he was pretty good looking.'

'Ew, Heather! How many times do I have to tell you: don't screw around with workmates. Anyway, I met his replacement this afternoon. Have you?' Ellie walked around to the end of the table and Heather followed her.

'I haven't met him yet, but I saw him from a distance yesterday when Jock was showing him around. Sex on legs.' Heather dropped her voice and her brown eyes sparkled. 'Just as well I don't follow your rules, because I fancy me a bit of Mr Fly Boy.'

'He wouldn't care for the nickname.' Ellie chuckled. 'He reckons he's only Mr Fix-it. I have to sort out his role with Jock tomorrow.' Ellie slid along the bench seat and let another workmate squeeze in, rolling her shoulders as the tension lifted a little. This was a part of the job she enjoyed, spending time with friends who loved the Territory as much as she did. She would trust these people with her life. Even Mike had been dependable once he'd cut the sleaze act.

It was an open question whether Kane would fit in here; they were a pretty tight group. If her hunch that he was ex-military was right, he should be used to working with a team, but after this afternoon she had a feeling he wouldn't want to. Terry, another of the Aboriginal staff, leaned towards her.

'Hey, Els. Welcome home. Got a new croc story for you!'

Standard conversation in the evenings; the guys all

knew she was terrified of the huge suckers and they loved to tease her, each yarn more exaggerated than the last. She'd been terrified of them ever since she was a child when she'd seen a fisherman taken at Cahill's Crossing. She and Dad had been fishing and he'd done his best to shield her from the sight, but the screams of the man as he'd been dragged off the causeway had stayed with her. But despite the shiver that ran down her back, Ellie wasn't worried. It was their way of saying they'd missed her. 'Okay Terry, spill.'

'I was over at Borroloola last week and a whole group of backpackers went missing the night before I arrived in town.' Terry looked at her over his beer, the sides of his mouth twitching.

Ellie frowned. 'A whole group? I didn't see that in the Darwin Sun online.'

'Jeez, Ellie.' Heather rolled her eyes. 'You're hopeless. You can't even leave the Territory without reading the paper to see if the place survived while you were away.'

'You can't talk.' Ellie gave her friend a friendly punch on the arm. 'I seem to remember you getting so homesick on that school excursion to Sydney that you cried all night and they almost sent you home.' She turned back to Terry. 'So what happened?'

'They were camping in tents on the edge of the McArthur River and the locals reckon that a monster croc came in and ate the lot of them.' Terry clamped his lips together and Ellie resisted the smile tugging at her lips. 'Ate all the food, the tents, everything.'

'Wow. That sure would give them indigestion.' Ellie widened her eyes. 'Are you sure you're not trying to wind me up already, Terry? I've only been back five minutes.'

Terry's dark eyes scrunched as he burst into a laugh. 'It's good to have you back on board, love.'

'It's great to be home, Terry. I missed you guys.'

Heather flicked her a glance and Ellie knew Heather sensed that her trip away had been difficult. She smiled at her friend and leaned over towards her but before Ellie could speak, a brawny arm came around her from behind. Steve, the barman, pulled her back against him and slid a kiss along her cheek towards her lips.

She pushed him off with a grin. 'Down, boyo!'

'Missed ya, darlin'. Beer or a wine?' Steve's voice was pure Irish, and his expression was cheeky. He hit on her every night and Heather had told her more than once that she was crazy not to take up with him, but Ellie had seen too many relationships go pear-shaped. Itinerant staff and good-looking tourists all out for a good time; it was a recipe for disaster – Mike was just the latest casualty. 'Beer please.'

Steve turned to get the drinks. He was handsome, but she didn't want to get involved in the casual sex that was often a part of this close-knit community of workers.

Her job was her life. She clung fiercely to the security of her routine, and she wouldn't risk it for any one-night stand. Maybe she was stupid and maybe she was missing out on some of the good times, but it hadn't killed her yet.

Chatter washed over Ellie as the cold liquid hit her throat. 'How's your mum doing?' Heather touched Ellie's hand and spoke quietly as the laughter and conversations continued around them. 'Things as bad as Emma said?'

'Worse, if it's possible. The doctor's changed her

medication and she barely sleeps.' Ellie stared out into the darkness as her throat closed up. The last of the light had gone quickly, and the tropical darkness enveloped the low forest surrounding the lodge. 'She's still hung up about Dad's death. She just can't accept that he took his own life. It's killing her. She does nothing apart from trawl the internet or sit on Em's verandah staring into space.'

'Oh, the poor thing,' Heather said sympathetically. 'It must be hard for Emma too.'

'Mum still swears that Dad got a big offer for the farm from some mining company a couple of months before he died. She thinks he was murdered to get him out of the way.'

'Really?' Heather shook her head. 'She's still on about that?'

'She's lost the plot. She's stuck with her murder theory to justify Dad's death to herself. Em and I even went through his papers again, trying to convince her to let it go. She feels so bloody guilty that she didn't see how depressed he was about money . . . or the lack of it.' Ellie swallowed, determined not to give into the ache in her throat. 'None of us did. When he got that bar job at the pub in Jabiru, I thought it eased the money situation and he still had time for the farm. He seemed happier that last weekend I saw him. I thought he was happy.'

'Poor Dru got home from school just after your Mum found him, didn't she?'

Ellie nodded and stared down into her beer. She still felt guilty about being away at the time – studying for her pilot's licence in Darwin. It was irrational, but there you go. Her mother had been distraught of course, and Emma had come home from medical school in Sydney and helped them deal with the paperwork, and the organisation of their father's funeral . . .and Mum.

Dru had been pretty much left to fend for herself and had gone off the rails in her last weeks at high school. The 'after' of Dad's suicide had been hard on all fronts. Emma had left Sydney uni and transferred to James Cook in Townsville so she and Dru could share cheaper accommodation when Dru took up her civil engineering course. But Panos buying the farm from Mum when he did, had helped all three girls follow their dreams.

'Els, come on. Stop stewing over it,' Heather said, rubbing her thumb over Ellie's wrist. 'You're home now and you can't do any more to help.'

The hollow ache moved down from Ellie's throat and settled in her chest. 'God, Heather, she's aged so much since I last saw her. She's thin and her face is so wrinkled, she looks like an old woman. And she's not. I know I should spend more time over on the coast with Emma and help out, but I hate it there. I don't know how Emma puts up with it. I couldn't get back here quick enough.'

'Don't think about it anymore,' Heather said. 'We can't do without you, honey. So how's Em? Still working at the local hospital?'

'Yes, in Dalrymple and she's got her own medical clinic too.' Ellie paused and drained the last of her drink. 'She says she's fine, but I know she carries her own guilt because she loses patience with Mum. She understands I love it over here and I have to work. Not much call for helicopter pilots in the rainforest near her and Mum. Although there'd be scenic flights out over the reef, I suppose.'

Heather stared at her. 'Uh-uh. You love the Territory too much to leave. Look at the great job and great friends you've got here. And you know we'd miss you too much.' She leaned forward and rested her chin in her hand on the table. 'What about Dru? Did you catch up with her?'

Ellie shook her head. 'Dru's Dru. Sometimes I think she wouldn't even have contact with us if it was up to her.' She pushed her glass away and looked up as Steve called out, holding up another beer over at the bar.

'Just one more.' She turned back to Heather. 'Your dad around tonight?'

'No, he had a committee meeting in the city.'

'I wanted to ask him about something I saw out at the old farm today. Have you heard anything about Panos Sordina moving back there?'

Heather shook her head. 'No, I haven't. I thought he lived in Darwin now. The last time I drove past, it looked deserted. But I'll ask. Dad always knows what's going on around the place.'

Heather gestured to Steve for another drink. 'You know what? I think it's time for a big night out. We need to welcome you back properly . . . and cheer you up. There's a band playing here on Sunday night. How about it?'

'Sounds like the happy fix I need.'

'And why don't you come out to Black Jungle Springs for a visit during the day? Dad would love to see you.'

'All right. I will.' Ellie felt the weight lift off her shoulders.

Heather could always make her feel better.

Heather tilted her head. 'Look who's here!'

She looked towards the entrance of the bar. The angular planes of Kane McLaren's face were softened by shadows as he stood there, seemingly deciding whether to enter or not.

Heather put her hand on her chest and pretended to swoon. 'Be still my beating heart. What. A. Honey.'

Steve stopped by the table with their drinks, then gestured in the direction of Heather's gaze.

'New guy needs to meet the crew.' He put the tray down and scooted over to speak to Kane.

Ellie looked down and focused on the glass of beer in front of her. This would be interesting. Heather watched the men, oblivious to Ellie's discomfort.

'Hey, maybe the hunk can come on Sunday too? Although Mr Fly Boy over there looks a bit too classy for this place. Maybe he's got high standards like yours. Though it might be fun trying to break him in.' Heather's eyes narrowed, and a cheeky smile tilted her lips.

Kane walked over to the group. Ellie looked up as Steve made the introductions.

'Kane, meet Terry, Heather, Ellie and down the far end of the table we have Roscoe and Amanda.' Everyone gave him a wave and Kane nodded.

Doesn't the man know how to smile? Mind you, all that grimness suited him. Heather was right. He was . . . fine. From his broad shoulders to the muscled legs outlined by the faded jeans that clung snugly to his thighs. His biceps bulged beneath the tight sleeves of his black T-shirt and his dark hair was slicked back from his face. The unshaven look just added to his appeal.

His air of authority was sexy, but she still remembered

how he'd doubted her ability to fly. Ellie had come across his type before. He was good-looking, but that didn't mean he was a decent guy.

Heather moved along and Ellie had to follow her along the wooden bench seat to make room for Kane to sit beside her. She picked up her beer and took a fortifying swig, before she looked sideways at him and nodded.

'Welcome to Makowa Lodge.'

'Thanks.' For the first time a brief smile crossed his face and an unwelcome little tremor skittered down Ellie's back.

'Hello, mate. Where are you from?' Terry stood and reached across the table to shake Kane's hand. This would be interesting. Ellie put her elbows on the table and waited for his answer, but Steve interrupted before Kane could reply.

'At least let the guy have a drink before the third degree starts.' Steve raised his voice over the greetings from the others seated at the table. 'Watch out, they're nosy, this lot. No secrets here. Beer for you, mate?'

'No to the beer, thanks. Just a soda water.' Kane's voice was quiet as he turned to Terry. 'I'm originally from Brisbane but I've been around. What about you guys?'

So that's all they were going to get. Ellie was conscious of Kane's thigh pressed against hers and she moved away a fraction as the guys told Kane they were all locals.

'Roster went up this afternoon.' Heather winked at Ellie and leaned across her to speak to Kane. 'You get a ground tour of the park tomorrow. I hear you've already had the one from the air today.' A sexy little laugh that Ellie knew was purely for Kane's benefit escaped Heather's lips. 'I'm stuck on office duty and you get to go exploring with Miss Ellie here.'

'What's the go?' Ellie ignored Heather's flirting. 'Did you say grand tour or ground tour?'

'Ground, sweetie. There's a car in the car park down at Jim Jim Falls.'

'How did it get there?'

Terry leaned over and spoke loudly above the noise from the now crowded bar. 'We had a medical evacuation last week. Some guy broke his ankle.' He shook his head. 'It wasn't just that he wasn't fit enough to make the trek. Would you believe he weighed a hundred and fifty kilos? The idiot jumped off a boulder at the end of the track and busted up his leg. Had to be choppered out.'

Ellie frowned. 'Are the falls open? Have the park staff finished the crocodile management already?'

'Yep, they opened the falls up the other day. Crocs are clear.' Terry drained his beer and stood up. 'But no one's had a chance to go down and get the car, so –' Terry's white teeth flashed in his dark-skinned face as he turned to Kane '– you get the pleasure of Ellie's company and get to see one of the best places in the park. And I get to go check on crocodile traps along the West Alligator with old Bill. I know where I'd rather be.'

Kane shot her a strange glance and heat warmed Ellie's cheeks as the laughter surrounded them. 'You have a nice day out on the water, Terry. At least you and Bill get to go out in one of the air-boats. We'll be stuck in a car most of the day.' She turned to Heather. 'How come you got office duty tomorrow?'

'No kids booked into the crèche and Jan has to go to Darwin, so I'm in charge.' Her grin was impish. and Ellie resisted looking at Kane to see his reaction.

None of my business.

'Well, if we're driving all the way to Jim Jim and back tomorrow, I think I'd better get an early night.'

Steve leaned across the table and placed a soda water in front of Kane. 'Do us a favour, Els? Be a doll and see to Kane tonight, would you?'

Ellie felt her mouth drop open. 'See to Kane?'

Heather giggled, and Kane's hands clenched on the table on front of him. Ellie waited for him to make a comment, but Steve continued. 'All I meant was, can you grab the key and show him where his room is, seeing you're going down to the staff quarters? He's in number eight, down the back along from your apartment. Keys are in the back of the till. Jan sent them over before she closed up the office.'

'No worries.' She stood and put her hand on Heather's shoulder as she swung her leg over the wooden seat. 'Night all. It's good to be back. I'll look forward to Sunday night.' She stood behind Kane and leaned down; it was hard to hear over the noise. 'Are you ready to come now or do you want to hang around and someone else can show you the way to your room?' She could almost read Heather's thoughts: Pick me, pick me.

Disappointment flashed across Heather's face when Kane stood up. 'I'll just finish my drink and I'll be right behind you.' Crossing to the bar, Ellie leaned across the counter and opened the till. The key was in one of the large change compartments. She reached over and pulled it out, then turned to find Kane had followed her. His gaze didn't leave her when she held out the key to him. An unwelcome tremble ran down her legs and she scowled, and then instantly regretted it. Just her hormones going crazy.

'Come on, I'll show you where your apartment is.' She forced a smile onto her face. 'I thought you'd been here a few days?'

Kane's fingers brushed hers as he took the key and Ellie looked down and saw that his nails were neat and clipped, with no grease staining his fingers. Certainly not the hands of a mechanic. She hadn't noticed when they'd been up in the air earlier.

'Yeah, but I only decided to take one of the apartments today.'

She strode off in front of him along the path to the staff quarters. 'Come on, I'm . . . I'll show you where to go.' Ellie had been about to say she was tired and wanted to get to bed, but that would have sounded rude, so she closed her mouth.

'Thank you. Appreciate it.' Kane's voice was close, and she stopped at the end of the path, surprised again to find him right behind her. His movements were stealthy, and a shiver ran down Ellie's back.

She didn't know the guy or his background. Just because he had a job at Makowa Lodge meant nothing. Most of the time, Jock was happy to take on anyone with the right certificates.

If he was ex-military, Jock would have jumped at the chance to add him to the staff. Generally, the retired service guys were great to work with, even though they never stayed long. Curiosity filled her, and she decided to ask Jock about him tomorrow. Kane's insistence that he was only there to look after the helicopters was a concern for her, so sussing him out with Jock wouldn't be snooping into his past. After all she'd be working closely with him, and it appeared he wasn't going to be forth- coming if the conversation at the table was any indication.

'What's the go with the roster?' His deep voice broke into her thoughts.

'We have to go down and retrieve a vehicle. One of the lodge guests got hurt.'

He ran a hand through his short hair. 'Yeah, yeah, I got all that. But why you and me? We're flight staff.'

'No, we're lodge staff. Our primary role is to take the tourists up on scenic flights, or at least mine is.' Ellie couldn't resist the dig. 'But at the beginning of the season, the bookings are usually light on, so we take on other duties.'

'As directed?'

'You got it. Read your contract, did you?'

'Well, as long as I don't have to do childcare duties, I suppose I can cope.'

Ellie couldn't help the bubble of laughter escaping her lips. 'I think that's the first thing we've agreed on today.'

Kane looked across at the narrow alley that led to the steps up to the staff apartments. 'Where should I park my Jeep?'

'You can bring it round the back if you've got a lot of gear to unload, but then you'll have to park it down behind the kitchens when you're finished.' Ellie pointed in the direction of the restaurant. 'Or in the main car park up the front. I'll show you where to put it after I show you where your apartment is.'

'Thanks. I haven't got much to unload.' He stepped to the left and walked along beside her. 'I travel light.'

Yup, a fly-by-nighter for sure. Well, Heather didn't

mind if they came and went. Ellie pushed away the thought.

'Just as well, because the staff digs are nothing flash. Just the basics. Most staff choose to live off site. But I've lived at the lodge since I started work here.'

'How come?'

'It suits me.' The gravel scrunching beneath their feet on the path was the only sound until they reached the staff quarters at the eastern edge of the complex.

'The kitchen car park's down that way.' When Ellie lifted her arm and pointed, the sensor light came on with a sharp click, bathing them in sudden bright light, and her breath came out in a soft oomph when Kane shoved her behind him in one swift movement. He faced out to the path, peering intently into the darkness and shielding her with his body. Her face was pushed against his back and she couldn't see a thing.

'What the fuck are you doing?' Ellie shoved him hard, but it was like pushing into a brick wall.

Kane fell back. 'I'm sorry. I thought that noise was . . . something else.' The bright light illuminated his face and there was something in his expression that Ellie hadn't seen there before. It was as though he was looking right through her.

'What? Don't worry, there are no crocs this far from the river, and the fence keeps the dingoes out.'

'Forget it. I was wrong.' He held her gaze, his eyes unsmiling. 'It won't happen again. I'll go get my car.'

***

By the time Kane reached the top car park, he'd calmed down and his heart had stopped racing. Christ, one small sound and he'd grabbed her. A bloody security light had clicked on and he'd thought it was a sniper.

He got into his Jeep and drove down to the car park Ellie had pointed out, thinking about how to explain it to her.

The psychologist had warned him this might happen. He'd dismissed it, refusing to admit that he might succumb to post-traumatic stress disorder. Kane disagreed with all that psycho mumbo-jumbo bullshit. It was a weakness he didn't accept; he was stronger than that.

It was mind over matter, that's all it took.

Move on. Get over it. Life goes on.

Getting in the helicopter this afternoon had been bloody hard. But he'd done it, so he supposed that was one achievement he could tick off the list on the way to getting his life back to normal. All he needed now was a shower to wash away his stress. He stopped behind the kitchen, hefted his kit bag to his shoulder and walked slowly up the steps to the verandah. Ellie's eyes were narrowed as she looked over at his car.

'That's your Jeep? That was you this afternoon?' she asked when he reached the top step.

Shit, what now?

'Out at the old mango farm on the Arnhem Highway. It was you, wasn't it?'

'Why? Is there a problem?'

She turned her head back to stare at him and her expression was decidedly unfriendly. 'You sprayed me – and my car – with gravel when you roared out of the gate out like a boy racer.' Her voice was icy, and it matched her eyes. They regarded him unblinkingly, as cold as flint. 'What were you doing there anyway?'

'None of your business. Wait a minute. That was you parked by the gate?' Now her hands were on her hips and her chin had lifted. 'What were you doing there?' he said.

'Looking.'

'Looking at what?'

'The house.'

'Sorry, I didn't see your car until I reached it or I wouldn't have driven so fast. Jock asked me to get to the base quickly.'

'Why were you there?' she persisted. 'At the house, I mean?'

'I was visiting my mother.'

'Your mother?'

'She moved in there with her husband last month.'

'Her husband?'

'Yeah. They moved here while I was –' He caught himself. No one needed to know where he'd come from. They generally turned him into some sort of a hero or something as soon as they heard Afghanistan. A hero was the one thing he wasn't.

Her brows drew together. 'Hold on, Panos Sordina is your father? I thought your surname was McLaren.'

'He's my stepfather. They've only been married a few years. And what's with the twenty questions?' Now she was getting under his skin. Not only bossy and sassy, but a stickybeak as well. Ellie pushed past him and headed along the verandah, without answering. He grabbed her arm; no one was going to treat him like that.

'Would you like to tell me what's bugging you?'

She stared at him as she turned. 'That was the farm where I grew up. Sordina bought it from my . . . my family.' A dull light came into her eyes as he held her gaze and she moved out of his grip. His fingers tingled where he'd held her. 'You're in number eight, third on the left.'

Without another word, she strode away and pushed open the door of the room three doors along the verandah from his. The door closed with a loud click behind her.

Kane shrugged and called out before he thought better of it. 'And it was a pleasure to meet you, too, babe.'

He made sure his voice was loud enough to be heard through the closed door.

# Chapter 4

*Thursday night*
*Darwin*

David Johnson didn't remember the elevator's descent to the lobby, just the sensation of the frigid air conditioning blowing on his neck when he stepped through the doors. He clicked the remote key control of his SUV, threw his briefcase on the back seat and climbed in, then sat there for a moment and let the heat warm him. The aftertaste of whisky lingered in his mouth. Never again would he drink it without reliving the feeling that crawled through him at Fairweather's threat.

David opened the window after he started the car, letting the hot wind of the tropical night blow through his hair.

He didn't care about Fairweather's threat to go to the media. That was part of his everyday life. But the threat to his family . . .

David took his position very seriously, and his integrity had seen him through difficult scenarios and many hard decisions. He was all about what was best for the Territory. He would play along with him and then vote as his conscience – and what was best for the Territory – dictated.

Blackmail wouldn't wash with him. Not now. Not ever.

He turned the car out of the parliamentary car park, waved to the security guard and headed for home as the words 'you have two weeks' pounded through his head.

Two weeks. Two weeks. Nowhere near long enough to give considered thought to the two issues and liaise with the committees.

How dare the bastard put me into this position? But the faces of his children kept filling his vision. David had no doubt that Fairweather would follow through with his threat. He'd seen the power the man wielded over the past two years and knew he would do anything to get his own way.

Anything.

A cold feeling settled in his gut as he drove along the deserted road. He slowed as the light turned to red in front of him. As he waited for it to change, David closed his eyes and took a deep breath. For the first time since he had been Chief Minister, he was unsure of the direction he would take. But one thing he was sure of; until the discussion took place about the mining exploration, he was going to send Gina and the kids out of town. She'd argue but that's the way it was going to be. When it was over, he'd join them, and they could have a family holiday for a few days.

The house at Cullen Bay was only a ten-minute drive from Parliament House, but it could have been worlds away. Although the place had all the latest security gadgets installed, they rarely used the system. One time they'd come home from a holiday and hadn't been able to find the control. They'd set it off and Gina had held her sides, laughing and the tears had run down her cheeks as the alarm had filled the neighbourhood. After that, they decided it was too much of a bother to switch on and off with the kids coming in and out all day. Most nights they forgot to turn it on.

That would be changing from today.

He parked halfway up the drive, because the paved area in front of the triple garage was strewn with toys. Andrew's bike was tipped on its side, where it had been left when something more interesting had caught his attention.

A small blow-up plastic pool was sitting on the grass at the edge of the driveway. The strong moonlight caught the small toys bobbing in the shallow water. Binny would spend her entire day splashing about in the four inches of water if she had her own way.

The house was in darkness and the night was quiet. He closed the car door quietly and grabbed his briefcase.

'David?' Gina's soft voice reached him as he closed the front door behind him. He locked and keyed the deadlock, jiggling the key to remove it from the rarely used lock. David loosened his tie and shrugged out of his jacket, dropping it on the white leather sofa in the living room. Gina always left a night light on when he had late sessions and committees.

'I'll be there in a minute. I'll just look in on the kids.'

The house was cool, and he flicked off the air conditioning switch as he walked through the living room. The low hum reminded him of his office and he didn't want that. Tonight he wanted to focus on his family.

The smell of chocolate cookies pervaded the house and he took a side-track to the kitchen on his way to the kids' bedroom. The cookie jars were full, and Gina had left the coffee pot on for him. He opened the jar and took two, shoving one in his mouth as he walked across to check the sliding door leading to the patio. It was unlocked, and he flicked the lock over.

Gina had grown up in a small village in Tuscany where doors were open for neighbours to drop in at will. There, life was slow-paced . . . and safe. Fairweather and his threats aside, it wasn't safe to leave the house unlocked at night in Darwin.

He'd talk to her about locking up later and try not to let it turn into a fight. He rubbed his hand across his eyes. All they seemed to do was have harsh words lately.

David knew he earned enough to provide a good life for them. The sticking point lately was that he was never there to share that life with Gina and the kids. Now that she was pregnant again, maybe it was time for a change.

Walking quietly down the hall, he looked at the long windows that reached from floor to ceiling in this wing of the house. It would be so easy for anyone to break in if they were determined. The house's glass walls and open plan had once seemed perfect for their lifestyle up here in the tropics. Now in one night it had become a place where danger lurked in every shadow.

'Fuck Fairweather,' he muttered under his breath. Two weeks. Binny was lying with one leg hanging over the side of her bed, her tiny foot just touching the tiled floor. David lifted her leg onto the bed, pulled back the light blanket and slid her up onto the pillow. She murmured as he reached down and kissed her warm cheek.

'Daddy?' Andrew lifted his head in the other bed and gazed at him, his eyes reflecting the soft night-light.

'Hey, tiger. What are you doing awake?'

'Waiting for you to come home.' As David reached down to kiss his son, two little arms fastened around his neck and held him tightly. 'We went for a walk to the harbour today and looked for your car, but we didn't see you. But guess what we saw?'

David's eyes burned even as the warmth of the little arms touched his skin. His family was living without him.

Endless late-night meetings, interstate trips, and now this.

'What did you see?' He pulled back and looked into the trusting eyes of his firstborn. 'A circus?'

'No.' Andrew sat back and spread his arms wide. 'We saw the biggest ever crocodile.'

'In town?'

'Yup.' Andrew was full of seriousness. 'We walked around the rocks and saw it in the water.'

'Wow.' David shook his head but didn't let his feelings show. Walking around the bloody rocks. Gina just didn't understand the dangers of living here. He ran his hand lightly through Andrew's hair and reached down to kiss his son. 'Can you keep a secret?'

The little boy nodded, and a grin crossed his face as David held out the chocolate cookie.

'We'll have a midnight feast.' David smiled down at his son who was the image of his mother. Dark hair that curled onto his neck, olive skin and almond-shaped green eyes, long lanky limbs. All of the features that had hit him like a freight train when he had first seen Gina on the catwalk in Milan. 'But brush your teeth as soon as you wake up in the morning or Mummy will know our secret.'

'I will, Daddy.' Andrew finished chewing and David pulled a clean handkerchief from his pocket and wiped his son's face. 'Just getting rid of the evidence. Now go to sleep and I'll see you in the morning.'

'Promise? Cross your heart?'

Determination filled David at the need in Andrew's voice. It was time to make some hard decisions about his career. 'I promise, and after I talk to Mummy, I might have a big surprise for you.'

He waited until his little son snuggled into the pillow and closed his eyes.

The sleep of the innocent.

It had been a long time since he'd slept like that.

# Chapter 5

*Friday*
*Makowa Lodge*

Ellie opened her eyes and watched the sunlight play across the wall of her bedroom. She'd left the slatted wooden blinds open to let the air circulate, and to wake up with the early light.

But she hadn't needed it. All night she'd tossed and turned through unsettling dreams. Images of her mother wandering between dead mango trees and past the crocodile-filled rivers in a khaki shirt and her old cardigan had woken her in the early hours. She'd still been awake when the sun rose but had drifted off into an uneasy doze.

Now she rolled over and groaned into her pillow. Her head was aching, and her eyes were scratchy.

She'd been looking forward to coming back to Makowa Lodge and getting back to work, but that was before she'd seen that ugly slash in the ground at the back of the old farm. It would be a few days before she could get out there again, but Ellie intended looking at it from ground level to see what was really happening. It was too close to the National Park for comfort. Her mother would hear the truth, if and when there was anything to tell, but first Ellie wanted to be one hundred per cent sure of her facts. Panos had been lying to her – she was pretty certain of that – and if there was exploration happening on his property she would fight tooth and nail to protect the park. No matter who owned the land, it must be subject to regulations.

She would go down to the farm to ease her mind and try to get rid of this niggling feeling that maybe – just maybe – some of Mum's theories weren't so farfetched. Why had she put those newspaper clippings of Panos and that man in the folder? And what about Kane McLaren and his connection to Sordina? Was it just a coincidence that he had turned up when he did? Or was he somehow involved? He was supposed to be a pilot, but he said he wouldn't be flying. Ellie shook her head and the smooth cotton of the pillow rubbed against her cheek as the thoughts circled her mind.

No, if he was involved with Panos, he'd have no reason to be working at the lodge. Or would he?

Ellie stared at the ceiling and watched the fan spinning lazily in slow circles, barely moving the air.

Why did Kane unsettle her so much? She'd worked with many pilots over the years, some of them difficult, and yet he'd somehow managed to take over her thoughts in the less than twenty-four hours she'd known him. He'd bothered her from the minute she'd introduced herself on the tarmac yesterday.

Was it his arrogance, and his attitude to her as a pilot? Why should she care what a macho engineer thought of her ability? She knew she was one of the best pilots in the Territory and didn't need to prove herself to anybody.

Today they would be together again, set to take the drive down to Jim Jim Falls and she'd just have to deal with it.

Ellie rolled out of bed and stumbled into the small bathroom, determined to get Kane McLaren out of her head. She scrabbled through the cupboard for some paracetamol capsules and popped two into her mouth with a handful of water.

Ten minutes later she walked into the staff dining room at the back of the lodge in search of her first coffee of the day. Kane was sitting at a table with an iPad in front of him. He glanced up and nodded as Ellie crossed to the coffee machine and she smiled tightly as she picked up a cup. At last her head had stopped throbbing. The noticeboard held a colourful poster announcing the band appearing in the Makowa Lodge main bar on Sunday night. At least there was something to look forward to.

'Come and join me.' The corners of Kane's mouth tilted up in a brief smile. So Mr Fix-it appeared to be in a better mood today. After her cup was full, she walked across and pulled out the chair opposite him.

His hair was damp, and he wore a khaki shirt the same as hers. 'Thanks for showing me to my apartment last night.' He was watching her intently as she checked out his work uniform.

It suited him.

'No problem. Did you get settled in okay?' Ellie closed her eyes for a second as the first slug of coffee hit her bloodstream. If he could be civil, so could she.

'Yup.' Kane held her gaze when she opened her eyes. 'Look, I was really tired yesterday, and I didn't expect to be up in the air so soon. If I came across as a bit of a cowboy, I apologise.'

'We have to work together, so if you've ever got a problem, be up front. Tell me what's bothering you, and then we'll get along just fine.'

'I will.' Kane pushed his plate away and stood, leaving most of the food untouched. Ellie glanced down at the congealing mix of bacon fat and runny eggs stuck to the plate he'd left on the table.

'A word of advice.' She looked up at him and his dark eyes held hers.

'Yeah?'

'Never ask for the cooked breakfast in the staff kitchen. Artery cloggers are all you'll get here. I keep cereal and milk in my room. I only come here for the coffee.'

Kane looked down at her, and his whole face lit up. It was as if another person had replaced the taciturn man of yesterday. 'Don't worry. I'm well used to those sorts of meals.'

Ellie tipped her head to the side, waiting for him to continue but he stood silently while she sipped her coffee. He was a good-looking man and she held his gaze a little longer than she normally would have. 'We'll have to get going soon. It's going to be a long day.' Heat ran up her neck; she'd been staring at him too long.

'I'm ready to leave when you are.' Kane had shaved this morning and he looked a good deal more civilised than the unshaven hunk in the unbuttoned shirt she'd taken up the chopper yesterday. Not that she'd been staring. Okay, maybe she had, but that didn't mean anything.

'I'll head across to the garage and get one of the four wheel drive vehicles out of the compound.' Ellie finished her coffee in one quick swallow and stood. 'Are you okay to drive down if I navigate? The last ten kilometres down to the car park is a dirt track and it's pretty rough.

You'll have to drive back so you might as well get to know the road on the way down.' She folded her arms. 'Or would you rather be a passenger?'

'You're the boss.' Kane shrugged casually. 'I'll come with you now.'

Ellie pushed her chair in as Kane picked up the iPad. The black headline on the screen caught her eye.

'Sordina meets with Aboriginal council. Gives an assurance that coal seam gas exploration will never impact on Kakadu.'

The hair on the back of Ellie's neck rose as she remembered the earthworks on the farm. This was precisely what her mother been harping on about for the past three years. The headline was ambiguous. Was the news item about policy or was exploration already being considered near Kakadu? She'd chase that news article up when they got back this afternoon. Kane shut the cover on the iPad. For a minute she'd forgotten about his connection to Sordina, but it seemed as though it was going to follow her everywhere. Ellie waited for him at the door and then she led him to the main office across the corridor.

As soon as they walked in, Heather came out of the small room at the back of the office and struck a pose in the doorway. Her khaki T-shirt was tucked into a short skirt and she was the picture of elegance. Ellie grinned at Heather before she looked down at her shorts and work boots with a grimace. 'Some of us have to work today.' She lifted the flap at the end of the counter and headed for the board where all the keys were hanging.

'Hey, girlfriend, I'm working. You're the lucky pair who get to go on a picnic.' Heather focused her attention on Kane. 'Morning, Fly Boy. Ready to head off into the wilderness today?'

Ellie rolled her eyes. God, Heather was so obvious. Maybe she just needed to chill out a bit. *Maybe I'm just too damned serious.*

Kane nodded. 'Morning. Yep, it's my first experience of Kakadu on the ground.' The smile he gave Heather was considerably bigger than the curl of lips he'd treated Ellie to.

'You're going to love Jim Jim Falls. Pure white sand and crystal-clear green water enclosed on three sides by towering, red granite cliffs. You'll see it from the air soon, but there's really nothing like being on the ground. You probably won't have time for a swim today, but maybe I'll take you there sometime and show you my favourite spot.'

Ellie smothered a smile and wondered if Mr Fly Boy had any idea what her friend had in store for him. She ignored the little niggle of jealousy that rippled through her as Kane held Heather's gaze.

Not that it was any of her business. Heather could make cow eyes at Kane as long as she liked. Ellie didn't give a rat's.

The coffee and the painkillers had already done the trick and her headache had eased. Just a slight ache remained behind her eyes.

'I've got another stop for you too.' Heather finally turned to Ellie and lifted a sheet of paper from the desk behind the counter. 'Yeah? Where to?' If they had another stop, they'd have to hurry to get on their way. Ellie took the sheet from Heather. 'Sandy Billabong. One of the campers spotted a water buffalo up there yesterday. Can you swing by there on your way to the falls? It's not too far off your route and it's a waste to send one of the boys so far just to put a sign up when you're going past.'

'Going past? It's twenty kilometres in the other direction.'

'Jock's instruction.' Heather shrugged and held out her hand. 'Give it here and I'll laminate it.'

'Looks like we've got a busy day ahead.' Ellie flicked a glance at Kane. The way he leaned casually against the counter, he looked like he belonged to the place already.

'Dad and Terry are going out there later this afternoon, but we need to get this up as soon as we can. There's heaps of tourists in the park already. Bumper to bumper caravans when I turned onto the main road this morning.' Heather put the notice into the poster laminating machine on the bench along the wall and waited for it to feed through before walking back over to the counter, holding it between her thumb and one finger.

'Which vehicle is booked out to us?' Ellie took the laminated poster from Heather with a smile.

'The new Land Cruiser. I made sure I nabbed it for you before the other guys got allocated a vehicle. Dad can drive the old one. He's used to it. And here, don't forget you'll need the keys to the rental you're picking up. The number plate is on the tag.'

'Thanks, you're a trooper.' Ellie took the keys from the hook beside the counter and added them to the keys Heather passed over before putting both sets in her pocket. She paused in the doorway. 'Will your dad be around tonight?'

'He'll probably stay back for a drink tonight after they come in. I'll make sure there's a cold beer waiting for both of you too. You'll need it after your long day.' Heather turned to Kane. 'Have a good day, Fly Boy.'

Kane waved to Heather and followed Ellie out of the office. 'You met Terry last night. Terry is Heather's cousin and Bill Jarragah is her dad,' Ellie explained. 'Some of our staff are subcontracted by the national park headquarters at this time of the year because there's so much to be done leading into the tourist season. If you're going to stay a while you'll soon get to know everyone and where they fit in. Do you know much about Kakadu and how the park works?'

He shook his head as they walked to the car park. 'Nothing.'

Ellie shot him a glance. 'You've got a lot to learn, then.'

'I do. And I'm keen. So lead the way.'

Ellie took a deep breath and filled her lungs with fresh air. The sky was clear and the faint smell of wood smoke from the burning savannah tinged the air. It was good to be home, but she could do without all these complications meeting her at every turn. She stopped walking and turned to Kane. She'd clear one of them right now. 'Remember when we flew back last night?'

'Yeah?' His eyes held hers as she turned around. 'Did you notice I flew over your stepfather's farm?'

'No. I was chilling for a while.'

Hmm. He might call it chilling, but Ellie had sensed he'd been strung out about something.

'There was some machinery down the back near the park boundary and the earth was all dug up.' She kept her voice casual. 'Do you know what Panos is doing down there?'

'No.' Kane shook his head slowly. 'I only called in at the house to see my mother.' A fleeting expression of sadness crossed his face, but it was gone in a flash. 'Why? What are you worried about?'

'Just that whatever's happening down there is very close to the National Park and the river. And I saw that article in the Sun on your iPad.'

'Ellie, look I don't have a very high opinion of my stepfather, so I wouldn't be surprised by anything he was doing. Next time I go to visit my mother, I'll ask her what's happening. Okay?'

'Thanks. Appreciate it. It's none of my business what happens on the farm. I know it's not ours anymore but –'

'But you care about the park? Don't worry, I've already picked that up.' His gaze swept around to the woodlands between the administration block and the river. 'It is a beautiful place and I'm looking forward to seeing more of it.'

'So are you going to stay around here long?'

'As long as it takes,' was the enigmatic reply.

'Come on, let's hit the road. I'll fill you in as we head out.' Ellie narrowed her eyes and the slight ache thudded behind her temples again. She sensed Kane was telling the truth about the farm, but still, there was something not quite right there. She dug in her pocket for her sunglasses.

'Sounds good.' Kane walked along the path beside her and Ellie focused her attention back on him. His voice was friendly – and deep and sexy – maybe she was overthinking things. 'How come you know so much about Kakadu? Have you worked here long?'

'As soon as I got my flying licence, I came back.'

'Came back?'

'I went to Darwin for a while. Plenty of jobs there but this is home to me.'

Ellie fought down the ache that was always just below the surface. Would there ever be a time when the grief eased? The anticipatory buzz of the day ahead had faded, and she pushed away the headache that was hammering at her temples.

'Do you miss the farm?' Kane asked.

'Yes.' Ellie hated talking about it. She'd been through the counselling with her sisters and despite the words that were supposed to heal, she knew she would never get over Dad's death until she knew why he'd taken his own life. What quiet demons had he been fighting that he couldn't overcome? It was so out of character for the father she had known and loved. Kane seemed to pick up on her reluctance to speak and he turned away and looked ahead as they walked along the path to the back of the lodge. Ellie's footsteps crunched on the gravel as she stepped off the path to unlock the gate of the compound where the vehicles were locked up.

Kane raised his eyebrows. 'A high level of security for a few vehicles?'

'It's to stop the cars from getting milked.'

'Milked?' Kane's brow wrinkled in a frown.

'Petrol sniffing is a big issue out here. It's a chronic problem among some of the Aboriginal kids. Worse further north in Arnhem Land, but we've had a few cars stolen from down here too.'

'Is the hangar secure?'

'We've never had a problem with the birds. The pump at the hangar is switched off at the central console each afternoon when we lock up. I'll have to show you where to do that. Better to be safe. Dad always said–' Ellie swallowed. The day seemed destined to bring memories of her father back. She passed the keys to Kane. 'Come on, we'll drive by the restaurant on the way out and I'll grab some lunch and water. They make picnic baskets up for the tourists, but we won't need the whole thing they usually do up. A couple of sandwiches enough for you?'

Kane nodded and climbed into the driver's side. 'I didn't realise we'd need to take lunch. How far away is it?'

'We'll be gone all day by the time we drive down and back. It's about thirty kilometres to the turn-off and then another forty along an unsealed road. But it's slow going; the last ten kilometres are little more than a sandy track.' She stepped up into the passenger seat and waited for Kane to start the car. 'I thought we might walk into the waterfall while we're down there.'

'Sounds good.'

'And we have to go north first to Sandy Billabong to put up the sign that Heather gave me. You really don't know much about Kakadu, do you?'

He shook his head.

Ellie shrugged, wondering again why he was really here. 'It's great working here.' She couldn't help the smile that tugged at her lips. 'It's the most beautiful place in the world. You're in for a treat.'

'It's very different from what I expected. Most of the feedback I've heard says it should be called "Kakadon't".'

'Yeah, I've heard that, but if people bypass it and don't visit, they miss out on one of the best places in the world.' Ellie pursed her lips and looked out the window. 'The most spectacular parts of the park are a long way off the sealed highway like our trip today. Some don't think it's worth the long drive, but you can make up your own mind.'

Kane put one arm along the bench seat and looked over his left shoulder as he reversed the car. 'So tell me why you moved away from the farm.'

'My father couldn't make a go of his mango plantation.' Her voice was clipped as she pulled out her stock answer and pushed away the sadness that always came when she had to explain what happened. 'He died. We moved. I trained, and I came back. Stop here.' She pointed to the building which housed the restaurant and when he pulled up, she jumped out. 'My life in a nutshell,' she said through the open window. 'Wait here, I'll be right back.'

\*\*\*

Despite the incident with the sensor light, Kane had slept all night without waking in the early hours as he usually did. Dreamless for the first time in months. He'd woken up feeling calm and rested but sitting beside Ellie Porter put paid to that now. The khaki shirt pulled tight over those lush curves as she moved on the seat, pointing out features of the landscape.

He'd seen a different side to her as soon as they parked at Sandy Billabong. The dour mood she'd been in since he mentioned the farm lifted when they'd turned off the main highway and headed east towards Djarradjin Billabong. Her face came alight as she pointed to some cabins in a cluster beside the dirt road. Kane caught a glimpse of a river behind them in the gap between the buildings.

'That's a culture camp run by one of the traditional

owners,' she said.

'What do you mean by traditional owners?'

'The local Aboriginal clans.'

Ellie glanced across at him and Kane took note of her relaxed position. Her legs were curled up beneath her on the seat and her arm rested along the back of the seat. He lifted his gaze from the tanned thigh close to his.

'The traditional owners make decisions in the management of the land, and many of them have in roles within the park.' She leaned her head back on the seat rest. 'Heather is descended from one of the clans, and Bill, her dad, is heavily involved with the protection of the park.'

'Protection from what?'

'Mining initiatives, development, basically anything that threatens the park. He represents the local clan on a couple of parliamentary committees.' Ellie's voice was quiet and she turned away, staring out of the window lost in her thoughts. They didn't speak again until they passed a narrow road and she indicated for him to take a right turn and pull up next to a big noticeboard on the other side of an area where long tussock grass almost reached to the top of the bonnet of their high vehicle.

She grabbed the laminated poster off the seat, opened the door and jumped down from the high seat, pulling a key from her pocket.

Kane opened his door and climbed down, watching as Ellie unlocked the glass door at the front of the noticeboard. He walked through the long grass to stand beside her.

'Any snakes around here?' He kicked at the sandy soil between the mounds of grass, grateful for his sturdy boots.

Plenty of holes and places for them to hide.

'Nah, they'll stay away. The main thing to worry about here is the crocs.'

Kane looked up at her, unsure whether she was teasing him. She pinned the warning onto the board and then slid the front panel back down and locked it. 'Want to have a look at the billabong while we're here? The bird life is amazing.'

'Sure, why not.' Ellie strode ahead of him and Kane followed, enjoying the view. He'd noticed Heather's posturing in the office and had been slightly amused by it, but he wasn't here to get involved with anyone. Still, that didn't mean he couldn't appreciate a tight butt and a fine set of legs.

Kane expelled his breath and lifted his gaze as a huge expanse of water dotted with all manner of bird life opened up in front of them. A mass of purple water lilies in full bloom edged the water, nodding over the flat lily pads. Beyond them, the billabong stretched as far as he could see.

'How big is this? I always imagined billabongs were like a small dam.'

'Sandy Billabong is almost three kilometres long. It's one of the biggest in Kakadu.'

Ellie stopped beside a wire fence that ran through the grass about three metres back from the edge of the water and Kane looked at it curiously. It was falling down, and in some places had been pushed flat to the ground. He could have stepped over it if he'd wanted to. 'That wouldn't stop a water buffalo in full flight, surely?'

Ellie grinned at him with a flash of white teeth. It was the biggest smile he'd had from her yet. A lazy swirl of desire ran through him and he kept his eyes on her face. Her lips parted softly as she held his gaze for a second before she looked away and across to the water. A faint hint of colour touched her cheeks.

'That's to keep the tourists away from the water. There are crocodiles here.'

'Are they really so dangerous?' It was hard to believe there was danger in such a beautiful place.

'Close your eyes.' Ellie's voice was soft. 'What do you hear?'

Kane glanced down at her before doing as she said. 'Nothing.'

'Listen.'

He tilted his head to the side and really listened. 'I can hear the wind.'

The soft cadence of her voice held him as she continued. 'Imagine being here at night. The moon is full and shining on the water, and everything is quiet, apart from that soft wind.'

'Very pleasant,' Kane said.

'Ten years ago, a young German girl and her friends were camping here. They fell in love with the natural beauty of this place, and one hot night they went for a midnight swim. Right here. Right where we're standing. She was found the next morning in the jaws of a crocodile, one hundred metres along the shore.' Ellie's voice hardened, and Kane opened his eyes as her warm fingers touched his forearm. She lifted her other hand and pointed to a sign at the water's edge.

DANGER.

The word was printed in huge red letters above three graphics: a crocodile, a person swimming with a red line through the figure, and a crocodile snatching a person from the water's edge.

She shivered and pointed past the sign to the grass on the other side of the flimsy wire. 'See that flattened grass?'

Kane stood close behind her and followed the direction of her finger.

A huge reptile was lying in the shallow water at the edge of the billabong about fifty metres away. Its nose and eyes were above the waterline, but the rest was a deep shadow beneath the surface. 'Holy shit. Look at the size of it. It must be at least four metres long.'

Ellie squealed and grabbed at his arm as if to pull him back. 'You've got a good eye. I didn't even see that one.' Kane steadied her against him and was pleased when she didn't move away from his hands resting on her shoulders.

He watched the creature for a few moments, intrigued to see such a massive creature in the wild, in its natural habitat. He went to step forward, but Ellie lifted her hand to stop him and shook her head.

'Please don't go any closer. 'Do you know how fast they can move?'

The fragrance of her skin wafted around him as she stood close. The same fragrance he'd noticed up in the air yesterday.

'How fast? They're such ungainly looking creatures.'

'Faster than you'd imagine. Remember what I told you. No matter how beautiful and enticing Kakadu appears, remember the danger lurking behind the beauty.'

Her eyes were wide, and Kane thought of another sort of danger, another sort of beauty, and her cheeks flared with colour again as he looked down at her.

The confident, sassy demeanour she'd put up yesterday had gone. Hell, if he didn't know better, he'd have said she was terrified. A protective instinct surged through him, the intensity hitting him unexpectedly. Kane dropped his hands from Ellie's shoulders and took a step back, unsettled by his response. 'I'll be careful.'

'Please.' The blush that had stained her cheeks a moment ago had faded into pallor.

'You really don't like those suckers, do you?' He tried for the casual response.

'No, I don't. I've seen what they can do first-hand and it wasn't pleasant.' She turned on her heel and he watched as she strode back to the car. Her shoulders were rigid, and she didn't even slow down as she threw a final comment at him. 'You need to develop a healthy respect for them. There's been too many deaths over the years when simple common sense could have saved a life.'

There was a splash and Kane switched his gaze from the curvy bottom in the snug-fitting cargo shorts back to the water. The crocodile had taken off towards the shore, slithering rapidly along the ground like a lizard. In one swift movement its massive jaws closed on a large bird that only seconds before had been pecking its way along the grass. The bird disappeared, and Kane shivered as the sound of crunching bones broke the peaceful silence of the idyllic scene.

He stiffened as the crunching was replaced by the unexpected sound of an out of control helicopter above. He squeezed his eyes shut and swallowed, clenching his jaw so hard it ached, waiting for the crash and the explosion, but it didn't come. For one fleeting second, he almost looked up, but a sudden weight dragged on his arms. Kane gagged as his throat filled with gritty sand and a hot, dry wind whistled around his head. Slowly opening his eyes, he looked down. Goose bumps rose on his arms, and the unwelcome familiar looseness weakened his legs. Hawk was in his arms, her eyes holding his, her jaw working trying to speak through the blood.

The out of control sensation whirled in his chest as anxiety took over his entire body. Perspiration ran down his neck as he fought for control. He had to get to the base. He had to save her.

Kane pressed the heels of his hands into his eyes. But the weight dragged his arms down and the smell of blood surrounded him. He dropped to his knees, clutching his arms to his chest. It's not fucking real. It's not really happening.

He opened his eyes. His arms were empty, and he was still standing. A bird called across the billabong and sweet, clean air filled Kane's lungs. He took deep gasping breaths as the soft breeze blew across the water.

He focused on the reflection in the middle of the billabong as the mid-morning sun caught the small waves kicked up by the light wind. Slowly, his breathing returned to normal and his heart rate slowed. He turned when he became aware of Ellie calling him.

'Come on, there's lots more scenery to look out when we get to the falls. If you think this is good, you are in for a treat.' Forcing his legs to move, he walked slowly back to the vehicle, all the while focused on his breathing. He hauled himself in.

Ellie looked at him curiously as she closed her door. She reached over to the back seat and passed him a bottle of water.

'Are you all right? Your shirt is soaked. Can't take the heat?'

'Thanks.' He accepted the bottle and took a long draught before turning back to her. 'Heat? Trust me, this isn't hot. Not by a long shot.'

Kane pushed away the fear as he clicked his belt in and turned the key to fire the ignition.

# Chapter 6

*Friday*
*Jim Jim Falls*

The drive down to Jim Jim Falls was quiet with only desultory conversation. Ellie occasionally broke the silence with a warning about upcoming corrugations or a kangaroo that she spotted on the side of the road. Mostly she looked out of the window at the scrubby landscape flashing by. For a while there, she'd been enjoying his company, and then for some reason he'd turned back into the sullen man who had been in the chopper with her yesterday.

She turned to him just before they were about to reach the end of the bitumen road.

'The traditional owners call this season Wurrgeng. The creeks drain out and the floodplains dry up. During the monsoon season, we can't even get down here.'

'Wurrgeng?'

'Yeah, there are six seasons in the Aboriginal year. The monsoon season is called Gudjewg.'

'Did you have to learn all that for the scenic flights?'

Ellie shook her head and looked at the sky. Smoke hung low over the looming escarpment. 'No. I learned it all from Bill Jarragah when I was a kid. He used to work with my dad, and he taught me a lot too. See the smoke? They're burning off the grasslands. It's a way of renewing for the next season.' Ellie pointed to the granite cliffs to the east. 'This time of year, we have spectacular sunsets. Have you been out on the lodge boardwalk at sunset yet?'

Kane shook his head and turned his attention back to the road. 'I only arrived here a few days before you got back.' His words sent Ellie's thoughts wandering back to her mother as she stared at the landscape flashing past. She'd ring Emma and get her to send over any more information that Mum had put together about shale gas exploration in Kakadu. She'd had another quick flick through the folder Mum had given her but apart from the newspaper clippings about Sordina, it was mainly general stuff printed off from websites about fracking in other places. There were a few mentions of a company called Black Coal Holdings, but there was no links between the documents.

Ellie reached up and tucked her hair behind her ear. She had the window wound down a little and the wind had blown strands of hair from her braid.

'What's wrong?' His voice broke into her thoughts.

She kept her gaze fixed on Kane as she considered whether to be up front with him. Even though his hair was cropped short, the ends were sun-tipped, and his tanned skin looked as though he spent a lot of time outdoors. His profile was hawkish and a little gaunt, with deep hollows in his cheeks. A web of laughter lines creased around his hazel-coloured eyes. Her eyes travelled down his tanned arms to the strong hands confidently holding the steering wheel.

Nerves shimmied in her stomach and tingled down a little bit lower. Ellie didn't like the feelings that rushed through her body when she looked at him. While she didn't know if she could trust him, the same as yesterday she instinctively sensed solidness about him.

Ellie swallowed and then bit her lip. 'I was just deciding

whether I can trust you to be honest with me.'

'About what?' Kane kept his eyes on the road ahead as the corrugations got deeper and the vehicle juddered to one side of the road.

She grabbed for the Jesus bar on the dashboard in front of her. 'About the farm.'

'I have been.' He wrenched on the steering wheel as they approached a wide corrugation and his biceps flexed.

'Do you think it would be okay if I went out there and had a look at what's going on?'

Kane shot her a glance. 'I can't see it would be a problem. Mum would probably appreciate a visitor too.' His hands were clenched on the steering wheel. 'She's not real well,' he said. 'And I think she's a bit lonely.'

There was no more conversation until the towering granite escarpments signalling the beginning of the gorge appeared in the distance ahead.

'Around the next bend, past the camping area, the road changes and it's four-wheel drive vehicles only.'

Kane nodded and moved back a gear, slowing the vehicle as they approached the sweeping curve. A sudden flash of white was the only warning as a large all-terrain vehicle came careening around on the wrong side of the road.

He pulled the wheel to the left and their vehicle came crashing down into the channel, Ellie's head bumping the roof.

'Christ, who gave that cowboy a licence? Are you okay?'

She rubbed it with her hand. 'Yes, I'm fine. That's another one of the not-so-natural dangers of the park. Sorry I should have warned you.' She shook her head. 'The tour buses take the road down to the falls, right through the dry season, full of backpackers and tourists. The worst part is, if we meet one of them on the next section of the road, one of the vehicles will have to back up to get past and I can guarantee it won't be them.'

Kane pulled back onto the road and slipped the vehicle into four-wheel drive mode as they passed the turnoff to the Garnamarr campground. Ellie watched his strong hands on the lever as the gearbox resisted for a moment. Finally, it slotted in and the tone of the motor dropped back.

'How come your mother is living back at the farm? I thought Sordina lived in Darwin. Isn't he a member for one of the southern regions of the city?'

'I can't really help you there.' Kane lifted one hand from the wheel and scratched his head, before he turned to her. 'I don't know why she is yet.'

'Watch the road.' She inclined her head to the road front of them.

'Yes, ma'am.' That broad grin was finally back, and he hadn't 'babed' her this time. 'To tell you the truth, I don't know Sordina that well. I'd only met him a couple of times before I –' Kane stared into the distance ahead of them '– when my mother married him. When I visited them in Darwin after they were first married, they were living right on the water at Cullen Bay.

But I've been away . . . for a few years. I must admit I was a bit shocked myself when I saw the state of the place yesterday. I'm not happy about her being there, especially when she's crook.' A pensive look crossed his face and Ellie could sense there was something more but she didn't press.

'Do you think he's going to try and resurrect the mango plantation?'

Kane shrugged and changed back another gear as the road ahead narrowed. 'I have no idea why he would want to. Mum didn't say anything about him taking up farming. But honestly, I can't imagine it. He's a city bloke. He loves the horse races. Always running off to put a bet on. Not what you'd expect of your local member.'

'That's the Territory for you,' Ellie joked.

'Is there anything else he might have in mind for the place?'

'Like what? Cattle or something? What other crops grow up here in this heat?' Ellie stared at him. It was becoming apparent that Kane knew very little about the area. But was he being truthful or just prevaricating?

She bit her lip again as he slowed the four-wheel drive when they approached the next bend. His slowing down was timely, and a curse left his lips as another tourist bus came around the curve in front of them, smack bang in the middle of the narrow road. Kane shifted the car into reverse, and his fingers brushed her shoulder as he put his arm along the back of the seat, sending a quiver down her arm. He looked over his shoulder as he backed to the side of the road to let the vehicle through.

'You're a quick learner.' Ellie nodded as the bus accelerated past them and tooted the deep horn as it went by. A blur of tourist faces flashed past.

'How far did you say we have to go on this road?'

The moment for asking any more questions was past. She'd bide her time and wait until another opportunity arose.

\*\*\*

Kane focused on the road without speaking. It had taken a while to regain his composure after that blasted panic attack at the billabong; the worst was the choking feeling when he had to fight for breath. The doctor at the base in Germany had offered him anti-depressants but Kane refused to believe that he had a problem. The doctor had looked at him over his glasses, so Kane had reluctantly agreed to take the leaflets on PTSD. Maybe it was time to read them.

'Another one.' Ellie's voice intruded on his thoughts. Yet another big four-wheel drive bus was hurtling towards them.

'Christ, it's like a freeway down here. How many tourists come down here in a day?'

'The tours start at daybreak and go all day. You'd be surprised at the thousands of visitors here every season.' She turned to him with a grin and his gaze lingered on her face. When she smiled the constant wariness in her expression disappeared. Her pale blue eyes held his for a minute before she turned away.

By the time they reached the small car park, the sky had clouded over. Kane looked at Ellie, raising his eyebrows in question. 'Are you sure this is the right place? Where are all the tourist buses?'

'Yes. We've timed it well. Between tours. Don't worry, the crowds will be back when the next bus arrives.' She pointed across to the lone car parked on the other side. 'That looks like the vehicle we have to retrieve over there.'

He parked beside it, and Ellie jumped out and checked the number plate. 'This is it.' She held the keys up. 'I'll drive that one back seeing you're used to driving the cruiser.'

Kane climbed out of the car and looked around. The car park was in the shape of a large square and was fenced in with low timber. A few trees lined one side and there was no sign of a river or a waterfall. Red dirt was furrowed in deep lines from the tyres of large vehicles and the dust clung to his boots as he followed Ellie around to the back of the four-wheel drive.

The sky was low and dark, but the air was still, as taut as a bowstring. As the first puff of wind rustled the leaves of the small trees along the fence, the distant sound of running water carried across to him. Ellie lifted her face to the sky and Kane watched as she took a deep breath with her eyes closed. She tipped her head to the side for a moment as though listening for something.

'There's no rain in that sky. We should be right to walk in if you want to.' Ellie had opened her eyes and her head was still tipped to one side. Her gaze was fixed on his face but her eyes were curious.

'To the waterfall?'

'We can have our lunch down at the falls before we walk back to drive back to the lodge. It's about a twenty-minute hike each way although it's a bit rough at the far end. Reckon you're up to it?' She leaned into the car and pulled out a small nylon backpack, slipping it over her shoulders. 'Unless you want to eat here and head back sooner?'

Kane sensed this was a test of some sort, and he shrugged. As long as he had time at the end of the day to go and visit Mum. 'Fine by me. Might as well see the waterfall after the long drive down here.'

Half an hour later, he was regretting his decision. Pain hovered over his hip like a knife. He hadn't expected boulders the size of small trucks. Ellie had left him behind and rock-hopped like a wallaby about fifty metres ahead, lightly jumping from rock to rock across wide gaps. By the time he pulled himself over the last stretch and the biggest boulders, the sun had come out and perspiration was running down the back of his neck. The heat and the pain in his hip had drenched his shirt. Finally he pulled himself over the last boulder onto the sand and looked around. They were in a massive clearing. Ellie lay back on a large flat rock watching his approach.

'Hell, this wasn't what I expected.' Up at the top of the escarpment, a single, narrow ribbon of water trickled down the rock face to a large pool. The water was dark green, but crystal clear. Kane let his gaze wander around the huge expanse of pure white sand edging the large pool. Towering red cliffs rose majestically on three sides of the gorge. Strolling over the sand, and forcing his leg to bend, he stepped up to the flat rock where Ellie was stretched out sunning herself like a lizard. Her long legs hung casually over the edge of the rock and her head was tipped back, making the most of the warm rays. Despite the pain in his hip, a rush of blood headed for his groin and he turned away. He lowered himself onto the hot surface and lay back, focusing on at the cliff top above him.

'High, isn't it?' Ellie sat up and passed him a small bottle of water as Kane caught his breath.

'Now I can understand how that tourist broke his ankle.' He looked back over the way they'd come in. 'Some of those big rocks aren't very stable.'

'Have a good look around, because we're sure to have the helicopters down here sometime in the next couple of months.'

'It must be a killer to bring a chopper between those cliffs.' Kane lay back on the rock and looked up at the top of the escarpment. 'Have you ever landed in here?'

'Sure have. It's a challenge, all right.' She laughed with a wave of her hand and the sound was pleasant. 'I think I came in here four or five times last season. I also helped the National Park bring the walkways back into Twin Falls at the beginning of the dry season. The cross winds are tricky, especially when they're blowing from the west.'

'I'll make sure your bird is in tiptop condition for you then.'

'How come you don't fly anymore?'

Kane shrugged. 'Personal decision. I enjoy the engineering side of the choppers.'

She tipped her head back to take a long drink of water. In contrast to her tanned arms, her slim neck was white, and Kane let his gaze linger on her lips when she wiped off a drop of water.

'If I hadn't been away, I probably would have helped out with the crocodile management before they opened the falls up.' She held his gaze and her tone was challenging 'If you're still around next year, you'll get to see it. We bring those big traps in by air, because there's no other way in. Hopefully we won't need to bring more in this season.' Ellie shivered. 'I don't know how people can swim here, even if they reckon the crocs have been "managed" out.'

'Is that why you've been away? Don't like doing it?'

She shook her head. 'Had some family stuff to do.'

'A swim sounds like a great idea.' The cold water would ease the blasted pain in his hip too.

'Oh, God, no. Please.' She unscrewed the cap from her water bottle and passed it over to him. 'Tip some of that on your head if you need to cool down.'

He returned her worried stare. 'Don't waste your water. If swimming bothers you that much, I'll just go down and have a splash in the shallows.'

Ellie grabbed his arm and Kane looked down at her long slender fingers as they circled his wrist.

'Please. Didn't you see the traps on the way in?'

'I was too busy watching where I put my feet,' he said. The warmth from her fingers was sending another lazy swirl of desire kicking to his groin. He lifted his gaze back to her face and a pleasant rush went through him as he caught her staring at his mouth. He realised she was serious. 'You really do worry about them, don't you?'

'You would too if you'd seen what they can do to a person.' Ellie let go of his arm and stretched across the rock to reach for the backpack. 'Sandwich?'

Kane nodded and took the packet she passed over to him.

She pointed up to the bend in the narrow river. 'The first traps are up there. All the areas stay closed to tourists until the wet season waters fall to a level where the crocs are less likely to be moving around. The National Park rangers have to see if any have moved in during the wet. They put baited traps and foam buoys in the water.'

'Foam buoys?'

'Yep.' She nodded. 'Crocs are curious creatures and will have a chew on a buoy. So they have to get rid of them before the tourists can come in. The traps are big and sometimes they'll put a big animal in there . . . maybe a donkey or a wild pig.'

'Sounds like complicated work . . . and dangerous?'

'Yep. Sometimes it's not successful because crocs can be territorial. There are stories of them travelling hundreds of miles to come back to a favourite spot.' Ellie looked at him and the colour ran up into her cheeks. 'I'm sorry. I tend to rabbit on a bit. Where did you work before you came here?'

'All over the place.' Kane avoided a direct answer. 'Any more sandwiches?' Ellie caught his eye again as she passed another one across to him but this time her expression was clear. She was well aware that he was avoiding anything personal. He didn't want to share. What he'd been through was his own business and the last thing he wanted was more sympathy. If it wasn't for his mother being ill, he wouldn't be visiting her either. He didn't want to hear any more questions about what had happened. Or any more accolades about his supposed heroic status.

Christ, he just wanted to forget it and get on with life. 'Come on, let's go back.' He wolfed down the sandwich and stood. Kane's pleasure in the day had dimmed.

The look that Ellie threw him as she slipped the backpack over her shoulders added to his mood. She opened her mouth as if to say something and then obviously changed her mind.

She didn't show him the crocodile traps as they walked back over the rocks and through the monsoon forest.

# Chapter 7

*Saturday*
*Arnhem Highway*

David had left their SUV at home in the garage last night and taken a bus to the airport where he'd picked up the rental car. Gina had booked and paid by phone with her credit card as he had instructed. He'd parked two streets away, walked down two blocks and come in through their back garden. This morning he got up early, retrieved the car and had bundled them and their luggage in before sunrise – the kids awake and excited about their adventure to Kakadu. Gina had watched, her lips set in a straight line as David had looked up and down the street, but it was as quiet as always. No one knew where they were going, and he'd made sure that not even a chance remark to neighbours could alert anyone who might enquire.

'Just a small precaution.' Maybe he was being overcautious, but he didn't trust Fairweather. 'You know what politics is like . . . and the media. This is a big week and I'm just being careful.'

'No, I don't know what politics is like. That's your life. And if you would tell me why or how we have to be "careful", I could be careful too, without having to travel away from home in the middle of the night.' Gina had stared at him, her beautiful eyes full of concern and David tried to reassure her.

'It'll be a good rest for you. One last chance to take some time for yourself before the baby. There's a day spa and a crèche for the kids. Two weeks of doing nothing. Order in room service, sleep when the kids nap. You can have a total rest. You'll enjoy the luxury suite by the pool. We'll have a good time.'

'We?' She was softening a little.

'I'll be with you both weekends. You can go off and get pampered and I'll sit with the kids this afternoon.'

The forgotten feeling of being the most important person in his wife's world came rushing back when Gina reached over and wrapped her fingers around his.

'No, *sei la mia anima gemella*. We will spend the weekend together before you go back to your office to whatever is so important.' Her voice was soft, and David smiled at her and squeezed her fingers.

'You know you are my soul mate too, *bella*. Don't ever doubt that.'

He'd thought of nothing but the safety of his family over the past twenty-four hours as he'd tried to prepare for the upcoming environmental committee meeting. The drive along the Arnhem Highway had given him a couple of hours to focus on the carefully worded position statement. Even though

Kakadu was a national park administered by the federal government, the government of the Territory still played a major role under the recent amendments to the Environment Protection and Biodiversity Conservation Act. The environmental impact

statement for the proposed mineral exploration on the northern edge of Kakadu had been submitted by Black Coal Holdings. 'Are we nearly there?' Andrew's loud whine pulled David's mind from the response he was drafting in his head. 'Daddy! Are we nearly there?'

David nodded absently, and the sound of a game resumed from Andrew's iPad in the back seat.

He glanced across at Gina; she'd dropped her Kindle and was dozing, her head on the leather headrest of the hire car. Her olive cheeks were lightly tinged with a rosy flush as the sunlight played on her face. She breathed softly through gently parted lips, and her hands were folded protectively over the soft swell of her pregnant stomach. She was more beautiful now than when he'd first met her.

A muscle clenched in David's gut. Was he doing the right thing bringing them down here?

The boundary change and the exploration licence votes could be brought forward. Maybe his vote wouldn't make any difference anyway? He wondered what Fairweather was capable of – how many others did he have in his pocket? Maybe he should have gone to the police after that comment about his children. But David didn't trust the influence that Fairweather had with the police either.

It could be the end of his career if the seabed mining approval went public before the approval was reversed. He'd set that in motion yesterday. David gripped the steering wheel and stared at the straight road ahead. Christ, he'd seen enough politicians across the country take a fall recently. The corruption commission hearings down in New South Wales had put paid to the careers of many.

'Daddy! How much longer? I need a wee.'

'Almost. Can you hang on for a few more minutes?' David pushed away the thoughts filling his head and tried to focus on his family. 'How about an ice cream when we get there, buddy?'

He had emails to read when he got there; his phone had been dinging non-stop all the way down the highway. Gina had offered to read them to him as she often did when he was driving but he'd shaken his head. She'd shrugged and given him a strange look, before turning back to her Kindle.

The possibility of spending time relaxing with Gina and the kids was becoming less likely every time his phone dinged, but David knew he needed to focus on family for the next two days. He didn't want to lose his wife's respect too.

The promise of ice cream quietened Andrew and there was silence from the back seat except for the low music from his game. They'd been on the road since dawn and were now only a few kilometres from the resort. Gina was not happy that he was going to leave them there when he headed back to the city – alone – on Sunday night.

'What if the baby comes early? Is there even a hospital out in the wilds here?' She'd widened her green eyes at him and placed her hand on her stomach. 'I'll be by myself with the children. I've only got eight weeks left. You do know that, don't you?'

'Of course I do, and no, it won't and yes, there is.' David had pulled her close and buried his face in her hair, inhaling the lavender fragrance that always calmed him. 'And it's not the wilds. It's only a couple of hours away from Darwin. You'll be fine.'

'Why all the secrecy, David? Why do we have to hide?'

The wheels of the car hummed on the tar as the sun rose in the winter sky, and the dawn light touched the charred savannah grasslands that had been burned off along the highway.

The morning mist hung eerily as the watery sun tried to break through the smoke-laden fog and David tried to forget the emails waiting for him, and his briefcase full of papers in the boot of the hire car as they turned right at Jabiru and sped down the Kakadu Highway towards Makowa Lodge.

\*\*\*

Gina checked into the lodge while David waited in the car with the kids. They'd paid for Friday night, so they could get an early check-in this morning. It was still early and there were no other guests at the reception desk.

'Welcome to Makowa Lodge, Ms Perini.' The pretty Aboriginal girl behind the counter had a deep, husky voice. She took Gina's credit card and swiped it over the terminal, before handing over the security card for the room. 'I hope you enjoy your stay with us. There are many activities on in the lodge, and there are brochures in the compendium in your room outlining the tours available.'

'Thank you –' Gina glanced at the girl's name badge '–

Heather.'

'And make sure you look at our day spa. It's won national awards.'

Gina smiled and nodded before she put her credit card away. 'So I have heard. I will, thank you.'

She decided to see if there was an appointment available at the day spa this afternoon. David could look after Andrew and Binny. Then they could have a romantic dinner in the room tonight after the children went to sleep.

David had parked the hire car in the middle of the car park and Gina put up her hand to shade her face from the sun. Despite the early hours, the heat was lifting in waves from the concrete. She smiled as the children's happy giggles reached her. They would make the most of the weekend away together and then she would try to enjoy the rest of the time when David was away.

She shook her head as he slouched down in the driver's seat and pulled the baseball cap low over his eyes.

'It's okay, James Bond, it's only me.' Gina opened the door and looked at him with a wry smile.

David flicked her a glance and didn't acknowledge her joke, and she turned away to the back seat. There was only so much she could take of this ridiculous behaviour. 'How about we go and find some ice cream after Daddy unpacks the car?'

The squeals from their two children showed her that someone still loved her anyway.

'Which building?' David started the car and she looked down at the security card.

'Over there. Block C.' Gina looked down at the lodge plan that the receptionist had given her and pointed to the building on the other side of the pool.'

'Good.' He reversed the car and drove across the car park before parking in the shade. The lodge was in the shape of a crocodile and they were in the wing at the end of one of the back legs. He came around, opened her door and held his arms wide as she stepped out. 'I'm sorry, sweetheart. I should have parked closer. I didn't think.'

'You haven't been doing much of that lately,' she said, but the feel of his arms around her and the steady beat of his heart against her cheek as he pulled her in for a hug softened her mood a little. 'I'm sorry. It's just that you have me worried with all this . . . this secrecy.'

David dropped his head and brushed a light kiss across her lips. 'You take the kids inside and I'll unpack.'

'What if someone sees you? Is that safe?'

David cupped one hand around the back of her head and pulled her close. Gina stared at him and a shiver ran through her at the expression in his eyes. Uncertainty and something else. This was not the man she'd shared her life with for the past ten years.

'Please don't hide things from me, David.'

He held her gaze for a minute and then let her go. 'I promise.' Gina opened the door and leaned in to unbuckle the children from their car seats.

David raised an eyebrow when he pulled out the first suitcase. 'You really need this much for a week?'

'Don't forget the other bag on the floor of the back seat too,' Gina said with an airy wave of her hand. 'It's full of toys.'

He grinned, and her stomach did a little flip. She was carrying their third child, and even with all the worry surrounding them at the moment, he could still entice her with that sexy smile. Problem was she didn't get to see it – or him – much lately. 'You should know by now what I'm like when it comes to travelling.'

'Everything but the kitchen sink, I know.' As his phone beeped with an incoming message, David put the suitcase down and moved away, his voice quiet as he turned his back to Gina and the children.

'Come on, you guys. Let's go explore our room while Daddy is on the phone.' She held the children's hands and looked at David, her stomach sinking as she listened to his conversation. 'Then we'll go and get our ice creams.'

'I could meet you there this afternoon.' David's words reached her even though he spoke quietly. He turned and held her gaze, and Gina's cheeks burned as she read the plea in his eyes.

'The bar where the cruise boats leave the harbour?' He glanced down at his watch with a frown. 'Yes, five o'clock will be fine.'

Gina turned away from David and left him to see to their luggage as he ended the call.

'Mummy!' Andrew protested as she hurried the children across to the building where their suite was located.

Dropping Andrew's hand, she swiped the card across the lock, her movement jerky, reflecting the anger that was building in her. So he'd intended spending the weekend with them and she'd fallen for his promise? The cold air of the foyer rushed out to meet her when she pushed the door open and Gina welcomed the chill on her burning skin. She sat the children on the floor inside the suite and went back to hold the door open while David made three trips back and forth from the car, filling the foyer with their luggage.

Not a word was spoken until he brought in the last bag, and Gina closed the door of the suite where she and the children would be spending God-knew-how-long until David decided they could come back home. She settled the children in front of a cartoon on cable television with a banana each, once again promising ice cream, and when they were settled, she went back into the kitchen. David was leaning against the stone countertop waiting for her. He opened his arms, but she ignored him, walking over to the kettle and filling it with water while she tried to contain her temper.'

'Where's your bag?' She looked at the pile of luggage stacked neatly inside the door.

'I left it in the car. I'll come back for the day tomorrow and spend it with you. I have to go to this meeting.'

She arched her eyebrow before turning away to rifle through a container of exotic tea bags. 'Don't bother. I'd hate for you to go out of your way for us.'

Gina closed her eyes as she waited for the water to boil and shrugged David's hand away when he gently touched her on the shoulder. She opened her eyes, staring out through the large window, and watched a family group cross the lawn to the pool area. She couldn't hear their laughter, but she could see the happiness on their faces as the couple watched two children run to the side of the sparking pool.

'You've changed so much, David.' She flinched as he slid his arms around her from behind and dropped his chin onto her shoulder. 'Tell me what's going on. Show me you can trust me. What you are showing me now is that we are no longer important to you and you have dumped us out here in the wilds where we won't bother you.'

His laugh held no amusement. 'It's nothing to do with trusting you. I just don't want to frighten you.'

Uncertainty made her chest ache as his voice shook and she turned around in his arms. 'Then tell me what it happening. Please.'

David dropped his forehead to rest against hers. 'I made a stupid mistake and signed a document I shouldn't have. Now I'm being pressured to uphold a decision in a committee meeting that may have consequences.'

'So?' Gina wrinkled her brow and waited for David to continue. 'Can't the other members of the committee see it is not a good decision?'

His breath was warm against her face and he didn't answer. Screams and laughter carried in from the television show in the living area and Binny's cute little chuckle followed soon after.

'David, you've always followed your judgement, and your integrity is one of the reasons you got to be Chief Minister at such a young age. You know that. How can you doubt you are doing the right thing this time?'

'I wish it was so easy. There's more than that.' He leaned back, and the fear settled into Gina's stomach as he held her gaze. 'A very powerful man has threatened to hurt the children if I don't recommend approval for a boundary change that could result in mining at the edge of the National Park.'

'Who has? What the hell are you talking about?' She pushed away from his gentle hold. 'How dare you not say that to . . . I mean . . . tell me that before. And you were just going to leave us here alone and go back to the city? Without warning me to be careful?' Gina sought the right words, her voice becoming increasingly shrill. When she was really upset, her English deserted her, and she would lapse into her native Italian. 'How dare you play with us, with *la nostra sicurezza*, with . . . with . . . our lives, just to run your precious Territory?' Her voice hitched on a sob and she pulled away from his hold. 'Our *bambini*, David. You risk them for what? A fucking piece of land?'

'Listen to me. No one knows you're here. It's safe here and –' David's voice was quiet, and it was his calm that fuelled Gina's anger even more. He ran his hand through his hair and then reached for her again, but she balled her fists and struck at his chest. David grabbed for her hand, but she folded her arms.

'Who are they?' Her eyes filled with tears as she stared at him, and she blinked them away. 'Tell me.'

'Keep your voice down.' The patience in his voice despite his commanding words pissed her off even more. How could he be so calm? She and the kids were just there for him to be with at his whim, and she knew they always came second to his precious political career.

'What are you going to do? Gina whispered and brushed away the tears that were now running down her cheeks. 'I know you so well, David, and I love you for your high ideals. You will do the right thing as I would wish you to.' She stared at him and her voice was cold. 'But if anything happens to our children, I will never forgive you.'

# Chapter 8

*Saturday*
*Makowa Lodge*

Kane pushed open the door to the administration block of the lodge and welcomed the cool air on his face. He lifted his hand and wiped away the beads of perspiration on his brow, although the sweat probably had more to do with the pain in his damned hip than the heat of the day outside. The walk into the waterfall yesterday had left him with a nagging ache down his leg, and he'd barely slept after he'd come back from a late visit to the farm – his mind fogged with pain and worry until he'd finally resorted to painkillers in the early hours.

Concern about what this job was going to require of him was interspersed with thoughts of his mother stuck in that rundown dump by herself, and the fact that Ellie Porter had somehow snuck through his defences.

He was hoping Jock worked Saturdays; he needed to ensure that he wasn't rostered on to fly anymore. That misunderstanding needed to be cleared up or he would be out of here in a flash. The office was empty, and he was relieved that Heather wasn't there striking her Marilyn Monroe pose in the doorway. She seemed like a friendly enough person, if a bit over the top with the come-hither glances.

Kane wasn't interested in making connections. As soon as Mum was on the road to recovery he was out of here. Where to, he wouldn't know that until he moved on. He had no interest in the social bonding that was always a part of isolated workplaces. It had been different in the Army; there you relied on others just to stay alive. They'd had good times together in the mess – as much as you could have in the middle of a war.

A single drop of perspiration ran down his cheek.

He squeezed his eyes shut but the flashback slammed in without warning.

'Look out. Lift up, lift up.' Hawk's voice was steady, but Kane sensed his navigator's fear in the same instant that the machine gun fire ripped through the oil lines of his chopper.

'Brace, brace.' His yell drowned in the thin, high-pitched scream as the bullets penetrated the airframe and smashed through Hawk's body. Surprise filled her eyes as her life drained away. The smell of her blood mixed with the acrid stink of the burning oil. Not my fault. Nothing I could –

Kane swallowed and forced the image away, focusing on the stand in front of him. Postcards, small stuffed animals and books about Kakadu filled the racks and he reached out and picked up a small green crocodile with huge teeth and a happy smile. He held it loosely, letting the soft fur brush against his fingers.

'Hey, there. Do you need a hand?'

He put the crocodile back on the stand and walked over to the high counter.

'I was wondering if Jock was about.' Kane glanced at the name badge on the woman's chest. 'Hi Jan. I'm Kane McLaren. I'm working over at the hangar.'

'Nice to meet you.' She held her hand out and he shook it. 'Sorry, but Jock's not here on weekends. He's got a place in Darwin and he won't be back till Monday.'

'Okay, thanks, I'll catch up with him, then.' He turned to leave, but like seemingly everyone else in this place, Jan was on for a chat.

'Are you staying in the staff apartments?' Kane nodded. 'For a while.'

'Where are you from?'

'Brisbane.' He glanced down at his watch and forced a friendly smile to his face. 'You?'

'Oh, I'm from Jabiru. A died-in-the wool-local.' She winked at him. 'Anything you need to know about the place, just ask.'

'Thanks.' He tried to think of something else to say but the art of social chit-chat had left him a long time ago. Rescue came in the form of a fluffy toy. There was another pile of them in a small basket on the counter and he reached out and picked up one of the soft green crocodiles. 'I'll have one of these. A memento of Kakadu.'

As she took it from him, his gaze dropped to the assortment of Cadbury chocolate blocks on display along the front of the counter, and he picked one up and passed it over to her. If he couldn't see Jock, he'd go for a drive back to the farm and see his mother.

The thought of spending the day alone in the lodge didn't appeal and it also meant there was more chance of running into Ellie. From now on, he'd shut himself off. Do his job. Look after the choppers and put his energy into taking care of Mum. And stay away from temptation – even though her apartment was only three doors up from his.

'Chocaholic?' Jan rang up his purchases and he shook his head as he passed over a note.

'Sure am.' He hated the stuff, but he wasn't going to say it was for his mother. That would open up a whole new conversation.

Two hours later Kane stood on the porch of the old farmhouse. He'd loaded his Jeep with groceries from the small IGA supermarket in Jabiru. Last night Mum had apologised that she couldn't offer him a meal because she hadn't been well enough to go shopping. He stared out over the dam and bit hard on the inside of his cheek, holding back the words that he knew would hurt his mother. What the fuck was she doing here by herself in this dump when she had a beautiful home on the beach in Darwin?

Susan sat behind him on an old sofa that looked as though the rats had been in the stuffing. Balls of white fluffy filling covered the verandah, and there were animal droppings scattered through it. Finally, he ran his hand through his hair and composed himself to speak.

'So Panos is taking up farming?' He kept his voice light as he walked over and sat beside her. Today her weight loss was much more apparent. On his first visit he'd tried to have a conversation about her illness, but she'd insisted she was fine and that the monthly visit to the hospital for her 'treatment' – she wouldn't give him any details – was only for a short time and she was on the road to recovery.

She shook her head. 'I don't think so. Why do you ask?'

'I heard there was some work happening here.'

'Oh, he said there might be some trucks; there's a new dam going in down the back. Who were you talking to?'

'One of the pilots at the lodge used to live here. She noticed them when she drove past the other day.'

'That would have to be one of the Porter girls.' Susan sat up straight and her eyes sparked with interest. 'Let me see. Was it Ellie?'

'Yes.'

'Oh, Kane. She's a lovely girl. Her father died about the time I met Panos. It was such a tragedy.'

'Tragedy?' He couldn't help himself.

'Her father committed suicide and the family was left with nothing but debt.'

'So how did Panos end up with the farm?'

'He bought it to help them out. One of the sisters was away at university, and the other one was about to finish school. That young Dru was such a wild one.' She shook her head. 'Their mother had a bit of a breakdown when Peter died, and Panos bailed them out financially.' She reached over and took his hand. 'All families have their hard times.'

Kane grunted an acknowledgement.

'Are you feeling better now that you've left the Army behind you?'

'Better? Me? I'm fine.' Apart from the flashbacks. 'It's you we have to take care of.' He took the opportunity that presented itself. 'Mum? Why are you here on your own? Where's Panos?'

His mother's hand gripped his and she turned away, but not before he caught the flash of tears in her eyes. 'We made some bad investments. You know? The GFC and all that.'

'And?' Kane held his tongue. His mother and Panos had married the first year he had been overseas on his first tour, which was well after the economic turmoil of the GFC.

She lifted her chin and this time she held his gaze

steadily. 'We had to sell our house at Cullen Bay to pay some debts that had accumulated.'

'Your house.'

'Our house. Panos is my husband. We owned this place, so it made much more sense to move here rather than buy a smaller place in Darwin.'

'So you're not here by yourself?'

'He stays in his electoral office in the city during the week and comes home weekends.'

Kane looked around innocently. 'So where is he? It's Saturday.'

'He had . . . he had . . . a meeting today, so he'll probably come tomorrow.'

'Good.' Kane's voice was clipped because he knew exactly what sort of meeting was on in Darwin today – it had been on the front page of the Darwin Sun this morning. There was a big winter meeting at the racecourse, and Panos would be there with bells on. He bit back the anger that stuck in his throat. Mum was in this dump, and her husband had left her here alone, as sick as she was? His mother always had been perceptive, and she turned to him, reading his thoughts.

'He calls to check on me every day, so I'm fine.' Her hands were icy as she held his hand. 'You worry too much.'

He'd be calling Panos as soon as he got out of here and giving him a piece of his mind.

\*\*\*

Despite the pregnancy bump in front of her, Gina all but floated back to the suite, gliding on the memory of the massage. After they had argued, David had picked up the hotel phone and enquired about a booking for her. She'd scrubbed at her eyes; if he could get an appointment, he could damn well look after the kids. She didn't want to be anywhere near him at the moment. Luckily, the day spa had been able to take her straight away.

'Mummy is going to have some time out while we have an ice cream. And then how about a swim?' David had held her gaze when the two children rushed across to him and wrapped their arms around his legs. Gina's mood softened marginally, though the fear still gripped her stomach like a vice. David tickled Andrew and he giggled, running away back into the television room. 'Then we'll come back here, and you can have a nap, okay?' He ruffled Binny's hair and she scarpered back into the living room behind her brother. Gina held David's gaze and put her hands on her stomach as the baby landed a good kick to one of her ribs.

'We'll talk later, I promise.' His voice was gentle but firm. 'All right. I'm sorry for yelling.

\*\*\*

The massage had been just what she'd needed, and calm had stolen over her as the long, firm strokes of the masseur had loosened the muscles in her shoulders, arms and legs. Gina laughed as the woman had held up the special pillow, so she could lie on her stomach. As she'd lain there with her eyes closed, some of her worry had dissipated. She had to trust David, but she was still angry that he hadn't told her earlier what was going on. The last thing she wanted was to be protected from reality. She'd had enough of being treated as a fragile female by her father – and her brothers – as she'd grown up, the only daughter in a boisterous Italian household.

The massage was followed a facial, and it was obvious that the staff didn't get many pregnant clients through the day spa as the technician adjusted the chair and Gina tipped slowly backward. She clutched the sides of the chair when her head tipped back lower than her feet, and a wave of vertigo hit her. 'Can you sit me up a bit higher please? Not good for the blood flow.' She placed one hand on her eyes and took a deep breath, placing the other hand on her stomach.

The young girl adjusted the chair and reached to the table at the side. All was quiet as soft fingers rubbed a cool cream into Gina's face. She closed her eyes and the room went dark as the girl laid rounds of cucumber and thin slices of cotton gauze on her closed eyelids.

'Your face is glowing, and your skin is quite full and firm.'

'Thank you. It's called pregnancy.' Gina smiled and settled more comfortably into the chair, relaxing as the girl's fingers gently massaged her temples. The time passed slowly as her face was scrubbed, masked and exfoliated. For a while, she drifted off into a light doze when she was left alone with only the soft harp music surrounding her.

By the time Gina returned to the suite, her mood was much improved. But if David had to be in Darwin by five, they wouldn't have long to talk.

She'd forgotten her security card, so she tapped at the door. There was no answer. Gina frowned. 'David?' she called softly. 'Open the door. I've left my key card inside.'

Maybe he's gone to sleep with the children? He'd said they'd have a swim and then a nap.

She tapped again, more loudly this time. She looked

down at her watch. It was almost two; he'd have to leave within half an hour if he was going to make Darwin by five o'clock. And she wanted to talk before he left.

She knocked loudly one more time and waited, but there was still no sound from within. Gina's newfound calm splintered. A frisson of worry tugged at her; it was out of character for David to risk being late for a meeting. Finally, she gave up and walked along the front of the building to the main doors that opened to the corridor leading to the pool. Maybe the three of them were still there; but if so, they'd be waterlogged by now.

Squeals and excited chatter reached her as Gina stepped through the door and held her hand up to her eyes. She looked around the two pools and over to the grassed area but there was no sign of David or the children. A chill ran through her blood. She gripped the doorframe, fighting the tendrils of panic that threatened.

'Are you okay, love?' An older woman in a pair of hot pink swimmers with a large sunhat perched on her head stood behind her.

'Er . . . yes. Thank you.' Gina forced a smile onto her face. She didn't want to draw attention to herself. 'I was just seeing if my husband was still out here with our children.' She raised a shaky hand to her brow.

'Are you sure you're all right? You're awfully pale.'

'Yes, yes, I'm fine, thank you. Just the heat.' Gina's heart picked up a beat, and she forced herself to take a deep breath. She was probably worrying about nothing. Maybe there was a playground somewhere. Yes, that was it. She turned and hurried back to their room, conscious of the woman's concerned gaze. Still no answer. Finally, she headed to the reception building.

Maybe David hadn't realised she hadn't taken her card with her. Maybe they were asleep inside the room. Maybe he'd taken them somewhere and left a note? She'd get another key card and check the suite.

As she crossed the garden to the covered walk that led to reception, Gina glanced across to the car park. The hair stood up on her arms as she realised their rental car was gone.

*Dio*, where are they? Surely he hadn't left for Darwin already. No that was ridiculous. She ran the last few steps and pushed the reception door open. Heather, the pretty Aboriginal girl was there and she looked at Gina curiously as she caught her breath.

'Hello, are you all right?'

'I've left my card in the room, and my husband is not around. You haven't seen him, perhaps, have you?' Then she shook her head, realising the girl wouldn't know what David looked like. 'No matter.' She grabbed the card with a muttered 'thank you' and whirled on her heel and hurried out.

The rental car still wasn't there as she crossed the lawn back to their building, but the noise of the television reached her as she pushed the door open.

Thank God.

'David?'

The living room was empty, and the blinds were drawn, the light from the television flickering in the dim room. Picking up the remote, she switched it off before hurrying down the hall to the children's bedroom.

Empty. And the same with the master suite.

A chill crawled down her spine. David's phone was charging on the table next to the bed. He never went anywhere without it. The whole apartment was cold. Gina rubbed her arms as she walked over to the control panel and switched the air conditioning off. Only silence filled her ears as she crossed the living area to the kitchen.

The mess in the kitchen showed they had been there, and she reached for the sponge, automatically wiping up some milk that had been spilt on the sink. When it was clean, she braced her arms on the cold stone benchtop, trying to calm herself as the baby kicked.

There was no point getting in a state. It wasn't good for the baby. She had to stay calm and work out what to do.

As she stood there, there was a noise at the front door and Gina's shoulders sagged with relief as she hurried up the hall. She paused; there was a strange scratching noise coming from the base of the front door. She listened . . . there it was again. It was as though someone was rubbing a rough piece of sandpaper on the timber. She walked over slowly and stood by the door and the strange sound continued. Stepping back, she crossed her arms protectively against her stomach as goose bumps ran down her arms.

Silence. And then another louder scratch. The door handle turned slowly, and Gina held her breath as the door opened.

'Oink, oink. I'm a baby pig.' Andrew crawled around the door on all fours. 'Mummy, I can scratch in the mud.'

'And me too.' Binny crawled in behind him.

The door opened fully, and David stepped over the two children, tossing the car keys onto the low wooden cupboard in the entry foyer.

Relief and anger bubbled up into her throat. The serenity of the massage and facial had long since fled. 'Where have you been? I thought you had to be in Darwin by five?'

He met her gaze, but Andrew stood and pushed between them. 'Mummy! We saw pigs, and crocodiles and ducks and funny birds.' He ran to the television and plonked himself on the floor, followed closely by his sister. 'Now can we watch Diego?'

She turned away from David before he could answer and picked up the remote from the kitchen bench. She switched on the television and turned to stare out the window. The afternoon sun was glinting on the pool and children were crying and splashing in the pool, but she could hear no sound.

David locked the door, walked across to the kitchen and stood behind her. 'A whole nature walk, and now nothing is as good as Diego.' He put his hands on her shoulders and dropped a quick kiss on the side of her neck. 'Mm. You smell good. How was your afternoon?

She turned slowly, and he dropped his hands and stepped back with a frown as her voice tightened.

'I thought you'd all been taken away. Taken by that man who threatened you.' Her voice was low, but the words sprayed from her tight lips like bullets. David reached for her again.

'No, don't touch me.' Gina turned back to the window, folding her arms across her chest. 'Just leave us. Go to your precious meeting. You're going to be late as it is.'

David put his hand on her shoulder and turned her around to face him, his touch gentle on her tense shoulder. 'No, I won't. I rang back and postponed the meeting. It can wait. I'll leave after lunch tomorrow.'

Gina blinked as unwanted tears filled her eyes.

David frowned as he looked at her. 'I'm sorry, darling. I thought we'd get back before you, but the kids were fascinated by the wild pigs and the crocodiles we could see from the boardwalk.'

Gina shuddered with revulsion. 'Will that matter, not going today?'

'No. I'll work around it.' He put his arms around her waist and pulled her close. 'I'm really sorry.'

Finally, she let her head rest on his shoulder.

'I didn't even think about you being worried. I thought you'd be enjoying being pampered.'

'I was.' She sniffed. 'Until I came back and couldn't find you at the pool. And your phone was here. You never leave your phone.' Another sniff and Gina lifted her hand and wiped her eyes. 'And then I saw that the car was gone. I was frightened.'

David rested his chin on the top of her head. 'My phone was flat. And I should have left a note before we drove down to the river.'

'That wouldn't have done any good. I didn't take my card to get back in.' This time she allowed a tremulous smile to tip her lips as she looked up at him. 'I had to go to reception and get another door card. It was just thinking about what that man said to you. I couldn't get it out of my head and I overreacted.'

David held her close and Gina's breathing eased as the warmth of his body soothed her.

'You do smell nice.'

David smiled as he held her gaze, before dropping his head and capturing her lips in a swift kiss. 'I left my bags in the car.' She glanced across at the children, now engrossed in the television show. 'I'll come with you. I left my Kindle in the glove box. Outside a storm was building in the north and the clouds that had threatened all day were closing in quickly. David held her hand as he grabbed at his cap and pushed it down hard as a gust of wind lifted the brim. They stood back and let a small red car go past before they crossed the road to the car and

David opened the boot.

'Daddy!' Gina turned as Binny's voice reached them. She was running from the building and heading for the road.

'Binny, stop,' Gina yelled.

'I wanna see the pigs some more.' The little girl stopped and teetered on the edge of the kerb.

'I'll get her.' David ran across and picked her up. There were no other cars apart from the one that had just passed them, but Gina's legs were shaking.

'No more pigs today,' David said.

Gina put her shaking hand to her mouth. She knew she was overreacting; there'd been no danger.

'No pigs?' Binny put her little hands on his face and turned his head to face her.

David shook his head. 'No pigs. 'Piggyback then.'

Gina swung around as a woman's voice called out: 'David Johnson. I thought it was you!'

***

Ellie had spent most of the day at the hangar, but no flights had been booked. Saturday was usually quiet as it was more often than not the changeover day for tourists. Kane hadn't been rostered on, but she couldn't help herself pulling up the electronic roster to see when they were next on together. Despite her expectations, she'd enjoyed the drive down to Jim Jim with him yesterday.

Pulling into the car park, she'd done a double take when the pregnant lady and the man in the baseball cap had stepped back and waited for her to drive past. It looked like David Johnson, but the cap and sunglasses hid his face, and she'd only got a side-on view.

She'd just got out of the car and put the keys in her pocket when a child's voice called out, 'Daddy!' She watched as the little girl sped towards the road, but the man ran across and intercepted her before she could step onto the bitumen.

It was David. He swung the little girl onto his back and crossed back to the woman who was waiting at the car. 'David Johnson. I thought it was you!'

He turned slowly, holding the little girl protectively against his chest. He frowned for a moment and then his face cleared.

'Ellie? Ellie Porter?'

'Long time no see. It's ages since I last saw you.'

He looked around the car park before he held out his hand. Ellie leaned in and kissed his cheek as the little girl took David's hat from his head and turned it around so that the brim was over the back of his neck

'I thought you'd be in Darwin. Aren't you an important politician now? Chief Minister, no less?'

'I'm just here for the weekend.' Again David scanned the car park before twisting his hat around. 'But I'm trying to have a family break. Don't tell anyone I'm here. You know, privacy and all that.'

Ellie laughed. 'Oh, David, I'm sure it's all around the lodge already. If you checked in, everyone will know.'

David dropped her hand and pulled at the collar of his polo shirt. 'This is my wife, Gina. We only came outside to get a couple of things and this naughty little madam followed us. Come on over to the apartment with us and we can catch up inside. Andrew, our little boy's over there.'

His wife was a beautiful woman with flawless, olive skin and almond-shaped green eyes. She glanced nervously at David before she greeted Ellie. David tipped his head back to the cute little girl who had her arms wound tightly around his neck. 'This is Binny, short for Belinda.' Hitching the little girl up his back with a roll of his shoulders, he said, 'Binny, say hello to Ellie. She's an old friend of your uncle Chad.' The little girl observed Ellie shyly as they all crossed the lawn to the building. Back before Dad died and they left the farm, Ellie had briefly gone out with David's youngest brother. They'd hung out at the Johnson house in Jabiru in the summer holidays until Dad found out that Mr Johnson was something important at the Ranger uranium mine. After that he'd said he preferred that she didn't go to their house. David was a good ten years older than Chad and she'd only met him a few times that summer when he'd come home for Chad's birthday. She'd forgotten all about him until years later when she read he'd been elected to parliament. She'd watched his meteoric rise to Chief Minister while he was still in his thirties and had followed his career with interest.

'Where's Chad these days?' Ellie asked.

'New York. Met a girl at uni and followed her back home to the States.' David put the little girl down and she ran through the open door. He stood back and waited for the two women to step inside before him.

Ellie whistled quietly as she took in the decor. It was one of the most expensive suites at Makowa. 'Wow. This is a bit different to my staff apartment.'

Gina turned to her and smiled. 'It is very nice. We're lucky to have the chance to stay here.' Her voice was lightly accented. A memory niggled at Ellie. Something she'd read about David marrying someone famous while he was overseas. Gina certainly had movie-star looks.

David looked from one to the other as if weighing something up. Ellie frowned, uncomfortable. 'Look, I won't take up any more of your time. I've got to drop some keys back to the office.' She nodded at David's wife. 'Nice to meet you, Gina. Have a nice break. And say hello to Chad next time you speak to him.' She turned to go.

'Ellie, no. Wait.' A significant look passed between the couple, and Ellie paused in the doorway.

'Can I beg a favour?'

'Sure,' she said slowly. 'What can I do for you?'

'I have to go back to the city for the week, and I was wondering if you could keep an eye out for Gina and the kids while they're here.' David had lifted the sunglasses, but his gaze was hooded. 'Just maybe drop in occasionally.'

Ellie nodded. 'Of course. How about a coffee one morning? Or even lunch?' She turned to Gina with a smile. If she found it strange that the Chief Minister of the Northern Territory was leaving his heavily pregnant wife here alone with two small kids, she certainly wasn't going to say anything. It was none of her business.

'I'll look forward to it. Call me when you're free.' Gina smiled and rolled her eyes as the little girl yelled from the room at the end of the hall. 'I'll really look forward to it.' She gave Ellie her number and then lifted her hand in a wave as she went to attend to the children.

'Bye.' Ellie smiled at David and turned to leave but before she could take a step, his hand gently gripped her arm.

'Ellie?'

'Yes.' She frowned as he slowly let her go.

His smile did not quite reach his eyes. 'Please don't mention to anyone you saw me here. Or that Gina and the kids are my family.'

# Chapter 9

*Sunday*
*Black Jungle Springs*

On Sunday morning Ellie rose early. She briefly considered driving out to the farm – Kane had said his mother wouldn't mind – but then remembered that she'd promised Heather she'd come out to Black Jungle Springs for the day. She still hadn't caught up with Bill Jarragah and she wanted to ask him if he'd heard anything about Panos Sordina and the development along the river.

She slowed her speed as the car crossed the last causeway across Stove Creek on the winding Old Jim Jim road. The causeway was almost dry – just a small flow of shallow water across the lowest point in the middle – but Ellie still glanced nervously to each side as the tyres sent a sheet of water arcing high in the midmorning sun. But there were no crocodiles basking in the warm winter sun this morning. When she reached the other side, a couple of Aboriginal children – probably Heather's cousins – ran along the side of the car smiling at her and waving. She didn't recognise them, and a pang of regret shot through her as she waved back. Between their rosters, she and Heather rarely had time off at the same time, and she didn't get out here very often anymore.

After turning off the sandy road, Ellie parked beneath the old Darwin woolly butt tree next to the falling-down fence at the Jarragah house, smiling as she looked up at the brilliant orange flowers. On one of her visits with her Dad, Bill had stood beneath the tree and shown her the buds. 'The orange flowers tell us it's time to start lighting fires, to clean up the country so we don't have intense wildfires late in the dry season.' Heather had rolled her eyes; she'd been more interested in the Dolly magazines that Ellie had in her bag than hearing about boring old trees.

'Ellie!' Heather pushed open the screen door and ran lightly down the steps to the car as she climbed out and stretched. 'It's so good to see you here, away from work. Just like old times.'

Ellie grinned at her. 'It's only two nights since we had a drink together.'

'Yeah, but you rushed off early and took Fly Boy away before I could get to know him.' Heather tipped her head to the side and examined Ellie as she reached into the car for her bag. 'How did the drive to Jim Jim go on Friday? Did you learn any more about him? I'm not stepping on your territory there if I make a move on him tonight, am I?

Ellie laughed at the barrage of questions and ignored the strange feeling that ran through her. 'Of course not. You know my policy: absolutely no sex with staff. I have to work closely with him, so he's all yours.'

'Did you check out the muscles in his arms?' Heather shook her fingers in front of her face. 'I wonder how big his – '

'Heather! You sound like we're in high school again.'

'I was only going to say I'd like to get a look at his six pack.'

'You were not. I know you too well. But just for the record, his abs are as good as the rest of him. When I first met him, he wasn't wearing a shirt.'

'Oh, lucky you. All I get to see is Terry in his work shirt and a tribe of kids in the crèche!'

Ellie walked around and opened the boot. 'I bought a cake from the kitchens.'

'Yum. I'll put the jug on.' Heather took the cake from her, and Ellie kept one eye out for snakes as they walked through the long grass to the house.

The screen door opened with a creak as Heather pushed it open, but the house was quiet and Ellie looked around. 'Where's your dad? Up in Darwin?'

'No. Still in bed.'

Ellie frowned. 'He's not crook, is he? I haven't seen him since I came back.'

'No, he had a late night. He's got a lot on his mind at the moment. Between you and me I've been a bit worried about him.' Heather dropped her voice to a whisper as footsteps padded along the dark hallway to the back of the old house. 'See what you reckon.'

Bill appeared in the kitchen doorway and Ellie frowned as he stretched one arm into the air and held onto his blue striped pyjama pants with the other. He'd lost a lot of weight in the month since Ellie had seen him and his chest was sunken. His face unshaven, with his hair unkempt, he looked every year of his sixty-plus age.

'Ellie. You're a nice surprise to wake up to.' Bill hitched his pants up with an apologetic smile. 'Sorry, I'll go and get dressed before we have a cuppa.'

'Hey, Bill.' She walked over and kissed his leathery old cheek, relieved when no smell of alcohol greeted her. For a brief moment, she'd wondered if he had gone back to old habits. She caught Heather's eye as he walked back down the hall.

'See.' Heather mouthed at her and Ellie nodded. He looked dreadful.

When the bathroom door closed, Ellie walked over to the sink where Heather was filling the kettle. 'Is he sick? Has he seen the doctor?'

Heather shook her head. 'No, he's got something on his mind and he won't talk about it. Lots of mysterious phone calls at all hours, and he leaves the room, so I can't overhear. He's been to Darwin about five times in the last two weeks. And every time he comes back he looks more worried than the last time.'

'I'm not surprised that he's so tired.' It was a good five-hour return trip from Black Jungle Springs to Darwin. 'I wonder what's going on.'

'I can't get it out of him.' Heather shrugged. 'But you know the way he is. When he's good and ready, he'll share. Now get the knife and cut me a huge piece of that carrot cake.'

The kettle boiled, and they sat down at the table together.

Heather reminded her about the band playing in the bar. 'Make sure you get dressed up tonight, Els. We don't get much chance to. And if you do, I can get dolled up and not look too obvious. Don't want to scare Fly Boy away.' Heather wiped her mouth and let out a gentle burp. 'Oops, pardon me.'

'That'll pull him in.' Ellie nudged her friend with her elbow. 'Treat him gently. If he comes that is. I get the impression Kane's not very interested in socialising.'

Heather burst out laughing. 'Aw, come on, Els, I'm not that bad.'

'You are too, Heath! You can be downright scary, especially when you're all dressed up. And when you put on that Mae West voice – the blokes have no hope.'

'I can't wait to get to know him better.' Heather waggled her eyebrows and giggled.

By the time Bill reappeared, shaved and dressed, they had demolished half the cake. He poured a tea from the huge teapot that Heather had placed in the middle of the table, into one of the enamel cups she had laid out. 'So what brings you to Black Jungle Springs, Ellie?'

'I actually wanted to catch up with you.' Ellie looked across at Heather apologetically. 'And you too, of course, Heather.'

'I thought the crocs in Stove Creek must have kept you away. They've been thick as flies this season. Bit of a worry.' Bill teased her as much as the other guys did.

'Yeah, we saw a monster one at Sandy Billabong on Friday.' She sipped her tea and looked at him. 'I needed to ask you something, Bill'

'What's up?' Bill blew on the tea before he drank it.

'I flew over our old place the other day and the back paddock was full of machinery. The ground's been dug up.'

The hot tea spilled onto Bill's hand as his cup tipped over. He swore, then got up and crossed to the sink to run cold water over his hand. He stood with his back to them. 'Dug up?'

'Are you okay, Dad?' Heather pushed her chair back but he waved her to sit down.

'Yeah, I'm okay. Cut me a piece of that cake, will ya.'

Ellie narrowed her eyes as Bill sat back down. He avoided her gaze as he rubbed his hands together nervously.

'So, do you know anything about it?' she persisted.

'No. I mean, yes.' Bill picked up his cup again, but his eyes were darting around the room. 'Yeah, I think they're getting ready to plant some new trees.'

'Who?'

'The owners, I guess.' Bill's bare foot was jiggling up and down on the old worn lino.

Ellie frowned. 'I think you're wrong. Panos Sordina told me he was putting in a new dam, but what I saw from the air doesn't look like a dam. Do you know anything about coal seam gas mining?'

Finally Bill raised his head and looked Ellie squarely in the eye. 'You don't live there anymore, so what are you so worried about?'

'I'm worried about what I read about in the paper, how close the exploration is to the park and the South Alligator river. Everything Mum's been saying.'

'What exploration? What's she been talking about?'

'You know . . . the fracking.'

Bill held her gaze. 'What paper was that in?'

'There was a report in the *Darwin Sun*. I read it online. It said that Sordina had met with your council. It was about coal seam gas exploration.'

'Just stay away from it, Ellie.'

'What are you saying?' Ellie glanced across at Heather as she waited for Bill to answer but she was staring at her father, her brow creased in a frown.

'I ain't saying nothing.' Bill lowered his voice. 'Just

forget about it and stay away from the place. Okay?'

'But Bill, you always taught us –'

'Fuckin' drop it, Ellie. All right?' He stood, and his chair fell to the floor with a crash. He picked it up and shoved it under the table.

'I have to go out,' he muttered. 'Nice to see you.'

Ellie and Heather stared at each other as he strode through the door without a backward glance. Soon they heard the rattling of the diesel motor in his old land cruiser, and he drove away.

***

Kane hadn't intended going to the bar that night, but the sound of the music drifting through the lodge eventually enticed him from his room. A couple of drinks and some good music would do him good, break the melancholy mood he'd been in since visiting his mother. He also hoped that Ellie might be there; he wanted to let her know how much he'd enjoyed their trip down to the waterfall.

He stepped into the shower and rubbed his aching neck; the muscles were tight beneath his fingers. He'd spent all day thinking about how to get his mother back to Darwin. He'd tried to call Panos a couple of times, but his stepfather hadn't answered, and Kane wasn't going to leave a message. Probably still at the bloody horse races. He couldn't understand how his mother had ever fallen for the guy.

Whatever Panos was doing, Kane was determined to get her back to Darwin where she was close to doctors and facilities. He was secure financially – the active service bonuses had let him build up a healthy investment portfolio – and it wouldn't hurt to buy an apartment and set Mum up in the city.

He pulled on a fresh pair of denims and a button–up black cotton shirt and headed for the bar. The grounds were well-lit and he was surprised by the number of people making their way to the entertainment area. Family groups dotted the lawn on picnic rugs and the tables inside were almost full.

'Kane!'

He turned as he heard his name called. Heather was waving from a table at the back of the room, well away from the low stage where the band had just finished a set. Steve, the barman, was sitting opposite her and the rest of the table was empty.

'Hey, we thought you weren't coming.' Heather leaned forward, and Kane got a flash of dark skin and generous breasts pushing out from a very low-cut shirt.

He looked at Steve. 'Night off?'

'Yeah, I was lucky. Usually have to work the nights the bands are on, but the roster was done, and I was due for a Sunday off.' Steve's eyes were fixed on Heather's cleavage and Kane stifled a smirk.

Be less obvious and you might get lucky, man.

He slid along the wooden bench beside Heather.

'How was your trip down to Jim Jim the other day?' Her arm pressed against his shoulder as she leaned into him.

'Amazing place. I would have liked to swim but Ellie warned me about the crocs there.'

Heather waved a dismissive hand and this time her leg

brushed against his. 'Ellie worries too much. I'll take you down there on your next day off and we can swim. It's safe.'

'Why's Ellie so scared of them? Did she have a scare?'

'Yeah, when she was a kid. It freaked her out for ages.'

Heather ran the tip of her tongue along her lips as she stared at him.

'She said she grew up on a mango farm on the way to Darwin.'

'Yeah.' Heather didn't elaborate, and Kane turned to Steve. 'Can I get you another beer, mate?'

'I'm right, thanks. The barman will keep an eye on us.' Steve kept his eyes on Heather as he answered.

'Hey, there's Ellie, too.' Heather waved towards the wide archway beside the bar. 'Els, over here.'

Ellie stood in the doorway, her gaze scanning the crowd. The light behind her made her light-coloured dress a little transparent, and she tugged nervously at the hem. She was nowhere near as confident as she would have people believe. She spotted them and made her way across the packed room. Kane couldn't take his eyes off her. Her hair was loose and curled over her shoulders, and her lips were shiny with a soft pink lip gloss. She'd done something with eye shadow, and her blue eyes looked huge.

When she reached the table, a waft of floral perfume preceded her as she slid across the seat beside him. 'You look gorgeous, Ellie.' Heather readjusted the neck of her top and flashed Kane a grin.

'You do.'

She lifted her eyes to his. 'Thanks. It's nice to get dressed up sometimes.'

The band launched into a cover of 'Eagle Rock' and the barman arrived with two jugs of beer and a dozen glasses tucked precariously in a tower under his elbow. By then, more staff had squeezed onto each side of the table. Kane was jammed between Ellie and Heather.

Conversation was difficult without yelling so he sat back and sipped his beer, content to watch the group at the table. They were obviously a close-knit bunch; there was a lot of good-natured teasing and they were all comfortable with each other. It reminded him of the mess on base. People comfortable in their own skin, private but knowing their mates well enough to trust. He pushed away the memory; the last thing he wanted was another of those damned flashback, panic things – whatever the psychiatrist and called them.

Dissociative episode. That's what the shrink had said. Substance abuse and sexual problems went hand in hand with it he'd been told. Well, he wasn't doing drugs and he hadn't had sex since the –

Since it had happened. Maybe it was time to make sure everything still worked. Prove there was nothing wrong with him. To himself as much as the clinical psychologist. The way Heather was trying to catch his eye and leaning into him, he knew he'd have no trouble scoring there. But his eyes were drawn to Ellie. Kane put his glass on the table and turned half sideways to face her. She was staring at the band, but he had a feeling her thoughts were a long way away. He leaned forward and touched her arm lightly. 'You okay?'

Ellie blinked and looked at him, and her blue eyes were full of confusion. 'Sorry, what did you say?'

'Are you okay?'

She nodded as the band launched into the chorus and the crowd on the makeshift dance floor cheered and sang along. The band was semi-decent and the pressure of Ellie's leg against his was pleasant, but it was impossible to talk, and Kane itched to get out of there. He'd avoided Heather for the past five minutes; the more beer she drank, the louder and more obvious she was becoming. Every time he looked to her side, her gaze was fixed on him. But as pretty and friendly as she was, there was no answering spark from him. Finally, the band took a break, and Ellie turned to him.

'Are you enjoying the music?'

'They're good but I think my eardrums are going to shatter.' As he spoke, Terry and the two girls on the other side of Ellie stood and headed for the bar.

'Want to make a break with me before we get jammed in again?'

'Good thinking.' Ellie grabbed her beer and followed Kane as he slid along the bench.

'Be back soon. Taking a break from the noise,' she called to Heather. Kane led her to the cleared grassy spot on the river side of the bar, his hip jarring as he strode across the concrete floor.

'God, that's better.' Ellie fanned herself with her hand. 'I'm not used to these nights.' Her cheeks were flushed, and Kane watched as she lifted her glass and drained the beer. 'That's enough for me. Two beers and my head spins.'

'Want to have a dance when the band comes back on? Work it off? I'd hate to see you with the head spins. Not a good look for a pilot.'

She paused for a moment, staring over towards where

Heather was holding court. Then turned back to him. 'Why not? One dance won't hurt. I can't remember the last time I had a dance.'

'What's going on?' He nodded over to the table. Heather was now watching them.

'Make sure you have a dance with Heather, too.' Guilt crossed her face and he finally understood.

'I'll see how the hip holds up.'

A few minutes later, the band struck up an ACDC song. Kane grabbed Ellie's hand and pulled her onto the dance floor. All thoughts of Heather, his mother and flashbacks disappeared as they gyrated, twisted and turned to the thumping music. His hip held up and he ignored the occasional twinge. Kane smiled as she reached for his hand and twirled herself beneath his arm. He didn't let it go when she twirled back around.

The music slowed and the band launched into a ballad. Kane held out his hands. 'A real dance?'

Her lips spread in a slow grin as she pointed to her feet. 'You'll be sorry. I might be able to use these feet to fly a helicopter, but I'm pretty useless on the dance floor.'

'I'm not real good either. I have a hip that occasionally gives up the ghost.' Kane looked down at her. 'But you look pretty good to me.'

Her cheeks flushed even pinker as she stepped in front of him and he took one of her hands in his, pulling her close, before resting his other hand above her waist. She barely reached his shoulder. Kane rested his chin gently on the top of her head and caught another whiff of that floral perfume. Her silky dress was soft and slippery, and a jolt of pleasure shafted through him.

Maybe it was time to start living again. 'What happened to your hip?'

He shrugged. 'Just a bit of an accident last year.' He waited for the stress to hit, or the heavy sadness, but all he felt was the soft, pliant woman in his arms.

'I love this song.' Ellie hummed along with 'Smoke Gets in Your Eyes' and the murmur of her voice sent a vibration through his chest. Kane let himself relax even more but disappointment replaced his contentment when Ellie pulled her head back.

Maybe it was a bit too romantic for her? Christ, he almost didn't recognise himself, but she smiled and put her hands on his shoulders and they rocked in time to the music. Pleasure flooded through him as her soft curves pressed against his chest. The song continued, and Kane closed his eyes, giving into the sensations that were coursing through him. He raised one hand to her neck and threaded his fingers through her soft hair. He opened his eyes, knowing he should have pulled away and she should have stepped back, but neither of them moved when their eyes met and held.

'Want to go for a walk on the boardwalk?' He held her gaze and she smiled.

'Sounds good.' Her voice was soft and husky. Seconds later, Kane had pulled her from the dance floor and led her towards the door.

Ellie was looking ahead and didn't see the look of pure venom that Heather threw her way as they stepped past the bar. Kane shrugged it off and followed Ellie onto the path that led down to the river.

They didn't speak until they reached the metal

boardwalk that skirted along the edge of the water. It was softly lit, and deserted; the only sounds the muted thump of the music and the occasional splash in the river.

Until the accident, Kane had always taken his pleasure when he'd wanted to. He realised he'd missed the smooth skin, the sweet scents and the soft lips. It had been way too long, and the desire that was coursing through him now had nothing to do with making sure everything still worked. It had more to do with this beautiful woman who was leaning back against the metal fence and watching him with a wary expression.

But when he bent his head down, Ellie stood on her toes and met him halfway. He'd intended to be gentle but as soon as their lips met, need ignited, and it was hot and hungry. Kane groaned against her mouth as Ellie slipped her hands beneath his shirt and ran her fingers down his back. She tasted like beer, but there was sweetness too as the soft moans escaped her lips. He ran his tongue over her bottom lip and her mouth opened wider beneath his.

But despite how much he wanted her, he was unsure of her intent. Maybe it was the beers talking. He pulled back and stared at her, at pale blue eyes shining in the moonlight.

Her lips tilted in a trembling smile. 'Problem?'

'Just checking we're on the same page.'

\*\*\*

Kane's lips had taken Ellie to a place she hadn't expected. The feelings racing through her were like the rush when she dipped her bird down in a low swoop. All she knew was that she had a need that had to be taken care of, and soon. Kane's muscles were hard beneath her fingers. She slid her hands down to his waist, struggling to get across what she was feeling.

*Am I crazy? I swore I'd never do this.*

She pushed Heather out of her mind. It had just been silly girl talk; she wasn't stepping on anyone's territory here. Hell, Heather should be pleased that she had finally let her defences down and given in to the moment.

And what a moment.

Her rock solid 'no colleague' policy had dissipated like the low evening mist hovering over the river beside them.

'Oh yes, we're on the same page.'

His mouth claimed hers again and their ragged breathing blended in with the sounds of the night. Finally, Ellie lifted her head and buried her face against his chest, barely able to breathe let alone think . . . or speak. If they didn't get back to one of their rooms soon, she wouldn't be responsible for what happened out here.

'How about we go back to my place?' he murmured, and a pleasurable shiver skittered down her back and settled between her thighs.

The two hundred metre walk back through the lodge grounds seemed to take forever. Kane held her hand tightly and pulled her along, and Ellie hurried to keep up, unused to the high heels she was wearing. He was as nervous as she was, fumbling for his key, dropping it twice before he got in the lock. But then the door opened suddenly, and she fell into the room, laughing as Kane grabbed her and pushed her up against the wall. He lifted her dress from the bottom and pulled it over her head, tossing it aside. A shaft of pure feminine gratitude filled her as he took in her lacy white underwear.

'Much nicer than the khaki work gear.' His mouth settled on the spot between her neck and her shoulder. Ellie closed her eyes, giving into the heat that had pooled between her thighs. She arched into him and sighed as his hands lowered and cupped her bottom. Lifting her legs, she wrapped them around his hips and he held her against the wall, letting the pleasure build as his hardness pressed against her.

'You've got too many clothes on,' Ellie murmured against the lips that had once again reclaimed hers. Kane lowered his head and unbuttoned his shirt with one hand, still holding her up with the other, and the strength of his biceps flexing beneath her fingers sent another bolt of desire heading south. Once again she remembered Heather, but this time it was barely a passing thought. Kane had breached her defences. In the cold light of day, she might castigate herself for what had happened, but for tonight, she was going to make the most it.

Thirst woke Ellie in the middle of the night. Her mouth was dry and she rolled over, only half awake. She froze and drew a breath when she realised where she was. Kane lay beside her, on his back, his arms stretched out above his head. His breathing was deep and even, and she allowed herself to look at him. In sleep, his face was soft and less . . . less angry. The wariness that he wore as a protective shell was gone. In the dim light, his long lashes feathered his cheeks and his lips were soft and slightly parted. The shadows beneath angular cheekbones were accentuated by the darkness of his stubble. The same stubble that had left her lips – and other places – tender after a couple of very thorough sessions of lovemaking.

Lovemaking?

A cold feeling began in her stomach and worked its way up into her chest. What the hell had she done? Her emotional self-sufficiency had been compromised and she'd broken her cardinal rule of not getting involved with someone at work. One tiny crack in her firm resolve, and here she was in bed with her fellow pilot – or engineer, whatever he wanted to say he was. Someone she was going to have to work closely with over the upcoming season . . . or for as long as he stayed.

And someone whom her best friend had made no secret of her interest in. How would she face Heather after this?

Ellie stifled a groan as she slowly swung her legs over the bed. In the dark, she tiptoed around finding her clothes, shoes and bag. She pulled her dress over her head. She held her shoes in one hand and shoved her lacy underwear into her bag as she made for the door, trying not to make a sound. Closing the door gently behind her, she padded barefoot down the timber verandah to her own room. The night was still, broken only by the occasional splash from the river and the soft breathy call of a tawny frogmouth.

Putting her shoes down outside, Ellie leaned on the door of her apartment, digging into the bag for her key. She had to fight for her balance as the door opened beneath her weight and she fell into her room with a small squeal.

Regaining her balance, she straightened and turned quickly, her heart thudding as a strange flickering illuminated the ceiling and the walls of the living room. She held her hand against her chest as her eyes became accustomed to the half-light.

Pictures of Dru, Emma and Mum smiled out at her as

the screensaver on her laptop rolled through the recent photos she'd taken over in the Daintree. Her breath rasped in her throat and her whole body tensed. She hadn't unpacked her computer since she'd been home. So why was it plugged in and open on the small bench between the kitchenette and the living room? Her pulse raced as she stood there, looking around. The door to her bedroom was slightly ajar and she was sure she'd left it wide open when she'd left for the bar. Someone had been in her room, and for all she knew they were still in there.

For a moment, she considered running back out onto the verandah and calling for Kane.

No. Holding her hands together to stop them shaking, Ellie took a deep breath and pressed herself against the wall, inching slowly towards her bedroom. When she reached the door, she paused and listened. There was no sound. Her heart seemed to be stuck in her throat as she leaned forward and pushed the door open, ready to take flight if she had to.

The bedroom was empty. And so was the small en-suite bathroom next to it. Her eyes scanned the room; everything seemed to be in place, not that she had anything valuable apart from her laptop. She returned to the kitchen and hit the space bar. The screen saver closed, and the screen switched to her email program. What the hell?

Maybe someone had been after her car keys, trying to steal her car. That was why the lodge vehicles were always locked in the compound at night. But no, the keys were where she'd left them. And why would they have turned the laptop on? And why would they have been looking at her emails?

She ran her shaking hands through her hair and then sat on the bed until the trembling subsided.

As soon as she was calm, she locked the door and headed for the bathroom. She needed a shower.

To dispel the fragrance of Kane's aftershave that lingered on her skin. To remove every trace of the stupid mistake she'd made.

As she stood beneath the water, her fear disappeared, and self-recrimination flooded in.

# Chapter 10

*Monday*
*Makowa Lodge*

Ellie was in the hangar office, trying to concentrate on the computer screen in front of her. Kane hadn't shown up yet and she wasn't sure yet what she'd say to him when he did. She hadn't had much experience lately with the morning after scene. She'd never had much experience full stop – especially with a work colleague.

There'd been no sign of him as she rushed from her apartment to let Jock know about the break-in. She'd also hoped to be able to sort out the issue of being the only pilot in the lodge. But Jock was in a meeting, so Jan had promised he would call as soon as he was free.

A groan escaped her lips as she tried to focus on the flight schedule. Bookings for scenic flights were coming in faster than she could schedule them. But at least the frustrating work situation had replaced the self-recrimination that had dogged her since she had left Kane's bed. It had even overtaken the nerves stirred up by her apartment being broken into. Nothing appeared to have been taken, and the only thing that had been touched was her laptop. She took a deep breath and relaxed her shoulders.

Everything combined to add to her cranky mood.

She'd passed Heather on the way to the office, and her friend had cut her dead before she'd had a chance to talk to her. Heather could be a bit precious sometimes, but Ellie certainly wasn't going to let one stupid mistake ruin their friendship.

Okay, so Heather's suggestion that she get dressed up had backfired. And she'd obviously made a mistake going off with Kane and having sex with him. But they were grown up and this wasn't a silly teenage game. Nevertheless, a frisson of guilt ran through her.

There was no point being angry with Kane either. She'd been a willing participant. It was her own rules she'd broken.

Now they had to work together, and she'd do her best to pretend it had never happened. He could do his job, and she'd do hers. Awkward but she'd get over it.

If Kane had half the regret as she did about last night, he wouldn't want to spend any more time than necessary in her company either. And the more she thought about it his connection to Panos, the more it bothered her. Bill's reaction to her questions and his unwillingness to talk yesterday had her antennae quivering. Something was going on and she was going to find out what it was. He hadn't showed up in the bar last night and she guessed he was going to avoid her, which made her all the more certain.

With a sigh she clicked the mouse and printed off the latest bookings' spreadsheet. Flights were heavily booked from this afternoon and they were back-to-back every morning for the rest of the week. She picked up the phone and called the office. 'Jan? Is Jock free yet? I really need to talk to him.'

'Come on over and wait. He won't be much longer.' Jan must have picked up on her mood as her tone was placatory.

Ellie locked the door to the hangar and headed over to the office, keeping an eye out for Gina and the children as she walked past the playground. That was something else she mustn't forget. She'd promised David to keep an eye out for them.

Heather, Gina, Bill . . . and Kane. A trip to the farm, and bloody flights all week. Ellie pushed away her rising temper as she pushed open the door of the administration block.

Jock was waiting for her in the front office. Although they'd spoken on Thursday, she hadn't seen him since she'd come back from her break, and she let her temper go as she hugged him back when he enfolded her in a bear hug. He'd been her mentor since she had done work experience here at Makowa Lodge during her final year of school and it was he who'd encouraged her to do her pilot training. She'd always suspected he'd been instrumental in getting her the job here, and she'd worked hard to show her appreciation.

'We missed you, Ellie. Sorry I didn't catch up with you before the weekend.' His Scottish burr washed over her, and Ellie's nose twitched at the smell of sweet pipe tobacco in his work shirt. 'And thanks for going up at such short notice the day you got back too. Appreciate it, love.'

She followed him into his office and dropped into the chair opposite his desk. 'It's good to be back. But we have a bit of a problem.'

'I know.' He held his hand up. 'It looks like the tourist season has started earlier than usual. The place is full, and flights are steady for the rest of the week.'

'More than steady. Are you aware that Kane won't fly?'

'I wanted to talk to you about that.' Jock frowned. 'Look, it's a long story, but basically I'd signed him up before I realised how adamant he was about not flying. There was a misunderstanding about the terms of –'

Ellie held her hand up. 'I know. I found that out the

other day when we went up together.' She didn't share that Kane had been reluctant to even do that. She was beginning to understand him, and it would have felt disloyal. 'So what are you going to do?'

'He's a damn good mechanic and he's willing to do other stuff around the lodge so I've talked to the Heli-Tour guys over at Cooinda. They have an extra pilot on at the moment, so if you're happy to be on your own, we can subcontract some of the flights out to them. Until I can get another pilot over here.'

'Sounds fine to me.' Ellie was pleased with Jock's solution. 'Kane is a good engineer and seems very experienced. He's really thorough with the birds.'

'Not a cowboy, eh?'

'Not a cowboy.'

'Be better if he'd fly, though. Maybe you can talk him into it. He's got the quals. Ex-military. There's a story there.'

'Always is, Jock.' So her hunch had been right. Ellie stood to leave and then remembered the break-in. 'Have we had any problems with security lately?'

He looked at her and shook his head. 'No, why? It's been pretty quiet since the new cop started at Jabiru.'

'I think someone broke into my apartment last night.' Jock frowned. 'You think? What did they take?'

'Nothing. That's the strange thing.'

'Any damage? To the lock?'

Ellie shook her head. 'No, nothing.'

'Are you sure there was someone in there?'

'I'm sure.'

'I'll give the police station a call and tell the staff to keep an eye out.'

'Thanks. I'll see you later.' She turned to leave but Jock called her back.

'Ellie? Go easy on him.'

She flicked her boss a curious look as she left the office.

Kane was in the hangar checking over the helicopters when Ellie walked in after grabbing a coffee at the bistro on the way back. Despite her feelings, a flurry of butterflies flitted around in her stomach. He reached up to wipe a mark off one of the windscreens and warmth shimmied straight down to her lower belly as the muscles in his arms flexed.

'They're both right to go up.' He jerked his head towards the two helicopters. No 'good morning, nice to see you, great sex,' but she was okay with his business-like greeting. He'd set the tone and she was more than happy to follow along.

'I might be a great pilot but I'm not that good.'

'What do you mean?' He leaned against the doorway into the office, pulled a rag from his pocket and wiped his hands.

'Taking both birds up at once.' She stared at him. The black T-shirt defined the muscles on his chest but thank God, they were covered this morning. She kept her eyes away from his biceps as he threw the rag onto the workbench.

'Look about last night, I wanted to say –'

Ellie cut him off before he could finish. 'I know. It was a mistake. Don't worry it won't happen again. Not wise when we have to work together.'

He shrugged, and disappointment flooded her as she wondered what he'd been going to say. 'I think you'll have to change your mind about flying. Have you seen the bookings for this morning?'

'Yeah, I have.' He returned her gaze, but without a smile. 'But you know what? That's not my problem. I told you I was hired as an engineer. I won't be taking any flights up. Not today. Not this week. Not ever. Talk to the boss if you don't like it.'

'I've already talked to the boss.' Ellie leaned casually against a table, striving for nonchalance. She let the words hang in the air for a moment. You could have cut the tension in the air with a knife. They were two different people from the man and woman who had sought pleasure in each other's bodies a few hours ago. She lifted her chin a fraction higher and held the intense gaze that was being levelled at her. 'You are a qualified pilot.'

'Sure am.' Now there was a glimmer of a smile around his lips and she held back the angry words that rose to her lips. The bastard was enjoying this.

'Military.'

'Clever lady.'

'No, Jock told me.' She folded her arms. 'So what's the big deal then?' Ellie kept her voice level. 'Are you going to fly here at all?'

'That, babe, is not your problem.' He turned away slowly as the gate opened and a middle-aged couple walked in.

'Hey there.' The guy had an American accent and he held his hand out to Kane. 'Steve and Jodie Wallace. You're taking us up at ten-thirty.'

Kane shook the guy's hand and then gestured to Ellie with a cat-that-got-the-cream smile. 'Good morning Steve. I'm the engineer. Miss Ellie here is your pilot.'

Ellie damped down her frustration as the guy looked at her with a sceptical frown. Every few days she encountered tourists who wanted a male pilot, but she'd got used to it early on. Whoever said sexism was dead?

'Hey, Steve, Jodie. Come with me and we'll get the paper-work going. Lovely morning to go up.' Ellie forced the happy tone into her welcome chat as she led them towards the office, ignoring the wink that Kane gave her as she passed him.

Bastard. She ignored the temptation to poke her tongue out.

He really brought out the worst in her.

\*\*\*

Kane was pissed off. On top of his confusion over why Ellie had left his room with no explanation – and had so easily dismissed it as a one-night stand – guilt burned in his gut every time she took off with another load of tourists. Just how many bloody people wanted to see Kakadu from the air anyway?

It wasn't his problem that Jock had stuffed up and hired him. Kane had made it quite clear when he'd been interviewed on Skype that he wasn't flying these days. Whether Jock had misunderstood, or whether he'd thought Kane would change his mind when he saw the set up here at the lodge, didn't matter. His contract stated it in black and white: he was the engineer. The looks Ellie had directed his way shouldn't have bothered him, but they did.

She'd taken seven flights back to back from ten-thirty; she hadn't even stopped for a lunch break. He made sure the other chopper was ready and waiting as soon as she came down each time. And he looked after each group as they arrived and had the paperwork done so all she had to do was take them up. She smiled and chatted to the tourists but the occasional glances she flicked his way were hard to read. She was as prickly as all hell with him.

Kane shrugged; the last thing he wanted to do was hurt anyone, and Ellie's vulnerability had already tugged at him. It had been a big part of the attraction last night. Something hard within him had softened a little when she'd drifted off to sleep with her fingers curled in his. He'd lain there for a long time watching her sleep before he drifted off.

It was bad enough that he hadn't gone to her when he'd woken up alone in his bed. As the sun cleared the horizon, he'd jerked awake to the noise of machine gun fire. Before he could make a fool of himself, he pulled on his sweats and went for a long run.

He was too damaged to inflict himself on anybody. Ellie deserved better. Someone she could rely on; he was not going to connect with anybody. Maybe he'd been an absolute louse the way he'd treated her today, but she was right – sleeping together had not been a good move.

I'm not worth it.

# Chapter 11

*Monday afternoon*
*Makowa Lodge*

By the time Ellie touched down after her final flight, she was exhausted. Seven back-to-back tours on top of the late night and shock of the break-in had left her frazzled. Despite that, she decided to go back to the farm to have a look at what was happening at the back boundary. Flying over it again today had made her more determined to find out what was going on. The gash in the land was wider than it had been on Thursday; it almost reached the South Alligator River that bordered the national park. As she flew over on the last trip, a flash of silver had caught her eye. She dropped a little lower and peered down. There was a series of pipes sitting vertically in the ground very close to the river. Funniest looking dam she'd ever seen, no matter what Panos said.

'Thank you, that was fabulous. We might do another one tomorrow.' The last couple gave her a wave as they headed across the tarmac to the gate and Ellie secured the chopper.

There was no sign of Kane and she ignored the twinge of disappointment that hit her when she glanced over to the hangar. The roller door was down and bolted. He'd already turned the fuel pump off and everything else was in order.

Glancing at her watch, she dug in her pocket for her car keys. Rather than going back to her apartment and getting changed she decided to go straight to her car. She'd put the phone on hands free and make a few calls until the phone dropped out of service.

The wind was picking up and the clouds were scudding across a bright blue sky. Ellie loved this time of the year. She took a deep breath as she hurried across the car park; it was good to be away from the smell of avgas. The humidity was low and the air was tinged with the smell of the burning grass around the lodge. She grinned to herself; spot on. It was only yesterday she'd seen the flowering Darwin woolly butt down at Heather and Bill's telling the indigenous people it was time to 'clean the country'.

The highway was busy, and she had to wait for a few vans and RVs to pass before she turned north. Gina's number was programmed into her phone and she pressed the shortcut button and put it onto speaker before she picked up speed.

'Hi Gina, it's your nursemaid calling. I'm so sorry I've not called in to see you yet. How are you enjoying your stay?'

A soft laugh came down the line. 'It is fine, Ellie. I don't expect you to babysit me – no matter what David said.'

'How about I come over after dinner? I have a chore to run this afternoon, but I should be back about seven or seven thirty.'

Gina's laugh trilled over the phone. 'No, you really don't want to. It's like a zoo over here then. Bath and bedtime. It'll turn you off kids for life. I'm planning an early night with my Kindle. I'm fine really.'

'How about lunch on Wednesday? I've got a couple of hours off in the middle of the day.' Ellie had taken note of the schedule when she'd pulled it up earlier.

'Honestly, you don't have to look after me. We're fine.' Gina sounded a bit embarrassed.

'No, I'd love to get to know you. How about I meet you

at noon? It'll be a nice break from all the flights we've got on this week.'

'Okay, then. I'll look forward to it.'

'I'll call if anything changes. Bye.' She disconnected and frowned. One call down, one to go. Clearing the air with Heather was a priority, but not something she really wanted to do over the phone. But it couldn't wait – she'd be finished work by the time Ellie got back. And her friendship was too important to let things get worse.

She hit the fast call button and waited for Heather to answer as her car sped towards Jabiru.

*** 

'Bill!' Terry threw an apologetic glance Kane's way and leaned over close to the older Aboriginal guy at the back of an air boat. They were inside a shed in the enclosed compound at the back of the lodge, and the boat was propped up on a long timber ramp that led down to the river.

'What?' The old guy lifted his head and stared at them. A dead roll-your-own was wedged between his lips and he narrowed his eyes as he looked at Kane.

'This is Kane McLaren,' Terry said. 'The new mechanic over at the flight centre. Jock sent him over to help you.'

Kane held out his hand as Terry turned back to him. 'Kane, this is Bill Jarragah, my uncle.'

The old guy finally straightened and held a filthy hand out to Kane. 'Don't need help.' His voice was gruff.

Kane nodded and shook his hand, ignoring the smear of grease transferred to his fingers. The guy's hands were as filthy as the stained overalls he wore.

'I thought you were having trouble with the motor?' Terry shook his head as Bill turned back to the boat.

Bill grunted and ignored them.

'Jeez, Uncle Bill. What's put the bug up your arse this week? You've been a real cranky old bugger lately.' Terry rolled his eyes at Kane.'

'I've sorted it.' Bill lifted his head again and gestured to the workbench that ran along the side of the shed. 'So quit your jabbering and pass me a thirty mil spanner.' Whether it was the problem with the motor or another problem he'd sorted was not clear.

Kane looked around the workshop, barely holding back a shudder. Every surface was covered with tools, bits of pipe and assorted pieces of metal, and the floor was littered with junk. It was a workplace safety nightmare and he was surprised. The rest of the lodge – the parts he'd seen – were immaculate. Even the gardens around the staff car park down the back were well cared for. This workshop was an accident waiting to happen. If the hangar had looked anything like this, he would have turned on his heel and walked out last week, contract or no contract.

To his surprise, Terry crossed to the end of the bench, reached into the assortment of junk and pulled out the required spanner.

He shrugged as he handed it to Bill and looked guiltily at Kane. 'Bit of a mess in here. Jock's given us till the end of the month to get it back in order, but we've been flat out with the crocodile management and the monitoring for salvinia.'

'Salvinia?' Kane hadn't heard of it.

'It's a noxious floating weed. We help out the national parks blokes with spotting it when we're out in the air boats.'

Kane nodded and looked around. 'If you want a hand with the clean-up, I've got some spare time. When I'm not rostered on anywhere else that is.'

'We'd appreciate any help we can get, hey Bill?' Another grunt from under the boat.

Kane wandered over to a second boat that was propped up at the front of the shed. He bent down to look at the motor and Terry followed him over.

'Really interesting set-up, these boats. I haven't seen one of these up close before. Is that a V8 engine?'

'Yep, they have automotive engines in them. You'll have to come out for a spin one afternoon. They get a good speed up.' Terry lowered his voice. 'Don't be put off by the mess. Bill's a damn good worker, but he stretches himself too thin. He represents our people on a lot of committees. He's a good man.'

'Ah, ya fuckin' bastard.' The clang of a spanner hitting the wire frame around the motor brought an oath from the lips of Bill, and Kane raised his eyebrows as he grinned at Terry. 'Do you think we should offer to help again?'

'Worst he can do is crack the shits with us.'

They walked back over to the airboat. It was good to be in male company. He missed the bond he'd had with the guys in the military. The friendships that were forged there drew similar characters together. Black and white outlooks, aggressive personalities and a workplace where expletives like Bill's filled most conversations.

Bill accepted their help without comment and by the

time he let out a grunt of satisfaction, long afternoon shadows were filling the large open shed. 'Thanks. Appreciate it.'

'Coming for a beer, Bill?' Terry wiped his hands and then passed over the piece of rag and Kane took it over to the sink in the corner.

'Dad?' The gate clanged shut and Kane turned around from the sink. Heather hurried across to the boat where Bill was topping up the oil. 'Can I get a lift home with you? My car's ratshit.'

Kane dropped the towel and walked out of the dark corner, and Heather smiled apologetically when she spotted him. 'Ah, I mean it won't start.'

Terry's white teeth flashed, and Kane hid a smile.

'Hi, Heather.' He stood beside the boat and looked down at her. 'What's wrong with it? Would you like me to take a look at it?'

'If you've got time that would be great.'

Bill straightened and wiped his hands on the front of his overalls. 'If you want to come home with me, you've got fifteen minutes.' For the first time since Kane and Terry had come into the workshop, Bill chuckled. 'But I'm warning you, I had a few roos in the wagon yesterday and it's got a bit of a stink up. No whinging on the way home, okay?'

Heather pulled a face and turned to Kane. 'If you can take a quick look, maybe I won't have to go in Dad's smelly truck.'

Terry laughed and shook his head. 'I don't know why you don't get yourself a ute like the rest of us, Uncle Bill.'

'Perfectly good Land cruiser wagon. It'll see me out.' He stepped back from the boat. 'Fifteen minutes or I go without you, missy.'

'Come on, Kane.' Heather held her hand out, but Kane ignored it and stepped past her to the gate.

'Where is it?'

'In the staff car park.'

Bill narrowed his eyes as he looked at Kane. 'Fourteen minutes.'

Heather and Kane walked quickly to the car park and she dug out her keys.

'Pop the bonnet and I'll have a look.'

As Heather closed the door and moved around beside him, he was conscious of her soft breasts pushed into his arm and he moved away. A bit too blatant for him. Besides, he'd stuffed up with a female staff member once already, and he had no intention of taking Heather up on her rather obvious offer. 'Where did you get to last night? You left early.' Her perfume washed over him as she leaned into him again. 'I didn't get a dance with you.

'Yeah.' His reply was noncommittal. 'Ellie left early too.'

'Did she?' If gossip was what she was after, he wasn't going to satisfy her need. He wasn't one to kiss and tell. He stretched away from her and reached into the engine. 'You were right.' He chuckled. 'It is ratshit. Looks like rats have chewed through a cable.'

'Bloody rats. It's happened before.' Heather turned around and leaned back on the front of the car and put her shoulders back to emphasise her breasts.

'This won't start until you get that cable replaced.' Kane stepped back and held the bonnet with one hand, waiting for her to move out of the way so he could slam it shut. 'Do you want me to get one and fix it for you?'

'Oh, that would be so lovely of you.' Her voice was soft and breathy.

'You'd better get a move on if you want a lift home with your dad.'

'Kane.' She reached out and put a hand on his arm, but before she could say whatever was on her mind – and he had a fair idea of what that was – her phone trilled.

Heather pulled it out of her pocket and glanced at the screen. Kane stepped away again as a small smile tipped her lips. 'Hi Ellie. Sorry, can't talk now. I'm with Kane.' Her voice lowered but Kane heard her soft whisper. 'My turn.'

# Chapter 12

*Monday*
*Porter Farm*

Shortly after Heather had cut her call short, Ellie reached over to turn down the radio and turned her small sedan off the highway. The thought of Heather with Kane shouldn't have bothered her, but it gave her a funny feeling in her chest that settled there until she reached the old farm.

By now they were probably in the bar having an after work drink. Bloody my turn. She tried to tell herself not to be petty. After all, she wasn't going to sleep with Kane again, so if he wanted to take up with Heather, that was fine by her.

It was.

As she drove up the rutted driveway, she briefly considered simply continuing nonchalantly past the house to the back of the farm, but old habits die hard. It was no longer her property, and she needed permission before she went wandering over someone else's land.

The place still looked abandoned, no black Jeeps roaring down the driveway today. The front door was closed, and the curtains were drawn across the front windows. The house sat sleeping in the late afternoon sun. There was no sign of Kane's mother. Maybe she was out? In the far distance, a small plume of smoke rose in a lazy spiral. Not enough to indicate a burn off, but enough to let her know that somebody was down at the back boundary.

Ellie parked the car at the front of the house, and slowly walked up the stairs onto the verandah. The old tank stand next to the kitchen still leaned at the same precarious angle. She and Emma had sat beneath that tank playing with frogs as the heavy rains of the wet season had clattered onto the tin roof of the house. Mum had been horrified and had scrubbed their hands and had spent days waiting for the warts to appear.

Another old wives' tale. There'd been lots of them. Most of all Ellie remembered the laughter . . . and the smells: the pungent smell of the tobacco from Dad's pipe, the ever-present sweet smell of the mangoes in boxes at the top of the steps.

Ellie swallowed, trying to force away the ache that stuck in her throat. Those memories felt real – real enough that she half expected to peer around the corner and see Dad heading down through the trees on the old tractor. Real enough to toss her school bag into the old sleep out and follow the day's cooking smells into the kitchen, where Mum would be standing in her gaudy apron, her hair held back in a rubber band, her cheeks flushed from the heat of the old wood stove.

Standing on the familiar verandah, just being here, was very different to standing at the gate looking in from a distance like she had the other day. That had been like looking through a filter, or at a photograph, something that didn't really exist. Now the creaking of the front step and the same old empty pots on the verandah took her immediately back to her childhood. Ellie hovered on the quiet edge of her memories and thought about turning around, getting into her car and leaving.

I can't. Now that she'd seen the earthworks she was going to find out what was happening. Panos had been lying to her the other day. She was sure of that. Bill knew something as well, but for some reason he wasn't telling either. She might have lost her father, but if this was a way to help her mother get out of that dark place that had ensnared her, it had to be done.

Taking a deep breath, Ellie forced her feet to take her to the front door. She raised one hand and curled her fingers, hesitating as she thought of what to say if the door opened. She straightened her shoulders; if Panos Sordina came to the door himself, she would be polite.

She knocked and waited.

Maybe there's no one here? Maybe she could just go for a walk through the old orchards and see what was happening. If anyone asked, she would say she was looking for something or someone. She'd figured out what if she had to. She turned towards the steps but the familiar rattle of the key in the front door made her stop. Turning back slowly, Ellie watched as the door opened and a tall thin woman leaned around to look at her.

'Yes?' The voice was soft and the expression wary. 'Can I help you?'

'Hello.' Ellie stepped forward and forced a friendly smile to her lips. 'My name is Ellie Porter. I used to live here, and I was driving past and –'

'Ellie! Come in, come in.' The woman pulled the door back and stepped to the side so Ellie could enter. 'My son mentioned that you might drop by sometime.'

'I don't want to intrude. I just wanted to –'

'Don't be silly. Of course you're going to come in.' She looked at Ellie curiously. 'You don't remember me, do you?'

'No, I'm sorry. You're Mrs Sordina?' She was not what Ellie had imagined.

'Yes, I am. But please call me Susan. I spent a couple of afternoons here with your mother when – before your Dad's funeral. You've grown up.'

A wisp of memory clung to Ellie's thoughts. Her mother had had a friend called Susan. But this thin woman didn't look like the woman she remembered at Dad's funeral. That woman had been plump with blonde, curly hair. She took a step forward and followed Susan into the house.

'It's time for afternoon tea. Would you like to have a cup of tea with me?' She looked at Ellie with a gentle smile. 'I'd enjoy the company.'

Ellie's throat closed up and she tried to think of a polite way to refuse. She closed her eyes for a second.

'Are you all right?'

She opened her eyes and swallowed the lump. Susan was looking at her with a frown and the strong light streaming through the large kitchen window from the west accentuated the deep furrows in her forehead and the dark shadows beneath her eyes. She could see where Kane got his cheekbones. As Ellie looked closer, she realised Susan was still in her dressing gown.

'Oh, I'm sorry. Were you taking a nap?'

'No.' A dismissive wave as she crossed to the sink and filled the kettle. 'I was having a lazy day. Reading in bed.'

All was quiet apart for the water spitting from the old tap over the sink. The kitchen was the same as it had ever been; if anything, it was in an even worse state of repair. Paint hung from the ceiling in loose peels, and there were a couple of large brown stains that indicated a leaking roof. Not what you want in the wet season in the Territory.

The familiar smells of her mother's cooking were long gone and a mouldy damp smell pervaded the air. No sweet aroma of mango chutney lingered, although there were still a few bright yellow stains on the old combustion stove and down the wall where the pots had once boiled over during her childhood. No matter how much Mum had scrubbed, the stains remained. Susan watched as Ellie's gaze moved around the room before she gestured for her to sit at the table. 'I know. The house is in poor condition. My husband has promised to get it seen to.'

But Ellie sensed a lack of conviction in her voice.

Why on earth are they living in this dump? Because that's what it was now. Neglected and run down. Kane had said they had lived in Darwin before and suddenly a memory pierced Ellie like a sharp needle prick.

'You're the Susan that my mother knew in Darwin. She used to visit you at the beach . . . at Cullen Bay?'

'Yes, that's right. We met at the CWA national conference the year it was held in Darwin. Your mother's mango chutney was famous. She scooped all the prizes at the show that year.'

'I remember now.' That school holiday they'd left Dad at the farm and had a girls' week away; she'd forgotten all about it. Typical – the good memories disappeared, and the bad ones stayed to haunt your dreams. 'We stayed at a caravan park near the showground and when Mum went to visit you, she dropped the three of us at a big shopping centre. Em, Dru, and I shopped all day.'

They'd bought make up and magazines and had lunch at the food court and felt very grown up. She smiled; that was her first taste of a cappuccino and her sisters had laughed as she'd spat the bitter flavoured milk into a tissue after ordering and trying to look mature.

'How is your mother?' Ellie looked up at the woman sitting across the table and the sadness on her face surprised her. 'I've written to her a few times over the years, but I didn't know if she was still living around here. She was a good friend to me when I used to come out here and visit Panos, but we lost touch when Peter . . . when your Dad . . .'

Ellie's pleasant memories evaporated like the steam that began to puff from the kettle on the old gas range. Leaning back into the chair, she held the other woman's intent gaze. 'She's doing okay. She's moved away.' It was all she could manage. After all, this woman offering her tea and kind words was the wife of the man who Mum blamed for Dad's death. Of course she wasn't going to send a chatty letter back.

Dear Susan, how are you? How's your husband. I don't have one anymore.

The kettle let out a piercing whistle and Susan pushed herself up slowly from the table. As she stood, her dressing gown gaped open at the front and Ellie caught a glimpse of long, stick-like legs beneath the edge of the knee-length nightie.

'Tea?' Susan pulled her gown together and retied the belt. Ellie nodded. All she wanted to do was get out of here, but Susan's loneliness was palpable, and she didn't want to seem ill-mannered. As the older woman bustled about lifting down a tea caddy and opening the fridge, Ellie's gaze settled on the small white boxes in the middle of the kitchen table. Medication – six boxes of varying size. She tipped her head to the side, knowing it was rude, but she couldn't help herself. 'Susan Sordina' was typed on each label.

She started as Susan placed two cups on the table in front of her. 'Would you like a biscuit? I'm sorry I don't have any home baking to offer you.'

Ellis waved her hand. 'That's fine. A cup of tea is plenty.'

Much more than she'd intended when she'd knocked at the door. All she wanted to do was get out of this house with its dead smells, stained walls and cloying memories. Susan gestured to the boxes on the table. 'They make up most of my diet these days. I've not been well, and I haven't had a chance to bake. Not even a CWA scone in the freezer.' She laughed but she caught her breath and for a moment Ellie thought the woman was going to cry, but she put her hand to her mouth and coughed. 'My husband works in Darwin, so I'm here by myself through the week. It's lovely having Kane visit, though. He came on Saturday and Sunday, but he was busy this afternoon, so it's nice to have an unexpected visitor.' Her breath was short and choppy.

'I'll call in again next time I go to Darwin.' The words were out before Ellie could think. Of course, if Kane was visiting there was no need to offer, but she felt so sad to see this woman looking so lost and lonely. Her smile was sweet and again, Ellie saw a flash of Kane in Susan's deep hazel eyes.

Susan's hand shook as she lifted her cup to her mouth. 'So Ellie, Kane tells me you're a helicopter pilot as well. What a lovely coincidence that the two of you should end up working together.'

Ellie lifted her cup and sipped the hot tea. Guilt trickled

through her as Susan's face came alight. Why guilt would hit her, she didn't know. She didn't have anything to hide.

'What brings you back to the old place?'

'I saw Kane's Jeep here the other day when I was driving back from Darwin. He told me you lived here.'

'So you decided to call in? That was so sweet of you. I'm so pleased there is a – a sort of – connection between us. Kane needs friends.' Susan looked over Ellie's head to the windows and was quiet for a moment. When she turned back she reached over and took her hand. Her grip was tight, and her fingers were like ice. Ellie looked down at the thin hand gripping her fingers. Susan's skin had a slight yellowish tinge and the veins stood out on the back of her hand.

'We're a fine pair. He's not been well either.' She gave a little laugh but there was no mirth in it. She sounded almost embarrassed that perhaps she was sharing something she shouldn't.

'I don't know Kane very well. We just work together.'

Except that we just had sex last night.

'No, you wouldn't. He is a very private man.' Susan bit her lip and stared at Ellie. The look on her face indicated she was about to share something.' Did he tell you what happened in Afghanistan?'

'Afghanistan? No.'

'He's getting better, and he is strong man like his father was. He's healing, I know he is.' She looked away and stared at the wall but kept a tight grip on Ellie's hand. 'I almost lost him, you know. I'll never forget the night our phone rang, and it was his commander, telling me his helicopter had been shot down. I thought he was dead.'

Ellie stared at Susan as Kane's refusal to fly began to make sense. She should have guessed it was something like that.

'He's so worried about my health, but he won't look after himself. And he's a man. He refuses to accept that the death of his crew has damaged him.'

Death of his crew? A surge of sympathy rushed through Ellie and she blinked away the moisture that suddenly threatened her eyes.

'He received a commendation you know, before he was medically discharged. He carried one of his crew through hostile territory, even with a shattered hip.' She lifted her face to Ellie's. 'She was dead before the helicopter hit the ground, but he still carried her out across the sand dunes.'

Oh fuck. No wonder he didn't want to fly.

'I didn't know any of that.' Ellie spoke slowly. 'But it explains his limp.'

'So.' Susan sat back. 'Knowing that he works with you has eased my mind. You'll make a lovely friend for him, my dear.' Susan's cup landed in its saucer with a gentle tinkle.

A lovely friend. Just the sort of things her mother would once have said, before the world became too difficult for her.

'I'll . . . I'll look out for him.' Ellie stood and carried both of their cups over to the old sink. She rinsed them and turned back to Susan.

'I noticed the orchard has been let go. I wondered if your husband was going to revive it.' She wasn't going to tell her she'd spoken to Panos already.

'No.' Susan shook her head. 'This is just somewhere for us to live for a while. Or it was supposed to be us. I'm afraid

Panos doesn't cope well with illness.'

Ellie's heart went out to her. 'Would you mind if I had a look around while I'm here? It's been a long time since I've been back.' She fiddled with the car keys in her pocket, feeling guilty for not being quite truthful. Well, it was the truth in a way.

'Not at all.' Susan stood and supported herself on the back of the chair.

She looked so ill Ellie wondered if she should really be here alone. 'Feel free to have a look around. My husband is having a new dam built down the back, so you might find some workers down there. There's been utes back and forth all morning. Tell them I said it was okay for you to go down there.' Susan's brow wrinkled, and her lips pursed as she looked around the kitchen. 'It would have been nicer to have a new kitchen instead of a new dam, but I suppose he thought there was no point.' Her tone was resigned.

'No point?' Ellie reached out and put her hand over Susan's on the back of the chair.

Even though her voice was sad, there was a sense of stoic acceptance there. Ellie's eyes filled with tears and an ache closed her throat at the next words to come from Susan's mouth. 'I haven't told Kane what a short time I have left. He's already been through so much. Please don't tell him.'

Ellie caught her breath and this time the tears spilled over onto her cheek. 'Should you be here alone?'

'It's the way things are.' Susan reached over and wiped away the tear on Ellie's cheek with the pad of her thumb. 'I will tell him. But it really eases my mind to know that he will have a friend when my time comes. You're a sweet girl, Ellie.

You remind me very much of your mother.'

Ellie shoved the sealed cardboard carton into the boot of her car. Susan had taken her around to the laundry at the back of the house and pointed to a shelf above the double concrete tub.

'This box was in the shed when we moved in. It had been shoved out there with some mango cartons, but it has your father's name on the outside. That's one of the reasons I wrote to your mother.' Susan covered her mouth and coughed again; a nasty rattling cough.

Ellie waited until she had caught her breath.

'Can you take it to her? I don't know what's inside.' Her breathing rasped around the words.

Ellie braced one hand on the old concrete tub as she reached up and tipped the edge of the small box, testing the weight. She levered the edge and balanced it on her palm until it slid off the shelf and she took a step back as she caught it. Dad's loopy writing with the distinctive curl on the Ps stared at back at her. Peter Porter. A childish giggle threatened. In their household the old nursery rhyme had always been 'Peter Porter picked a peck of pickled peppers'. Ellie remembered how indignant Dru had been when she'd come home from school one afternoon and told Dad he had the rhyme wrong. He'd smiled his gentle smile and ruffled her hair.

'Thank you. I'll tell Mum about it when I speak to her.'

But not before I look inside.

Susan had walked her back around to the front of the house and watched as she put the box in the boot. She stood there as Ellie opened her car door. 'It was so sweet of you to call in. If you are going past again, I'd love to see you.' She straightened, gripping the edges of her dressing gown together with her claw-like hands. 'I know. Next time Kane comes over, perhaps you could come for a drive with him and I'll cook dinner for both of you.' Her face brightened as though the thought of having something purposeful to do pleased her.

The ache took a tighter hold on Ellie's throat and she nodded. 'I will.'

I haven't told Kane what a short time I have left. He's already been through so much. The love in Susan's voice tore at Ellie's composure. Life was bloody cruel.

The track to the back boundary had been recently graded. Ellie glanced to the side as she drove the three miles from the house through the orchard to the corner where the property was edged by the South Alligator River. The three small dams were full from the wet season just gone, and the brown water was dotted with an abundance of wild birds and whistling ducks. The irrigation pumps next to the dams were rusted, and the dead mango trees bore testament to the fact that the dams were no longer used for irrigation. Everything was dead and brown, including the thick tussock grass in the paddocks which was in need of a decent slash or burn – a cleaning of country. Ellie wished she could hop on a tractor and slash it herself, but those days were gone.

Her small sedan crested the hill that overlooked the final dam that was fed by the river. She drew in a gasp and hit the brakes. Pulling across to the side of the track, she opened the door slowly and put her hand up to her eyes to shade them from the late afternoon sun. The dam was bone dry. Huge cracks splintered the mud at its base. Old plastic containers littered the flat dry surface, exposed by the drying up of the water.

'What the – ?' A large motor started with a roar and Ellie strode across the road into the orchard, and climbed the next hill, taking care to stay behind the stand of scrubby trees that delineated the back of the orchard from the river flats on the eastern boundary.

There was no sign of the huge trucks from last week, but three white utilities were parked at the bottom of the hill. A three metre high wire fence enclosed a large square from the base of the hill to the river and the gates were closed, the padlock big enough for Ellie to see it from where she stood. It was the red scarred earth she'd seen from above, but it looked much wider from the ground.

'New dam, my arse,' she muttered. Something serious was going on here, and it had nothing to do with mango farming or a new fence. The machine over at the edge of the river backed up with another roar of its engine and a puff of smoke was followed by the squealing of steel on steel. Along the length of the back of the fence was a square pit lined with black plastic. It was half-full of discoloured water. The pipes she had seen from the air towered to the height of a house roof. Ellie took a step forward and peered through the dust that rose and obscured her vision. She frowned and wrinkled her nose as a strange odour filled her nostrils – a mix of gasoline and kerosene.

'Hey! Stop right there!'

Ellie jumped and put her hand to her chest. Her heartbeat ramped up and she swallowed down the fear that burned in her throat. A huge guy with tattoos circling his neck was marching across the paddock towards her. His eyes were too small for the face that was set in a scowl. The sun glinted off his shaved head and the earrings in his right ear flashed as he closed the distance between them. He would have looked more at home on a motorbike than on any of the earthmoving machinery down the hill.

She thought quickly. 'Oh, hello. Maybe you can help me?' She let out a nervous giggle, but the nerves were for real. The pungent smell of sweat and body odour filled her nostrils as he came to a stop only inches from her side. He grabbed her arm and held it tightly as she tried to twist out of his grip.

'Who the fuck are you? What are you doing here?' His voice was deep and tinged with an Eastern European accent.

'I'm lost.' She put on a timid voice. 'I'm looking for the jumping crocodile show, but I must have I missed the turn. There was no one home at the house down the road, and I saw the smoke down here.'

He turned her around and let go of her arm, only to push his hand into the small of her back. 'This is private property.'

'There's no need to be like that. I'm only looking for the crocodile park.' She cleared her throat and met his gaze.

'You're a tourist, huh?'

His gaze lowered and stared at her chest. Too late she realised she was in her work clothes and her khaki shirt was emblazoned with the Makowa Lodge logo.

'I'm new here and I wanted to see the jumping crocodile show.' She stuck to her story but in truth it was the last thing she wanted to see. Many locals wanted to see the jumping crocodile show banned and she agreed with them. A man had been killed last dry season when a four-metre crocodile had jumped up and snatched him from his tinnie.

'Like I said, get in your car and piss off.'

Ellie's temper fired. 'There's no need to be like that. What's going on down here, anyway?'

She flinched as his large sweaty hand grabbed hers again and he dragged her down the hill to her car. A white ute was parked beside it; she hadn't heard it over the noise of the machinery she'd been watching.

'Get in your car and leave or you'll be charged with trespassing.' He shoved her roughly towards the car.

Her hands shook as she shoved the key into the ignition and started the car. With a spray of gravel to rival that of Kane's exit last week, the wheels spun as she turned the car towards the highway.

Before she reached the top of the hill she glanced back.

The man held a phone to his ear.

# Chapter 13

*Monday*
*Arnhem Highway*

Ellie's lips trembled as her hands gripped the steering wheel. What she had seen beside the South Alligator River confirmed her worst fears. The ground was ripped to pieces; the soft red soil now slashed into huge channels by the machinery parked inside that wire-fenced compound. And that tattooed guy had terrified her. What the hell were they doing down there that needed a thug to guard it? But she knew. She'd read enough of Mum's files and seen enough photographs to know that hydraulic fracking was underway.

But how had it been kept so quiet? There'd been nothing in the paper about it – except that denial from Sordina. Did anyone else know? Maybe this was why Bill had been so cagey the other day. Something was seriously wrong here and it was up to her to put a stop to it.

The communication towers at Jabiru appeared in the distance and when she reached the turn-off, Ellie took a left into the small township. She pulled over to the side of the road near the bakery and hurried inside.

She bought a takeaway coffee from the young Aboriginal girl and then hurried back to the car. Her hands were still shaking as she balanced the cardboard cup on the bonnet and ripped open three packets of sugar to sweeten the drink. She needed something to calm her nerves and help her think rationally.

Taking a slug of the coffee and scalding her mouth in the process, Ellie pulled out her mobile and pressed the shortcut to Call Connect. Her hands were shaking too much to look through her recent calls for the number she wanted.

'Town and name please.' The call centre operator came on the line before she could think.

'Ah . . . Darwin. The electoral office of Panos Sordina.'

'Do you want to be connected?'

'Yes. Yes please. Put me through.'

The call was put through and Ellie tapped her hand on the roof of the car impatiently.

Eventually a woman answered the phone. 'Good afternoon, can I help you?'

Ellie kept her voice calm. 'I would like to speak to Mr Sordina please.'

'What shall I say it is in relation to?'

She fought for composure. 'Tell him it's Ellie Porter calling. Peter Porter's daughter.' That should get the bastard's attention.

It was only a moment before the call was picked up. 'Ellie.

What can I do for you?'

Ellie gritted her teeth. For a moment the words wouldn't come, but then they tumbled out in a rush. 'I'm going to give you one more chance to tell me the truth. What is really going on at the back of our old farm?'

Silence. And then he spoke and his voice sounded reedy. 'You mean the new dam?'

'That's no dam you're building.' To Ellie's dismay her voice broke. 'Panos, what the hell is going on? Don't you know it's the boundary to Kakadu?'

'Ellie. Calm down. I have no idea why you are so upset. I'm putting in a dam. If you've flown over, you'll have seen for yourself how dry the paddocks are. '

'Don't lie to me. I've just come from there. I met your wife. God only knows why you've left her down there on her own. She obviously has no idea what you're up to, but I'm not a fool. My mother has said for years that you were after the place, even before Dad died.'

'Ellie. You're seeing shadows where there are none. My wife is a sick woman. I don't know what she told you, and I don't know what you think you've seen, but –'

'I'm going public with it. I don't care if I have to go on Territory television or radio, or both, I'll do it.'

'Don't be silly. Let me come and see you. I can explain everything. There's no point stirring up a media frenzy and then be made to look like a fool.' His voice was wheedling.

'Too late, Panos. You've already lied to me twice.'

'Ellie, stop. Give me a chance. You know I was your father's best mate. I wouldn't do anything to hurt your family.'

'What are you talking about? It's not my family I'm worried about.'

'Listen.' A tinge of desperation laced his voice. 'I did the right thing by your mother when your father died. I deserve the chance to explain. Let me come to see you.'

'When and where?'

'I'll be down at the farm next weekend. I'll meet you then. Okay?

'All right.'

'Give me your number. And I'll call you.'

Ellie recited her number and pressed end without saying goodbye.

The drive back from Jabiru seemed to take so much longer than the trip there, and by the time she got back it was dark. She stood at the window of the tiny kitchenette in her staff apartment and trickled water into the tray of herbs on the windowsill. It was a wonder these plants were alive the way she neglected them. Not that she needed to grow them – she ate in the bistro most nights – but just the fact that she could tend to something growing filled the empty void in her.

The propagation and nurturing of the small pots reminded her of the days when she and Dad used to hover over the seed trays in the old shed, waiting for the first tiny green shoots to break through the dark soil.

High five, Els. She curled her fingers into a fist. For a moment she could almost feel the sting of her father's hand against her open palm as they celebrated another frail green tendril pushing through the soil to the light. Dad had taken so much pleasure in the cycle of life: a winter sunrise promising a clear day to bathe the trees in warmth, the colours of the flames when they'd burned the dead branches at pruning time, the tendrils of mist that hung over the lush green leaves in the wet season when the clouds had almost seemed to skim the tops of the trees. She remembered the feel of the soft red soil running through their fingers as they tested the acidity levels, the clods that they had patted down around the small trees.

They hadn't always lived on the farm. Ellie had a dim memory of moving there before she'd even started primary school. Dad had thrown in his job as an accountant in Melbourne and bought the five hundred acre property. He'd been determined to make his fortune in the tropical fruit market, but he'd missed the boom of the eighties and no one had told him about the vagaries of the weather – the fruit yield dropped dramatically if the winter was too warm or the spring too wet. He found that out the second season they were there. But simply knowing and loving the cycle of the seasons didn't make for a bumper crop each year. In the fifteen years they'd been there, the long-awaited fortune hadn't ensued, and Dad wasn't enough of a farmer to diversify. It had been easier for him to take up the part-time job at the pub in Jabiru. The debts had grown, and then there'd been another winter heat wave in the year he had . . . died. Ellie shook her head slowly, trying to lift the veil of nostalgic melancholy that had wrapped itself around her as she stared unseeingly at the herbs. The box that Susan Sordina had given her was sitting on the small sofa in the living room. She wandered over and stared down at it, wondering what had been left behind at the farm. She reached out to lift the lid, but the top was taped down securely with masking tape. As she stared at Dad's loopy writing, tears filled her eyes and she turned away, putting her hands up to her face.

Taking a breath, she scrubbed at her eyes before ripping the masking tape from the top of the box. A lever arch folder sat inside. Ellie lifted it out and her breath caught in her throat as she flicked it open. School reports. Emma Porter, Ellie Porter and Drusilla Porter – Jabiru Primary School. Commendation certificates. She flicked through the papers and smiled. Dad had been so proud of them, and he'd held a little family ceremony at the dinner table each night that one of the three girls had brought something home from school. Another memory that had disappeared in the grief of his loss. But there was nothing there to explain why he'd taken his own life.

# Chapter 14

*Tuesday*
*Makowa Lodge*

The morning had been a bit quieter than yesterday, although Kane had started work early to prep one of the choppers for a sunrise flight. Ellie had taken two couples up on the Magela Valley tour to watch the sun come up over the majestic stone formations. At least they looked majestic in the brochure. The only parts of the park he'd seen – apart from the rescue flight the other day – had been from the ground.

But he'd spent a lot of time looking at the photos around the office after he finished servicing the choppers between flights. Maybe, just maybe, he'd ask her to take him up for a look around one day when it wasn't so busy.

When they next had a conversation that was – she'd said barely anything to him at all this morning apart from 'Right to take up?' or a quiet, occasional 'Thank you'. She wasn't smiling much either, and Kane couldn't help the suspicion that he was at least partially responsible. They shouldn't have left things the way they had yesterday.

When he'd called Mum last night, she told him that Ellie had been to visit, but she had not said a word about it this morning. It had been very kind of her to go out there; seeing his mother over the past week had brought all sorts of regrets to the surface. He'd not been in touch with her as much as he should have after she'd remarried. He'd been punishing her for letting go of the memory of his father. Kane knew now that he had been unfair. He had no right to judge her, and no right to stop her from being happy.

Afghanistan had put things in perspective. Life was too short to judge others for their life choices. Mum had suggested he come to the Territory for a while, but finding her so ill and thin had shocked him to the core.

But he was still determined to see Panos when he came home next weekend; the sooner he could talk them into moving Mum back to Darwin and away from that rundown old farmhouse, the better. If it meant he had to help them out financially, so be it.

After five days, Kane was also beginning to settle into the lodge. The rest of the staff were friendly, the job was relatively stress-free, and he was feeling more comfortable with where he was – especially since he'd helped out in the workshop yesterday. If he could make his peace with Ellie, he could see himself staying at Makowa Lodge at least for one season.

Maybe. Then he'd think about where he'd go after that. His time in the Army had been structured and this newfound flexibility about where he went and how long he stayed was going to take some getting used to.

Maybe it was time to find a home base for a while.

Maybe he could even start to think about flying again.

One day.

But his first plan today was to brighten Ellie's day and see if he could coax a smile from her. Time to make amends for the way he'd treated her yesterday.

He judged the time perfectly and was walking out of the bistro just as the helicopter buzzed overhead and headed for the tarmac. By the time she'd shut the chopper down and the tourists had left, he'd put the pizza box and the coffee on her desk.

Kane pulled out the other chair and straddled it as she walked into the office. 'I thought you might like to have an early lunch. I couldn't resist the smell of pizza coming from the bistro.'

The look she gave him was cautious.

'You've worked your butt off these last two days.' He spread his hands out in a placatory gesture. 'This is a peace offering to make up for the cranky bastard I've been. And to thank you for dropping in on Mum yesterday.' One step at a time. He'd apologise for the other night when they'd eaten.

For a moment, he was unsure what her reaction was going to be. She turned to the pizza box and lifted the lid, and an angelic smile crossed her face as she closed her eyes and inhaled.

And damn if that wasn't sexy. The surge of desire set off a warning in his brain. Don't go there again.

'How did you know?' Her whole face lit up and her eyes were dancing with amusement.

Kane put his fingers to each side of his head. 'Hmm. Let me read the lady's mind. Double anchovies, no olives and a vanilla latte.'

Ellie's laughter hit him square in the chest. 'So you've been doing a bit of research over in the kitchen. Very thoughtful of you.' Her voice was dry. 'Apology accepted. I'm sorry. I've been a cranky bitch too.'

'Nothing like pizza to clear the air.' Kane glanced up at the clock. 'And if I've read the schedule right, you've still got an hour to enjoy it.'

He waited for Ellie to take the first piece. He smiled as she pulled a piece of pizza up and bit off the long pieces of dangling melted cheese that were hanging over each side.

'Delicious,' she mumbled with her mouth full. 'I'm starving.'

'Only way to eat pizza. With fingers and straight from the box.'

They munched their way through the pizza in companion- able silence and Kane gradually let himself relax.

Ellie finished her coffee, and then stifled a burp with her fingers spread over her lips. 'Sorry.'

'Just one of the guys.' He laughed as he closed the empty box. 'Now I feel right at home.' He reached over and removed a string of cheese that was stuck to her chin.

'Ladylike too, that's me.' A faint colour stained her cheeks. 'That was really thoughtful of you. I love pizza and I don't get a chance to have it at night. They close the pizza oven after lunch.'

'Don't they realise pizza is one of the food groups?'

Ellie nodded. 'Oh yes. It's an essential part of my diet. What's your favourite?'

'I'm a man. What do you think it is? Meat lovers, of course.' She leaned back and folded her arms, but Kane avoided temptation and kept his eyes above chest level. Although he was so very tempted to look down. The feel of her soft breast in his hands the other night . . .

He cleared his throat. 'So yours is double anchovies, no olives?'

'Promise not to laugh?' Ellie's grin widened. 'That's my second favourite. They don't do my favourite here.'

'So?' He tipped his head to the side. 'What is it?'

'Potato and sour cream.' She shook her head slowly. 'But I have to go to Darwin to indulge in that one.'

'That's not a pizza. That's a vegetable.'

'It's to die for. You'll have to try it.' Ellie sat back in her chair and covered a yawn. 'I always get sleepy if I eat a big lunch.'

'You've been busy since you came back from your holiday.' He held her gaze and Ellie swallowed. She took a deep breath and sat up straight in the chair.

'Kane?'

He nodded.

'About the other night.'

He held up his hand and held her gaze 'Let's just agree to move on. It was a mistake. A very pleasant mistake and I'm not going to say I'm sorry for that.'

She stared at him and he saw her swallow again. Christ, was he responsible for her nervousness? He didn't think he could feel any worse than he did.

'I want to ask you something and I want you to be honest with me.' Her voice was steady.

'About Heather? I heard what she said on the phone, and honestly, there's nothing there, Ellie.' He moved his chair closer to hers and an unfamiliar feeling settled in his chest. An emotion was pushing there, and he tried to ignore it. Like a hatchling trying to break free of its shell, waiting to see what the world would hold in store for it.

'No.' She frowned at him. 'Not Heather.' Her voice was sad, and Kane had always been a sucker for sad. He reached over and took her clasped hands between his.

'What's on your mind?'

'Tell me a little bit about your –' She shook her head '– oh, I don't mean anything private, nothing personal. Just talk to me about you and why you're here.'

Kane brushed her knuckles with the back of his hand. 'I was in the Army until recently. I came back to Darwin to see my mother, but she'd moved. So then I came to work at the lodge because I wanted to be closer to her. I didn't know she was sick. I'm really not happy about her living out there by herself. I offered to move in with her, but she said no. Reckons it was too far for me to drive every day.' He looked away and stared towards the river and flinched as the high-pitched squeal of a bird carried across the tarmac. 'Thank you for visiting her. The farm is very different to what I expected.'

'It's been empty for five years. No one's lived there since we moved out when my father died.' Sadness crossed her face. 'I enjoyed visiting your mother. I had forgotten that she knew my mum. But she did seem lonely.'

'I've been trying to contact Panos about her living out there by herself.'

A strange look crossed Ellie's face. 'How much do you know about him?'

'Panos? Honestly?' She nodded.

'He's a scammer and a gambler, and I have no idea why my mother married him.'

'My dad spent a lot of time with him before he died. It was a strange relationship. Dad had never been one for the pub and I guess when his friendship with Panos took him away from us, I resented it. Maybe I'm being too hard on him now.'

'I doubt it. He's a shallow man and I'm amazed that he

got elected.'

Ellie let out a little sigh. 'We're on the same wavelength. There's something else too.' Kane touched her hand again. 'What's wrong?'

Ellie looked away. 'I'm scared. I know something illegal is happening at the back of the old farm. I saw it with my own eyes, and then I was chased off the place by a thug after I visited your mother.' Ellie closed her eyes and let the words pour out, the words she'd held to herself for so long. 'My father died five years ago. The coroner ruled his death was suicide, but my mother never accepted it. And lately, I'm beginning to wonder if she's right.' Her voice hitched on a sob that she swallowed back.

Kane's hand gripped her shoulder and she turned slowly into the warm comfort. Her eyes were now awash with tears and Ellie lifted her hand and brushed them away with an angry swipe.

'I knew Sordina was a weak man the first day I met him.' Kane's voice was hard. 'The way he's treated my mother is disgraceful. Dumping her out in that farm house is –'

'Unforgiveable. And more than that, there's something odd going on down the back and I know Panos is lying about it. It all ties in with some stuff that my mum's been worried about.'

'If there's anything I can do to help, just ask, okay?'

The sweet smile that crossed her face hit him in the gut. 'It's good to talk to you. Really talk. I came here on the understanding that I was an engineer and I'm sorry that this misunderstanding has made it so hard for you this week.'

'Do you ever fly?' Her eyes were clear and steady as

she held his. Kane was tempted to look away but that would have been the cowardly thing to do. She deserved as much honesty as he could give her.

'No. Not anymore. But that's a whole different story. Maybe for another pizza day.'

And maybe not.

Ellie frowned as she looked over his shoulder. 'The next tourist has just come through the gate.'

Kane was relieved. A new level of friendship had been established and she'd opened up to him.

'I'll go and check the chopper for you.' He stood and picked up the empty pizza box.

He knew Ellie was watching him as he walked out and dropped the box into the rubbish bin. He'd already checked the bird when she'd come down from the last flight and refuelled it, but hell, that was his way.

# Chapter 15

*Tuesday afternoon*
*Darwin*

Everything had been going fine until Ellie Porter started sticking her nose in. The drill site was away from most of the regular scenic tour flight paths, and no-one would ever have cause to go down the back; it was almost two kilometres from the highway gate to the eastern boundary. None of the tourist boats travelled that far down the river. The place was miles from anywhere. It should have been perfect. But she had to start snooping. And when Fairweather heard that she had been out there – and there was no doubt he would – there would be consequences. It was a complication he didn't need. He didn't know what he would say to her on Saturday, but that could wait. In the meantime, there was another problem to deal with.

'What box, Susan?' As Panos pressed the phone to his ear, he could feel the blood thumping through his veins.

'Oh, just a small box I found in the shed.'

'What was in it?' His words were like bullets.

'I have no idea. It wasn't mine to look at. It had her father's name on the top.' Susan's voice trembled. 'She was really happy to take it.'

'I bet she fucking was.' He'd seen no box in the shed. It would have been burned if he had. No matter how hard he tried not to think about it, Panos knew he was responsible for Peter Porter's suicide. He might as well have put the noose around his neck himself.

'Panos? Have I done something wrong? I didn't mean

to upset you.' Susan's voice was teary, and a bolt of regret jarred through him. He rubbed his forehead with his fist and his anger eased a little.

Susan was his wife and he'd loved her when they'd got married, but he'd loved the money she'd inherited from her first husband just a little more. She put others first, and her martyrdom always irritated him. And now despite her illness and the loss of their beautiful home in Darwin because of his gambling, here she was, feeling sorry for Ellie Porter because her father was dead.

Peter Porter's death haunted him. He had been found hanging from a beam, a tumbled pile of mango crates beneath his dangling legs. Eyes bulging, red spots on his cheeks. In the recurring dream, Peter called Panos to help him, his hands reaching out. A dream that made him jump to Fairweather's bidding every day since. He had hoped he'd get away from him when he'd married Susan's money, but a visit from Mick, Fairweather's frightening offsider, had put the fear of God into him. It had been a clear warning: do as he was told, or he would end up dead too.

Lately, that was looking like an attractive option.

Panos ran his hand over his eyes, trying to blot out the memory; he didn't want to think too much about what Mick had meant.

'Panos?' she repeated softly.

'I'm here.' He tried to inject some life into his voice. 'I'm sorry I snapped, darling. You know how hard it was for me when Peter died.'

'I know, Panos.'

'Are you feeling okay?'

'Yes. I'm not too bad. It's been nice to have some visitors.'

He'd been waiting for this to happen ever since the call from security that someone from Makowa Lodge had flown over the drill site. Ellie Porter would not let it go. They should have put the new barbed wire fence at the front gate, but that would have been like telling passers-by 'Illegal Drilling Taking Place On This Property.'

He should have gone to the farm and spent the weekend with Susan, but his guilt kept him away. The guilt about trying to convince Peter to sell, the guilt about Susan having to live in that dump, the guilt about what was happening down the back, they all gnawed at his insides like the cancer that was slowly killing his wife.

So he'd slept on the couch in his office, eaten at McDonald's around the corner, and taken a small measure of pride in the fact that he'd stayed away from the race meeting.

He'd have to go to the farm soon or find a laundromat. Especially if there was any chance of a face-to-face meeting with Fairweather. Last time they'd met, he'd looked at Panos as though he'd crawled out from under a rock.

'I'll be home on Friday night. I'm pleased you had some company. I'll call you tomorrow night.'

'Love you, Panos.'

'Ditto.' He stared into space as he ended the call. In his own way, he did love Susan. She was a kind woman and had never uttered one word of complaint about their situation. He didn't deserve her.

Only a few minutes passed before the call he was dreading sounded on his other phone. He looked at it as it chirped out the happy ringtone, and dread clawed at his throat. The ringtone did not reflect the caller on the other end of the line. When Mick had given him the phone that was to be used only for contacting Fairweather, it had been set up for his use, but Panos had not been brave enough to change any of the settings. So the happy tune stayed; it was almost obscene.

The music got louder.

He had to pick it up. And he would have to meet with the cold bastard; it was inevitable. Panos needed more money.

And I deserve more. This deal was worth millions to Fairweather. If he wanted Panos to do his dirty work and secure more committee votes, it was going to cost him.

His hand reached out in front of him, slowly, tentatively, as though the phone would rear up and bite him.

'Yes?' He injected confidence into his voice.

'Panos.' The voice was soft and the cold spread through his whole body. 'I've received a very disturbing call from the site.'

'Which site?'

'Don't play with me, Panos. I know Ellie Porter has been out there. You've just spoken to your wife about it.'

Christ help me. He's tapping my phone as well?

With Fairweather's reach, Panos should have realised all of his calls would be tracked but for God's sake, he'd only hung up a few minutes ago.

'So what are you going to do about it?'

He cleared his throat. 'I was just pondering the situation when you called. Susan said Ellie had visited her. Maybe she didn't see anything.'

'You're lying to me, Panos.' When Fairweather spoke,

his words were like chips of ice. 'I know you've spoken to Ellie Porter. Twice. In fact, I have transcripts of both calls in front of me. What do you think is in that box?'

God help me. 'I don't –'

'Think back carefully. Did you give anything to Peter that had the company name on it?'

'No.'

'Are you sure?

'One hundred per cent.'

Fairweather paused, and then seemed to come to a decision. 'You have one way to redeem yourself, and one way only. She knows too much, and she's threatened to go public with it. You let me down with her father. You won't let me down gain.'

Perspiration rolled down his neck and a sharp cramp clenched Panos' bowels.

'Helicopters can be very unsafe. Especially over the wild gorges of Kakadu National Park.' Fairweather's voice hardened and Panos looked at the drop of perspiration that had rolled off the end of his nose and landed on a piece of paper on the desk. He watched as the circle spread and blurred the text.

'I don't understand.' The numb feeling had spread to Panos' mouth and for a moment, his vision clouded at the edges. A strange, stretching numbness pulled at his cheeks.

Am I having a stroke? Please, God.

'I'm really not very happy with you, Panos. For the past six years, I've continually bailed you out of the problems you've made for yourself. I've been very patient, but now it's time to repay that debt. Even if it you have to be up there with her and bring the bird down yourself, her helicopter will crash.

Do you understand me?'

'I can't do that.' Panos shook his head from side to side. He was dead either way. 'You will.'

'No.' His voice was a bare whisper. 'What did you say?'

'I can't do this anymore.' Panos sniffed, not surprised to feel the tears on his cheeks. 'I can't. It's over. I'm out.'

'I am disappointed, Panos.' Fairweather's voice was even, almost chatty.

'I'll get a loan. I'll hand over the property. I'll sign it over to you. It's yours anyway, we both know that. That'll clear all my debts.'

'Oh no. I'm afraid it's far too late for that.'

'I'll –'

'Goodbye, Panos.'

The cold silence of the disconnected call surrounded him as Panos dropped the phone and lowered his head to the cold leather-topped desk.

# Chapter 16

*Tuesday night*
*Makowa Lodge*

Ellie pushed open the door to her apartment and kicked her heavy boots off as soon as she was inside. She'd picked up a hamburger at the bistro on the way past and the smell of the onions was making her mouth water. At this rate she'd have to ramp up the exercise. Pizza for lunch and hamburger for dinner. At least she'd managed to resist the hot chips.

The lunch with Kane had sent confusion spiralling through her again. When he'd reached over and wiped that piece of cheese from her chin, it had taken every ounce of willpower not to reach up and hold his hand against her skin. She'd tried to ignore the warm feeling that coursed through her blood every time their eyes had met. Instead she'd lowered her eyes and focused on the pulse in his neck, remembering the steady beat of his heart against her cheek as she'd lain in his bed.

She didn't trust these unfamiliar feelings. As she crossed to the sink to wash her hands, she glanced up at the clock. Half an hour to eat and then Skype Emma and Mum, and Dru. Maybe hearing about the family stuff in that box would cheer Mum up. After wiping her hands, she dropped the towel on the sink, and bent down to pull a plate from the cupboard. The aroma of the onions won out and she unwrapped the burger, unable to resist taking a bite before she took the plate into the living room.

Ellie stopped dead in the doorway and grabbed for the

plate as the hamburger slid to the edge.

The sofa was empty. She put the plate on the coffee table, casting her mind back to the night before, and trying to remember exactly where she'd put the small box. Standing with her hands on her hips, she slowly scanned the room before continuing into the bedroom. The top drawer of the chest of drawers was open and her underwear was hanging over the edge. Her neck prickled as she walked over and bent down, picking up two pairs of her lace panties from the floor. Her mouth dried, and she threw them back down to the floor. Ragged cuts had been sliced through the crotch of each pair. They were the same as the set that she'd worn out to the bar on Sunday night. Hands shaking, she walked quietly over to the small bathroom and peered in. The shower curtain was pulled closed across the small bath. She always left it open because she hated the feel of the wet plastic against her skin when she showered. Slowly, she reached out, poised to run.

The soft plastic slithered against her fingers as they curled around the edge and she yanked the curtain back.

Nothing. No one was there.

She checked that the windows in the bathroom and the bedroom were locked before she walked back to the living room. Leaning over each end of the sofa, she looked for the box on the floor, but there was no sign of it.

Lowering herself to the soft cushions, she sat straight and looked around, trying to see if anything else was missing. But nothing was out of place. Only the box and her underwear. A shiver ran through her at the thought of someone touching her panties. The furniture melded into a blur of colour as she stared at the wall, ignoring the food in front of her. The clock ticked in the silence as the greyness of uncertainty enveloped her. It was time to start taking a bit more care. A lot more care. After a few minutes, she picked up the plate, took it into the kitchen, and tipped the cold burger, which was now sitting in a congealed pool of juices, into the small bin under the sink.

Her stomach roiled as she walked across to the table and opened her laptop. Someone had been in her room again. The metallic taste of fear and doubt filled her mouth.

She fought for calm as she logged on and set up a group call. The musical tones of the Skype call signal broke the silence as she waited for her sisters to pick up.

'Ellie!' Dru's blonde curls filled the screen. 'You're early. I just got to the office.'

'Hey, Dru. Have you got time a chat? Em's not picking up. She mustn't be home yet.' Ellie managed to speak naturally, and her calm voice surprised her.

'Yes but be quick. I've got an unexpected meeting.' Dru's voice was as clear as if she was in the room with her.

Holding the laptop in front of her, Ellie walked over to the door and checked it was locked. Dru always had unexpected meetings when they tried to set up a family call. Even when they tried to talk at Emma's place a couple of weeks back, whenever the discussion turned to Mum's issues, there'd always been something she had to do or a call she had to make. It had been like that since Dad's death, but she and Em still always made the effort to include her.

Ding! As she stared at the computer screen, an email notification came in from Emma.

Ellie chewed her lip thoughtfully. Dad had always laughed when the computer dinged when an email had arrived.

He hadn't been savvy with computers, but she'd sent up an account for him a few months before he died.

'Dru, you're the computer whiz. How long do email accounts stay active if you don't use them?'

'As long as the service provider exists. But with something like Gmail or Hotmail, they're pretty much there forever. Why, what's up?'

Ellie stared at the screen. Dru was only half paying attention and was focused on something on her desk and Ellie knew she wasn't interested in the past. And she could do nothing to help way over in Dubai. 'Nothing important. Have you settled back to work after your holiday?'

'Yep, work's good. How about you?'

How about me? Broke my rules and slept with a guy I work with. Someone has been breaking into my room. And then there's the old farm. Ellie shook her head as she stared at Dru's big blue eyes and the office window behind her sister. Even over the connection, she could see the smog of Dubai hanging in the air. 'Yes, really busy. The lodge is full and –'

'Look, Ellie, I'm really sorry, Sam is waving at me from his office. Obviously a drama of some sort. Give my love to Mum . . . and Em. I'll email you. Bye.'

The screen went blue before Ellie could even reply. She jumped as a tree branch scraped against the corrugated roof.

Why would anyone be interested in a box of old school reports? Maybe there was a petty thief on the prowl. But why would they take the box and leave her laptop and the other minor valuables alone? And why would they go through her underwear drawer? She thought of the thug who'd chased her off the farm.

Maybe it was some sort of warning. Her uniform had indicated where she worked, and it wouldn't be hard to find out where her apartment was.

The Skype call chimed again, and she pressed answer.

Emma's happy smile filled the screen. 'Hey, sis. You look tired.'

Ellie closed her eyes for a brief second and drew a breath. 'Hi Em. I am a bit. Mum there too?

'She'll be here in a minute. We're going across to the cafe in the village for tea. Mum's idea.'

Ellie frowned, surprised. 'Wow, Mum's idea? What's happening over there?'

'I took her down to the new clinical psychologist at the hospital in Port Douglas on Friday, and he's eased her medication right back. I don't know what he said to her, but she looked brighter as soon as she came out of the consult.'

'Shit.' Ellie bit her lip, not knowing what to do. The last thing she wanted was to put Mum back again.

'What do you mean shit? We've been waiting for this to happen for five years.'

'I know and it's wonderful to hear.' Ellie hesitated. 'Where is she now?'

'In the shower.' Emma's face filled the screen as she leaned in closer to the camera on her computer. 'You, okay?'

'I'll be quick before she gets out. Tell me as soon as you hear her.'

'What's wrong?'

'You're not going to believe this, but I think she's been right all along. There's something going on at our old place. I saw it with my own eyes.'

'Something like what?'

She quickly filled Emma in on everything she'd seen; first the trucks, then the earthworks and suspicious construction next to the river, and finally her trip to the farm, including meeting Susan Sordina and being run off the property.

'Ellie, I don't like the sound of this. It makes sense of something else I was going to tell you too.'

'What else?'

There was a long silence at the other end. 'Em?'

'After you left I read some of the emails Mum got from one of the action groups. Right now, there's a parliamentary committee looking into exploration applications in the north of the Territory. For fracking and seabed mining.'

'Are you serious?'

She glanced across at the living room window and saw her face reflected back at her. The sudden realisation that anyone out there could see her clearly in the brightly lit room sent a shiver down her spine. She jumped up and pulled down the rarely used blind behind the curtains.

'The emails were from a guy at Mary River. He said there's been a heap of discussion over the past month about moving the border of Kakadu south to allow for hydraulic fracking up on South Alligator River, but it's been kept quiet. A company called Black Coal Holdings is pushing for a licence to drill. From all accounts there is a big shale gas deposit there. And I looked at the map.'

Ellie shook her head. No way. 'The South Alligator River is part of the border of the old farm.' Her mind was spinning with the implications. 'Why hasn't there been an uproar about this? There's always been opposition to mining in the National Park and it is traditional land across the river. Remember all the demonstrations at the Ranger mine when we were kids? And Panos owns the farm so where does this Black Coal Holdings company come into it? I'm going to see Bill Jarragah again tonight. He must know something.'

'You mean Bill who used to work on the farm?'

'Yeah, Heather's dad. There was an article in the paper the other day about Sordina meeting with his Aboriginal council. He's been acting strangely ever since.' Ellie took a deep breath. 'Do you know what fracking does to the environment?' She'd read up on it when she'd been looking for the article she'd seen on Kane's iPad.

'No, only what's been in the emails to Mum.'

'Even though they reckon it could be really good for the economy, there are so many risks involved. It's scary stuff. Read some of the articles on the internet. The chemicals they use can leach into the water table. They've even blamed earthquakes and global warming on fracking in other parts of the world.' She turned to pace back the other way. 'God, I cannot believe this. I wonder if Dad knew about the gas deposits.' A memory of a conversation tugged at her mind.

Emma's voice was firm. 'Promise me you won't go back to the farm. I have a bad feeling about this. You don't want to alert them to anything.'

'Them? Who?'

'Whoever's behind it. Whoever owns that company. There's so much money to be made out of all that stuff in the ground. Are you sure you want to stir up trouble?'

Ellie burred up. 'I love this place and there's no way I'm

going to let the environment be destroyed. I don't care that it's on our old farm, I'd fight it wherever it was.'

'You're so like Dad.'

'I'm sorry, Em, but I can't sit back and watch this happen. There's too much apathy in the world today. This is Kakadu, a World Heritage site, for God's sake.'

'I know. But I'm worried about you. I just wish you'd move over here with us and leave it all behind. You could get a job flying out of Cairns to the reef.'

'I don't want to leave here; you know that. This is my home. I love the Territory.'

Ellie pinched her nose hard until her eyes watered. 'There's something else. When I was out there today, Susan Sordina gave me a box of Dad's stuff.'

'What was in it?

'School reports and merit certificates for the three of us. It was taken from my room today while I was at work.'

'What do you mean taken?'

'Someone broke into my room.'

'Have you reported it?' Emma's voice was almost a squawk. 'And who'd be interested in that old stuff?'

'I haven't had a chance, but I will. And I don't know why. It had Dad's name on the lid. Maybe they thought there was something in there.'

Something incriminating. Damn, I hate thinking about all this. And talking to Emma about it, made it seem so real. The past all came slamming back with a vengeance. The fear, the grief, the uncertainty. Now she could understand the confusion her mother had felt for the last five years. That unbearable feeling of being let down by the person she'd loved so much. And always the question: Why?

A pang of regret settled in Ellie's chest. They should have been more understanding. They should have listened, and not assumed it was the grief causing Mum to make up crazy stories.

'Holy hell, Ellie. You be careful.' Emma held her gaze.

'Em, you know how we went through Dad's papers when I was staying with you? Do you know if Mum ever looked at Dad's emails? I know he had a Gmail account. I remembered helping him set it up.'

'I don't know. How about I broach it carefully over dinner?'

'Thanks.'

'Em?' Ellie dropped her hand from her face and slowly shook her head from side to side as she stared at her sister's face filing her screen. 'Mum can't be right about Dad's death, could she?'

'I honestly don't know, Ellie. Look, I've got to go. She's coming.' Emma dropped her voice. 'When we get home tonight, I'll see if I can find anything else in her stuff. If I do, I'll email it all to you. Promise me you won't do anything stupid? Please? And be careful.'

'I'll be careful. I'll call if Bill knows anything, too. Tell Mum I'll ring her tomorrow.'

Only when Ellie logged off and closed the laptop did she realise that she hadn't mentioned Kane at all.

# Chapter 17

*Tuesday night*
*Makowa Lodge*

Ellie had a shower, trying to clear her mind and shake off the heavy feeling that filled her. But she was quick, because every little noise, every branch hitting the outside wall had her jumping.

She pulled on a pair of jeans and a long-sleeved T-shirt and left her hair loose. The temperature had dropped a little and she shivered as crossed the lawn, aware of the shadows between the buildings. Was the intruder who had stolen the box still around? She turned along the path that ran behind the kitchen and froze as she caught a flash of white in her peripheral vision. Pressing her hand to her chest she took a deep breath; her heart was pounding. The wind gusted but it was only a white plastic bag blowing from the garden. Muttering to herself, she reached down and carried it across to the bin at the back of the building.

Light shifted in the trees ahead as she stepped back onto the path, signalling the approach of a car. The light intensified as the headlights shifted to high beam bathing her in bright light, almost blinding her. The engine stopped but the lights stayed on highlighting her like a rabbit caught in a spotlight. Ellie put her head down and hurried along the path to the bar, irritated by how jumpy she was. She glanced back to the car park as she reached the bar area; it was still there, and the lights were still on high beam.

Kane was beside the bar chatting to Steve and he lifted

his glass in a greeting. He took a sip of his beer and leaned nonchalantly against the wooden counter, but his eyes stayed on her.

Ellie lifted her hand and pushed her hair back over her shoulder, wishing she'd braided it. Her heartbeat had settled but now Kane was there to add to her confusion. She was aware of his eyes on her as she crossed the lawn, stepping carefully around the family groups sitting on the grass. She flicked a glance over at Heather, who was talking to a man Ellie hadn't seen before, but Heather looked away.

'Hey there. Would you like a drink?' Kane's voice was soft. 'Everything okay?'

'Yes. A soda water would be great, thanks. My throat's dry.' Ellie forced a smile to her face. 'My nerves are a bit frazzled.'

Kane leaned forward and took her hand just as Heather looked across at them. 'What happened?'

'Someone's been in my room again.'

'Again?'

'Why didn't you mention it before? Anything stolen?'

She bit her lip as she stared at him. 'Just a box of old stuff that your mother found at the farm. Nothing important.' She looked down as Kane's thumb rubbed soothingly along the back of her hand. 'The scary part is that they went through my underwear.' Kane frowned as he took her hands and squeezed them.

'That's off.'

'It's rattled me a bit. I wondered –' She cut off her words and watched his fingers as he gently wrapped them around hers.

'You wondered?'

'Nothing.' She swallowed. 'When your mum gave me the box I thought there might have been something in the papers to shed some light on his suicide.' Ellie bit her lip and shook her head. 'But there wasn't. I guess I was clutching at straws. There's been some crazy stuff happening this week.'

Kane's eyes were intent as she looked up at him. 'What do you mean?'

Ellie filled him in on the activity she has seen at the back of the property and the information that Emma had conveyed on Skype. 'Don't get me wrong. I don't hold with Mum's theory but I called Panos, and since then someone's been snooping around in my room.'

'And you think there's a connection?'

Ellie shrugged. 'I really don't know what to think.'

'I passed a guy near the steps of the apartment block this afternoon.' His eyes narrowed. 'He was carrying a small box.'

'Did you recognise him?'

'Not really. I just assumed he was someone on the staff I hadn't met before.'

'What did he look like?'

'Tall, well built, short-cropped blond hair. He nodded, and I didn't think anything of it.'

Steve finished serving the guest on the other side of Kane and interrupted them. 'Drinks?'

'Just a soda water for Ellie please, mate.'

Steve picked up the post-mix siphon and made an elaborate show of pouring a drink for her, and Kane inclined his head towards Heather's table. 'Want to sit down and chill for a while? I think you need to tell me a bit more about what's going on.'

'Not yet. Let's leave Heather in peace for a while.' Ellie relaxed a little. He was so much more comfortable around her since they'd cleared the air over lunch. More natural, with no macho posturing to hide behind. And it was a relief to share her worries.

'One soda water with a twist of lime.' Steve laughed as he passed her the drink and she rolled her eyes when she saw he'd put an umbrella in the lime slice.

'Have you seen Bill around, Steve?' She couldn't see him over at the staff table where he usually sat.

'He was over there with Heather a little while ago, but I think she put the skids under him. She's found an unsuspecting tourist already. How long is it going to take you ladies to realise that I'm the best catch around here?' The Irish accent thickened, and a mournful look replaced his smile as he looked at Kane. 'Don't try and get lucky with the locals here, mate. Waste o' time.'

'We just have high standards.' Ellie fought the heat that was running up her neck into her cheeks and Kane looked across to the window as though there was something interesting out there all of a sudden.

Ellie frowned at him as a knowing smile crossed Steve's face. As Kane stared outside, Ellie was struck again by the authority that emanated from him. Even in his casual chinos and collared shirt, he exuded confidence. He turned back suddenly, and she realised he'd caught her staring.

'How was your afternoon?' Ellie sipped her drink and looked over to the tables. This time she caught Heather's gaze, but her friend looked away again.

'I sorted out the hangar and ordered a few parts. That last guy had really let things run down.'

'Mike was a bit casual in the hangar.'

Kane's face closed, and his voice tightened. 'There's no excuse for that.'

'True. But we managed.' Ellie tilted her head to the side. 'You know, I do appreciate how thorough you are with the birds. It's good to know they're in good hands.'

'You'll get used to the way I operate.'

'In everything you do?' Ellie smiled up at him.

Steve shook his head. 'Ha! Now I know the secret. You have to be more than a simple barman to get Miss Ellie here to flirt with you.' She hadn't realised that Steve was still there. She'd been too focused on Kane.

Kane's smile was lazy, and a tremble rippled down Ellie's back. He lowered his voice. 'Were you flirting with me?' He tapped his lips with one finger and Ellie tried hard not to focus on his mouth, although it was a pleasure to see him smile. Those lips had taken her to heaven and back on Sunday night. 'Me, flirt? No way.' She kept her words light. They were putting on a show for Steve but each of them knew the subtext. 'Come on, let's go sit down and wait till Bill comes back.' She picked up her soft drink and followed Kane across to Heather's table. The table was almost full; a few other staff had joined Heather. The tourist guy had moved on.

Ellie looked around before pausing behind Heather. 'Where's your Dad?'

'Don't know where he's got to.' Her voice was short, and Ellie reached out and put her hand on her arm.

'Can we talk?'

Heather shrugged and looked away. 'Whatever.' Finally she turned back to Ellie but her brow was wrinkled in a frown. 'Why do you want see Dad?'

'I want to ask him about something.' Ellie slid in beside Heather and watched as Kane walked around and took the empty space opposite her.

'What about?'

'Nothing important. Just some business stuff.'

'He'll be back soon.' Heather shrugged and turned her back but Ellie wasn't going to let a lifetime friendship be jeopardised by one silly mistake. She leaned over closer to her. 'Come for a walk with me while I wait for him.

'Why?' Heather looked from Ellie to Kane and finally she stood.

'We'll be back in a minute.' Ellie gave Kane an apologetic smile for leaving him at the table alone. 'Mind our seats.'

They strolled over to the river and stood on the boardwalk, but Heather didn't speak. She stared out over the dark water and Ellie jumped as the boardwalk swayed beneath their feet and she crouched down. A huge black pig was rutting in the reedy grass beneath them as a dozen or so little piglets sniffed around in her shadow. The strange sound of the Makowa whistling ducks on the side of the muddy riverbank filled the air with a cacophony of sound. Small birds zipped through the leaves that overhung the boardwalk, catching the mosquitoes that were beginning to buzz around their heads.

'Look, I know you're royally pissed off with me, but it just happened. I never meant to hurt you.' She stood up and looked at Heather. 'We were both carrying on like adolescents anyway.'

'Okay. I was being a bitch.' Finally Heather turned to her. 'I'm sorry. If the truth be told it was good to see you letting your hair down on the dance floor with him that night. You've been way too serious lately.'

Ellie smiled as relief flooded her. 'Thanks. I've had a bit on my mind this week, and I'd hate to lose my best friend over a one-night stand.'

'So he wasn't as good as his looks promised?' Heather laughed when Ellie shook her head, embarrassed.

'No . . . yes . . . I mean, I don't kiss and tell.'

'Hey, you used to when we were at school.'

'We're all grown up now, Heath, but still friends?'

'Of course we are.' Heather bumped her shoulder. 'Come on, Mr Fly Boy will be getting lonely. 'So why just a one-night stand then? Give yourself a chance to practise.' A small smile lifted her lips as the moonlight shone on her face. 'But if you –'

Ellie grabbed her arm. 'Come on, girlfriend. Let's go back and keep him company while I wait for your Dad.'

Kane had been pleased to see Ellie walk in; if he was honest, she was the only reason he'd come to the bar. She'd been in his thoughts most of the afternoon. No, more than that. Ellie Porter had been in his head ever since he'd first laid eyes on her climbing into her helicopter. If he'd thought sleeping with her was going to help him forget about her, he'd been dead wrong there. And now with his protective instincts flaring to life he had no chance; the thought of someone breaking into Ellie's room worried him.

After Heather and Ellie took off outside, he sat at the

table soaking up the relaxed atmosphere. It was a long time since he'd let himself just sit and chill; it was cathartic clearing his mind and listening to the conversations around him.

When they came back, each with a smile on their face, Ellie sat beside him and Heather headed for the door.

'I'll go and see what's holding Dad up,' she called out.

The familiar feminine smell of Ellie, as her thigh pressed against his, set Kane's body aching with need. His libido was not paying any attention to his resolve of not getting involved and he tried to withdraw into himself a little.

'Have you talked to your Mum today?' Her brow wrinkled in a frown as she looked across at him. 'I was worried about her after I saw her yesterday.'

'She's okay.' He knew his voice was terse but, hell it was bloody hard not to put his arm around her and pull her close. 'I don't want you to think I went down there to pry, but she talked about you.'

Kane ran his hand through his hair. He knew exactly what his mother would have said. 'I suppose you got the war hero story. Don't believe a word of it. That's the sanitised version of a monumental fuck up.'

'She said you were healing.' Her voice was quiet.

Kane stared hard at her for a moment and she held his gaze without blinking.

'Look. It's not my business. Where you came from or where you'll go to next has nothing to do with me.' Her chest rose and fell as she took a deep breath, and Kane realised she was affected by his proximity as much as he was by hers. 'But she asked me to be your friend –' she gestured around the room '– so I guess this is what friends do.' Ellie hesitated and then put her hand his arm. 'Your mum didn't look well.'

'No, she's not.' Usually Kane would have left it at that, but as Ellie's concerned eyes held his, he suddenly felt the need to share. Before he could voice his deep concern about his mum's health, Ellie continued speaking.

'Your mum looked out for mine when Dad died. If there's any way I can help out, please let me. I'd like to.'

'Thank you. I'm going up to try and get her back to Darwin tomorrow. To look at apartments. Fancy a drive?'

'What time?'

Kane noticed Ellie's hesitation. 'After lunch. We're both on the same shift, which will make it easy. You've got three flights to take up in the morning.'

'Yes, longer flights . . . and yes I would love to come. I'd like to help out if I could.' She stared up at him and he couldn't look away from her blue eyes. 'I'm having lunch with someone, but I'll make it an early one unless you want to get away before noon?'

'No, as long as we get away by one that's fine. I've lined up a couple of places to look at around four o'clock. If Mum's up to it, we can have an early dinner and drive back? Maybe I can tempt you with a potato pizza?'

Ellie smiled up at him and nodded.

Heather came back and stood behind Ellie. She looked as surprised as he was; they'd been in their own little world there for a moment.

'Hey, Kane. Excuse us for a minute? I just need to talk to Ellie again.'

Their voices were low, and Kane turned back to survey the crowd. Most of those couples with children had left and the bar was emptying out. He thought about going back to his room. A couple of nights out was more socialising than he'd done since before the crash in Afghanistan.

Closing his eyes, Kane blocked out the sound of the room around him and thought back to that last night in the desert. He waited for the usual surge of adrenaline to settle in his chest, but he must have been more relaxed than he thought. There was a pang of sadness, but none of the physical symptoms that usually took over when he thought about what had happened. He let himself test the memory – slowly – like opening a photograph album and flicking through the pages. Taking slow, easy breaths, he let his muscles relax. His pulse stayed steady and his heart beat slowly in his chest. Dirk and Jerry had been playing cards, and Hawk had been strumming on her guitar. The conversation was animated, with the usual swearing when someone got a bad hand.

If they'd known it was their last night of their lives, what would his crew have talked about? Would they have questioned what they were doing in this godforsaken desert fighting a war that could never be won? Kane waited for the guilt to come slamming in, but it stayed away. The usual pain blocking his throat didn't come. It was sweet relief; the violence of his reactions when he was feeling that pain frightened him.

He opened his eyes slowly and looked around. There was no point wishing he could go back; he couldn't change what had happened. In a way he was pleased Ellie knew some of his background – maybe he was beginning to let go a little bit. Kane straightened his posture and stretched his legs out in front of him as he looked across at her. A comfortable, almost mellow feeling had settled in his bones.

She and Heather were still deep in conversation as they walked back to the table and a lull in the crowd noise let their words carry across to him.

'Do you want me to come with you?' Ellie was looking up at her friend with a frown. 'Just be a bit careful out there.'

'Let me go and see if his car is in the car park. Maybe he changed his mind and went home. The old bugger refuses to turn his mobile on so I can't text him.' Heather headed towards the door.

'Everything okay?'

Ellie glanced at Kane. 'We can't find Bill. Heather's car's still out of action and she needs a lift home. I'm going out to help her look for him.'

He jumped to his feet. 'Not by yourselves. I'll come with you. I said I'd fix her car, but the cable hasn't arrived yet.

'She's just gone to check the car park.' Ellie bit her bottom lip. 'How will she get home if he's gone?'

'She'll probably stay. It's a good hour out there on a dirt road.' Ellie frowned.

'What's wrong?'

'It's not like Bill. He's really not been himself lately.' Ellie came to an abrupt stop on the lawn beside the covered area of the bar. Heather was standing in the doorway, her face wet with tears. Ellie ran over and put her arms around her.

'What's wrong?' They led Heather away from the noisy crowd.

Heather hitched a sob. She turned and looked up at Kane. 'Can you help me?'

'What's happened?' Ellie kept hold of Heather's arm.

Her voice broke. 'I don't know what to do. His car is still in the car park. His keys were on the ground and there's a big smear of blood on the door. Really big. And on the ground too.'

Ellie threw a worried look at Kane.

'Show us where his car is. Maybe he's just hit a kangaroo or something on the way in.' Kane kept his voice calm, even though all of his senses were on full alert.

When they reached the old battered Land cruiser – and it did look like it had hit plenty of wildlife in its day – Kane crouched down beside it and ran his fingers over the smear of blood on the driver's door. It was still wet. The dark maroon stain covered the chrome of the door handle and ran down in a broad splatter of drops to the ground where a large stain covered the gravel.

'Maybe he cut his hand when he tried to open the door.' He looked around. 'Where were the keys?'

'On the ground over there.' Heather pulled them from her pocket. The leather of the key ring was damp with blood.

Ellie nodded. 'Kane's right. That's what's probably happened. He's probably gone to the office to get the first aid kit. Come on, we'll go and look for him.'

'As long as he hasn't passed out on the way?' Heather hurried away towards the administration building, closely followed by Kane and Ellie. The office was in darkness and the door was firmly shut; the only light shone through outside from the glass in the drinks refrigerator inside the door.

Heather walked across to the staff entrance and tried to turn the handle. Kane put his hand on Ellie's before she could follow. 'Is there anything else I should know about Bill?' He was surprised at the level of Heather's distress.

Ellie shook her head as Heather walked back to them. 'Later,' she said in a soft voice.

'Is there somewhere else around here he might have gone for help?' Kane directed his question to Heather and she shook her head.

'Everyone lives offsite apart from you and Ellie.'

Kane was surprised; he'd assumed that the staff apartments were full.

'Most of the staff live at Jabiru,' Ellie explained. 'And most of the Aboriginal staff have homes in the settlements along the river. So there's really no one here apart from me who Bill would go to for help.'

'Maybe he went down to your apartment?'

'Maybe he did.' Heather turned swiftly and followed the path to the back of the lodge. They hurried after her.

'What were you going to tell me before?' Kane kept his voice low as their footsteps crunched on the gravel.

'Bill used to drink a lot. We used to find him passed out all over the place, but he's been to AA and he's been dry for a long time.' Ellie leaned over and whispered close to his ear as Heather walked ahead of them. 'She's probably worried that he's passed out somewhere now. He's been acting a bit strange this week.'

'If that's the case, I hope he's nowhere near the river.'

'Oh, God.' Heather's harsh gasp filled his ears and she stopped dead at the end of the path. Kane pushed past her and ran across to the figure lying prostrate on the path at the bottom of the steps near Ellie's room.

'Look after Heather.' Kane crouched beside the

unconscious man and placed his fingers on his neck, searching for a pulse. He let out a relieved breath as the strong beat pulsed steadily against his fingertips. 'He's alive.'

Kane rolled Bill into the recovery position. He sat back on his heels for a moment and pulled his own shirt off, rolled it up and placed it beneath Bill's head before he ran his hands gently over the man's body, looking for the injury that had caused the blood to be on the car door. The sounds of a car's wheels moving slowly over crushed stones at the edge of the road behind the staff apartment block distracted him and Kane glanced up as the headlights swept across them. It was then that he saw Bill's hand.

'Whose car is that?' Heather's voice was thready.

'It's a Mercedes. I saw the badge on the back when it turned.' Kane looked up as Ellie put her hand on his shoulder but he barely registered her touch on his bare skin.

'Is he drunk?' she asked.

Kane shook his head. 'I don't think so.' He'd leaned forward to sniff Bill's breath but there was no smell of alcohol coming from him.

Bill moaned and tried to sit up but Kane put his hands on his shoulders. 'Stay there, mate. I just want to check you out.'

'Do we need an ambulance?' Ellie's voice was calm.

Kane shook his head as he turned and stared up at Ellie, his stomach clenching. The blood was starting to get to him.

'It would be quicker to take him to the medical centre ourselves, wouldn't it?' He swallowed and kept his voice steady as he searched the ground around them, but he couldn't see what he was looking for. Ellie nodded as she looked at

Kane, picking up the warning he was trying to convey.

'What's wrong with him?' Heather crouched beside them. 'It's okay, Dad. We're here now.'

'His hand is hurt. I think he's lost a fair bit of blood and that would be why he passed out. We need to get him to the hospital.'

Kane looked across the car park, remembering the sound of the car slowly driving away. He wasn't ready to tell them that one of Bill's fingers was missing.

***

After binding Bill's hand with a bandage from the first aid kit in Ellie's car, Kane drove to the medical centre. Ellie and Heather sat in the back of his jeep and they'd supported Bill between them as they'd sped up the dark highway.

'What did you do, Dad?' Heather asked but Bill just shook his head and stared ahead, his bound hand pressed against his chest.

'Were you looking for Ellie? Is that why you were down the back?'

'Button it, Heather. Enough with the questions, can't you see a man's in pain?' Bill dropped his head to his chest and closed his eyes.

There was no traffic on the road and it only took twenty minutes to get to Jabiru. Ellie had called ahead and one of the resident doctors met them in the emergency department.

'I'm going to admit you, mate.' The doctor finished his examination and patted Bill on the shoulder. 'I'm going to give you a good slug of local anaesthetic and antibiotics while I do what I can. And you can tell me exactly how you managed to rip your finger off.'

Bill tried to sit up but the doctor's hand stayed him.

'I can't stay. I have to be in Darwin tomorrow afternoon.' Bill jutted his chin out and Heather stepped forward.

'I'll look after Dad when I get him home.

The doctor shook his head. 'I won't put him in for surgery till the nursing staff comes on at seven in the morning, but he needs to stay here tonight. It's more than a few stitches. The rest of you might as well all go home and get some sleep.'

Kane and Ellie waited in the car while Heather had a few moments with her father. Ellie sat in the front with Kane, and Heather was quiet in the back seat as they headed back to the lodge. Ellie turned sideways in the seat and looked back at her friend in the last, dim light from the street lights before they turned onto the highway. Heather's hand was over her eyes.

'Did your Dad say any more about what happened?'

'No.' Heather rubbed her eyes. 'But he told me to stay with you and not go home.'

'That's a good idea. It's way too late for you to drive out to your place,' Ellie agreed. 'But I still want to know what happened.'

'Leave it Ellie, it was just an accident. Like we thought.'

'How could it be an accident?' Ellie finally gave into the fear

that had settled in her chest. 'The way Bill was the other day, and with what's happening at the farm I –'

'Dad talked to me about that after you left.' Heather's voice was sharp. 'He said you're imagining things, just like your mother.' Ellie clenched her hands on her lap as anger surged through her. 'It's something to do with the Aboriginal council or the environmental committee, isn't it?' It was dark now and Ellie couldn't see Heather's expression.

Kane reached over and squeezed her hand. 'What happened the other day?'

'Bill warned me off when I asked him some questions.'

'Like he said, Ellie, just drop it. It was an accident.' Heather's voice was short.

There was no more conversation until they got back to the lodge.

Ellie pushed opened the door of her apartment. Kane raised his hand and stepped in first and flicked the lights on. 'It's okay. All good.'

'You can have my room. I've got an early start. I'll sleep on the sofa.' Ellie frowned as Heather nodded and walked past her into the bedroom. The door closed behind her with a loud click and Kane raised his eyebrows.

Ellie crossed the living area and stood by the bedroom door. 'Something sounded a bit off, didn't it?'

'It did.'

'I'm not going to let it go.' Ellie pushed open the door and sat beside her friend as she lay back on the pillow with her hand over her eyes. 'What's going on, Heather? I know there's something. Why would someone do this to Bill? Has he been threatened?'

Heather's eyes flew open and she stared at Ellie. 'What?'

'I think I know what's going on.'

Heather's face closed. 'You heard Dad at our place.

He's right. Just stay out of it.'

'For fuck's sake, Heather. Someone tortured him tonight. They cut his finger off. What the hell is going on? Why are you both acting so strangely?'

'It was an accident. No one cut his finger off. You have a vivid imagination, Ellie.' Heather rolled over and turned her back. 'I'm tired. Just forget it. Dad's got things under control.'

Ellie closed the door quietly and crossed to the small kitchenette. She looked over at Kane, who was standing just inside the door. 'A cuppa or something stronger?' She lifted her eyebrows and waited for him to answer. He'd been to his room and changed his shirt while Ellie had been in the bedroom with Heather.

'Coffee would be good, thanks.'

The kettle boiled with a soft whoosh. Ellie poured the water and let out a soft sigh as the aromatic orange fragrance of her tea calmed her jangling nerves. She carried the two mugs across to the door and waited for Kane to slide open the screen door. He seemed to understand that she wanted to sit outside in the quiet dark of the night. The air was still and only the occasional ominous splash from the river, and one stray birdcall broke the silence. The sounds of Kakadu were about the only thing she could rely on lately.

Ellie looked over the top of her cup as Kane stared into the darkness. 'What do you think really happened to Bill?'

Kane swung around in his chair and put his cup down. 'He refused to let the doctor call the police. He's insisting it was an accident.'

'He's lying.'

'Of course he's lying. Injuries like that don't happen by

accident. Not opening a car door. What's going on? Who would do this to him?'

'It's too much of a coincidence, isn't it?' Ellie shook her head from side to side, tears welling in her eyes. 'He's a good man. He wouldn't do anything wrong.'

'Ellie.' She jumped as Kane reached over and took her hands that she had clenched in her lap. 'I want you to be careful. It's way more than a coincidence.'

'This is a tourist park, for God's sake. A resort where you're supposed to have a good time. Not the back streets of the Darwin waterfront.' She stifled the sob that rose in her throat and met Kane's eyes squarely. 'I'm sure Bill's hiding something and it has to do with the work at the back of the farm. His "accident" worries me. Now I think Heather knows something too. That thug scared me and someone has been in my apartment twice now. And now that I've have seen the drilling with my own eyes, I know Mum is right about the fracking.'

'And maybe about . . .' She couldn't put her doubt about Dad's death into words and her breath caught. Kane held her close and his hand was warm in the small of her back.

'Why would Bill be involved in anything to do with the farm?'

'He's on the committee that's involved in protecting the environment. They make decisions about mining licences. I may be making a big leap in my thinking but what if he was attacked as a warning?' Ellie drew in a shaky breath and swallowed. Her throat was dry from all the emotion coursing through her. 'There's no other reason for anyone to hurt him.' After his out-of-character behaviour with her on Sunday, Ellie knew she was right. Bill had got wind of something happening there. Maybe he was being warned to stay out of it. Whatever it was, she was going to get to the bottom of it.

For years, Ellie had held it together, not wanting to lean on Mum or Emma. A great sense of desolation filled her and she put her elbows on her knees and dropped her face into her hands.

'Shit, oh shit.' She muttered the words in frustration.

Finally she lifted her head and met Kane's gaze. She knew he'd been watching her, she could feel his gaze on her. She needed someone to help her find out what was going on; she couldn't do it by herself.

Ellie held his eyes and saw only concern and kindness. She let her gaze travel across his face and he stared at her as she examined him. His short hair was brushed back from his high forehead. Laughter lines that spoke of happier times were traced in small white creases in his tanned face. But his eyes were hooded and she could see the touch of dark shadows beneath them.

We all carry our own secrets and our own grief.

Kane stood slowly and held out his hands. Ellie took them and he pulled her to her feet. He embraced her and the feeling of safety she'd experienced in his arms came rushing back.

His steady breath blew gently on her hair as she leaned into him. 'Don't worry. I'm with you on this. There is something going on. What Heather said about your mother was cruel but I got the feeling she was trying to upset you so you'd stop asking questions.'

'So did I.'

They stood in the dark on the verandah and the world grew quiet around them. Kane fingers drew lazy circles on her back and Ellie trembled as the warmth of his hands pressed against the thin fabric of her top.

'It's a long time since I held anyone like this. Even before the accident in Afghanistan, I promised myself I wouldn't get involved with anyone. It was too dangerous and too hard. I saw how some of my crew suffered when they had to leave their families behind for each deployment.'

Ellie rested her cheek against Kane's chest and let his voice soothe her.

'I can't bear to think what their deaths did to those families. I'll tell you about it one day, but it's why I won't fly.' His voice was steady but Ellie could hear the emotion behind the words he uttered. 'I'm glad you visited my mother yesterday. I don't know exactly what's wrong with her, but it's not right that she's there on her own. I don't care what Sordina says. I'm going to insist she goes back to Darwin closer to medical care.'

'She does look very weak.' Ellie's voice shook. It was hard holding back what Susan had confided.

'You know, I lost touch with Mum for a while after she remarried. I suspected he was marrying her for money but she wouldn't have a bar of it. She's always seen the good in people.' His voice was bitter. 'I guess I've been proved right now. When we're in Darwin I'll go and see him. I'll find out what's going on at the farm.'

'Thank you.'

Neither of them spoke for a while. Ellie put her head back down onto Kane's shoulder. He smelled of mint and a woody aftershave and she drew in her breath, enjoying the feel of his arms around her; comfort given and comfort shared.

'It will be a long way to go and see her if she moves back to Darwin. Will you stay working here?' Ellie swallowed, thinking how much she would miss him when he left.

The sounds of the night surrounded them as the nocturnal wildlife became more active. Slowly Ellie drew back; as much as she'd have liked to, she couldn't stand there in his arms all night. She tipped her head to the side and looked up at Kane. 'Listen. The northern bullfrog.'

His eyes were dark and anticipation ran through Ellie as he held her gaze. An indefinable change hovered in the air between them as a smile tipped the corner of his lips. Kane's expression softened and his voice was low.

'I don't really have frogs on my mind at the moment.'

He lowered his head and the diamond stars were blotted out as his cool lips brushed against hers. She stood on her toes and let her lips cling to his as he pulled her closer to him.

'Where are you going to sleep for what's left of the night?' She smiled as she held his gaze. 'My sofa.'

'Come down to my room?' His smile was gentle and a warm feeling rushed through Ellie's chest.

# Chapter 18

*Wednesday*
*Makowa Lodge*

Ellie woke alone in Kane's bed, a light blanket thrown over her. He had simply held her as she had lain beside him and they'd talked until almost sunrise. Finally she had drifted off to sleep with his arms around her and her head on his shoulder. She felt safe and complete for the first time for a long time.

Friendship. That's all it was. She wasn't going to read too much into it. Yeah, it was different to the moves that guys like Mike and Steve tried. Friendship was good, but that still didn't account completely for the lightness in her step this morning. Back in her own apartment, she looked in on Heather but she was still asleep. She had a quick wash and pulled her khakis on, and then left a note asking Heather to call before she left for the medical centre. She left her car keys on top of the note so Heather wouldn't have to take Bill's old cruiser.

Keen to get over to the hangar to see Kane, Ellie called into the office to pick up the scenic flight bookings for the day, and skimmed a quick glance down them. Another two had been added overnight, but she'd still be finished in time to catch up with Gina for lunch. The anticipation of going to Darwin with Kane buzzed through her.

'The tourist season has begun with a vengeance.' Jock's voice interrupted her and she looked up at him with a smile. 'You're handling it with the way Jan's sending some of the flights Cooinda's way?'

'So far, so good.'

'You've got five on this morning?' Jock rubbed his chin and smiled at her apologetically.

She glanced back down at the bookings. 'Yep. Four couples, and then a guy on his own. All good.'

Ellie was pinning the schedule to the board in the hangar office when Kane strode in, dressed in his khaki lodge shirt and cargo shorts. She pressed the last pin hard to control the pleasant tremble that ran through her.

Friends.

He walked in to the office with a smile and put his hands on her shoulders. The warmth of his fingers burned through the thick cotton of her shirt. He swooped down with a grin and kissed her briefly, and Ellie couldn't help the smile that tugged at her own lips.

Okay, maybe more. The feeling fluttered to her lower belly and legs.

'Sleep well?' His voice was bright and she knew he was feeling the same buzz as she was.

She nodded.

'How's Heather this morning.'

'Still asleep when I left. I'll check on her later. I asked her to let me know when she goes to the medical centre.'

'I called them. They wouldn't tell me how Bill was but they did let me speak to him. He's still insisting on going to Darwin today.' Kane nodded at the flight schedule on the wall. 'Busy morning ahead?'

Ellie glanced up at the schedule and nodded. 'Not too bad. Two flights back to back and then I'll have a break and go and see if Heather's okay, before the last three.'

Kane brought his hands back to her shoulders and laughed when Ellie jumped. 'Sorry, I could get addicted to having my hands on you.'

Her laugh was self-conscious. 'It's new to me.'

He inclined his head to the list in her hand. 'You okay to take that many flights up?'

'Pfft. I'm used to it. You'll be earning your pay in a few weeks.' She realised what she'd said. 'I mean, you'll be checking the two machines ten times a day.'

\*\*\*

The first couple had booked the short scenic light over Ubirr Rock in the South Alligator region.

As well as being the highlight of a scenic flight, guided ground tours wound through the low scrub to the rock. The Aboriginal rock art gallery was protected and wonderful to experience, but for Ellie there was nothing to equal swooping over the river and the wetlands up to the high escarpment and then back to Ubirr Rock. It was one of her favourite flights and the tourists always enjoyed the experience. The traditional owners managed it jointly with the Territory government; it was another committee Bill was on. Ellie frowned as she worried about what had happened last night, but the 'oohs' and 'aahs' and questions from the passengers kept her focussed on the flight. Gradually a feeling of contentment filled her; it was the most settled she had felt for a long time. Knowing that Kane would be waiting when she brought the helicopter down added to her good mood.

After they had done the circuit, Ellie turned the chopper

back towards Makowa Lodge. She took the eastern flight path, deciding to avoid flying over the old farm.

The next flight took her to the south of the park, and the early morning passed quickly. Ellie took a break before the next flight that was booked in for ten o'clock. She secured the bird – there was no sign of Kane – and headed back to her apartment, picking up two coffees from the bistro on the way.

Heather was sitting in the sun on the verandah. 'I was just about to text you. You don't mind if I borrow your car and drive into Jabiru to pick up Dad?'

'That's why I left my keys out for you. Is he ready to come home?'

'Yeah. He'll be ready in an hour. I'm sorry I snapped at you last night.'

'No problem. Did he say anything else on the phone?' Ellie probed gently.

'Just that he's ready to come home as soon as the doctor checks on him again.' Heather pulled a face. 'You know for a while I thought he'd gone back to his old habits.'

'He gave us a scare, that's for sure. What time do you start work?'

Heather glanced down at the phone in her hand. 'I'm at the crèche from one-thirty, so I'll have time to pick up Dad and bring your car back. He's got to go straight to Darwin for a meeting.'

'Will he be okay to drive?'

Heather shrugged. 'You know what Dad's like. Can't be told anything.' She shot Ellie a nervous smile. 'Thanks for the bed, Els. I hope me being here didn't . . . er . . . cramp your style.'

Ellie pulled a face at her. 'No style to worry yourself about. Kane and I are just friends.' She rolled back the cuffs of her long-sleeved shirt; the morning sun was hot. 'He's a nice guy, now that he's got over trying to show his testosterone and establish his place in the pecking order.'

'We'll see.'

Ellie gave a noncommittal grunt and headed for the stairs. 'Make sure you lock the door and pull it shut when you go. Leave the keys with Jan when you get back.' Normally she wouldn't worry too much about security but the events of last night had made her more than a little nervous. 'I've got three more flights to take up this morning and then I'm having lunch with a friend.' She flashed Heather a big smile. 'And then I'm going to Darwin to help Kane out with some family stuff.'


On the way back to the hangar, Ellie detoured around the pool, looking out for Gina and the two children. She wanted to ask Gina to have an early lunch but there was no sign of them on the lawn; she'd send her a text between flights.

The hangar was deserted; Kane wasn't in the work bays or out on the tarmac. Ellie frowned. He'd checked both helicopters before the first flights this morning, but she wondered where he'd got to now. Her next flight wasn't scheduled for another twenty minutes, so she logged onto the computer in the office to check her email in the browser.

Sixteen messages including one with a multitude of attachments from Emma. Ellie nodded with satisfaction as she whispered softly under her breath. 'Thanks, sis.'

She'd known Emma would get straight onto it. Em,

always the steady reliable one. Ellie knew she was the dreamer.

Ellie scrolled through the file names, not wanting to download them on this computer. She was keen to open the attachments, but she'd have to wait until tonight. Newspaper articles, parliamentary minutes and a file named Fairweather. She flicked an email back to Emma: 'Thanks for the stuff. Did you ask Mum about the Gmail account? Busy day ahead for me. Love Els.'

She glanced at her watch and peered out into the foyer looking for her next booking. The guy was running late. Passengers were supposed to arrive fifteen minutes before the flight time to complete the mandatory paperwork before they went up.

She was about to give up when the sound of the door to the office opening broke the silence.

A tall, well-built blond man strolled through the door and his eyes narrowed as he caught sight of her. Ellie had to force the welcoming smile onto her face. Sometimes you could just pick a difficult customer.

'Mr Henry?'

He nodded and she picked up her clipboard.

'Just some paperwork to fill out and we'll get going.'

You had to take the good with the bad in this job.


Ellie skirted around the pool again on her way over to the office. Mr Henry had been one of the most difficult passengers she'd ever had. The questions about the R22 hadn't bothered her; it had been his insistence on taking over the T-bar so he could 'fly the bird' that had made it a difficult flight.

In the end she'd given in for a few seconds when he'd become unpleasant. She hadn't liked the way he'd looked at her either. Cold and calculating. When they'd come back down, there'd still been no sign of Kane, and she'd hurried the guy out even though he wanted to stay and chat. He made her feel uneasy; being in the hangar by herself was not on, and it was probably against some safety regulation anyway. They'd have to sort that with Jock. She frowned as she headed towards the pool. Kane was rostered on and should have been there.

Gina was sitting in the shade on a sun lounge, looking cool and elegant as she watched her two small children wading in the nearby baby pool. Despite her pregnancy, she wore a red bikini with a sarong tied over her bump. A floppy straw hat and huge sunglasses completed the picture. Ellie waved and called out to her as she hurried past. 'I'll be back soon. Just have to drop the keys off to the office and then get changed.'

Gina put down her Kindle and waved back with a smile.

The reception area was busy so Ellie went into the back room and hung the hangar keys on the board.

Jock wandered in as she was about to leave. 'Kane asked me to tell you he had to leave for Darwin earlier than he planned.' Disappointment rocketed through Ellie. 'Oh, okay. Thanks, Jock.'

'He's had to go away for a couple of days, so we'll sub flights from today till the weekend. I've organised for the Cooinda engineer to help us out for a couple of days. I'm not prepared to lose the bookings.'

Ellie's head flew up and her eyes narrowed. That explained why he hadn't been around since her first flight this morning. Maybe he'd changed his mind about her going with them.

'Anything wrong?'

'Yeah, his mother's been taken to hospital and he's gone across to be with her.'

A weight descended on Ellie's shoulders as she remembered how sick and lonely Susan had looked on Monday. She knew that Kane would be worried about her and she made a snap decision. 'Jock? Can I beg a favour?'

He cocked his head to the side and stared at her. 'What?'

'There's no more flights booked today. I know I've got this afternoon off, but . . . do you mind if I take tomorrow morning too? I need to help someone out.'

'I do owe you for the extra hours last week.' Jock looked down at the roster on the side of his desk. 'You can have the morning. Be back on duty at four tomorrow for the afternoon sunset flight. You can do a short afternoon shift. I'll get one of the boys over from Cooinda to do the once over on the birds in the morning.' He looked at her curiously. 'Is everything okay?'

'Yes, I just need to be a friend.' Ellie tore out of the office and hurried back to her apartment, hoping to catch Heather before she left for Jabiru. She'd need her car. She swung around the corner and stood with her hands on her hips, scanning the car park behind the building. Too late, her car was gone.

'Shit.' She'd have to wait until Heather got back before she headed to Darwin. She walked slowly back to the office and collected the keys from Jan.

She pulled out her phone and checked the time: eleven-thirty. She had almost two hours to kill before Heather would be back. Ellie flicked through her phone and found Gina's number. Her fingers flew over the letters as she sent a text.

'Ready to eat?'

The reply came back almost immediately. 'Yes. Where and when?'

'At the pool bar. Stay there'. Ellie knew it would be easier for Gina if the children were somewhere they could play and the pool bar brought food orders in from the bistro.

She sent Heather a text to tell her to leave her car in the front car park when she came back from picking up Bill. She walked slowly up the steps, wondering if she should tell Kane that she was coming. But she couldn't anyway; she didn't have his number and she didn't want to ask Jock for it. What she was going to do was private and nothing to do with them being workmates.

Ellie changed out of her khaki shorts and work shirt into a summer dress suitable for visiting at the hospital. She grabbed a light jacket, locked the door of her apartment and walked back over to the pool area. The gate squeaked as she lifted the childproof lock and pushed it open. Gina looked up with a smile, pointing to the phone she held against her ear. Ellie walked over to the children and crouched down on the grass beside the sandpit, giving Gina some privacy to finish her call.

'Hey, guys. Want some lunch?'

Binny looked at her with green eyes identical to her mother's. 'Ice cream?'

Andrew shook his head. 'No, Binny. Hot chips, then ice cream.' Ellie laughed, sure she was being conned. Binny ran for the gate and Ellie jumped up to chase the little girl whose little legs pumped furiously as she covered the distance across the manicured lawn.

Ellie turned to reassure Gina that Binny was fine, and heard her laugh out loud and exclaim in what sounded like Italian.

Her eyes were sparkling and her lips were tipped into a pretty smile. Gina beckoned her over when she finished her call.

Ellie held Binny's hand as she walked over to Gina. 'Hi, you look happy about something.'

'I was talking to my mother . . . in Italy. She misses us all so much.'

'Oh, that's nice.' Ellie pointed to the phone. 'Hey, I love the phone cover.'

'It is pretty special.' Gina held it up with a smile. 'If I tell you who gave it to me, will you promise not to think I am – how do you say it – big-headed?' Her accent was more pronounced in her excitement.

'Of course.'

'The last time I worked a fashion show in Milan, Giorgio gave it to me to try to persuade me to stay. Isn't it beautiful?' She held it out to Ellie. 'It's a little big for my new phone but it's too pretty to put away.

'Giorgio?' Ellie picked it up and looked at it closely. There were hundreds of small crystals covering a silver leather flap.

'Armani.' Gina's cheeks coloured and Ellie laughed. 'Wow. That is pretty special. I wouldn't be using it. I'd leave it in the bank!'

'Giorgio couldn't understand why I wanted to leave Italy in the middle of a good career. But my choice was easy. Modelling or David? No contest.'

Ellie wondered what it would be like to love someone so much. She'd had the occasional boyfriend at school but since Dad had died, she'd found it very hard to commit her feelings to anyone. She guessed – if she was honest – it had to do with a fear of losing someone else. It was easier not to get involved; then you couldn't be hurt.

'Ellie?'

She realised Gina was staring at her. 'Sorry.'

'Everything okay with you? You look sad.'

'Yes, all good.' She smiled over at the children who had climbed back into the sandpit in the shade. 'So I hear it's hot chips and ice cream for lunch.'

'Vegemite sandwiches is more like it. Come and sit with me for a while before we eat. I'm so pleased you ran into David last weekend.' Gina chuckled and patted the empty lounge beside her, before her expression turned serious. 'Do you have time to stay and chat for a while?'

'I do. I've got a trip to Darwin this afternoon. I'm sorry it took me so long to catch up with you. It's been madness here.' Ellie sat on the lounge and kicked her sandals off, stretching her legs out. 'How long are you here for?'

'David will be back on Saturday and then maybe we have another week. Hopefully by that time he –' Gina cut her words off and shook her head – 'so a few more days of rest for us.'

Ellie looked at her curiously, but respected Gina's privacy. David's attitude had unnerved her a little last weekend. He's was very serious and uptight about something; but it was none of her business. Em had always told her she was a soft touch, always taking on everyone else's worries.

Is that what I'm doing with Kane?

She turned to watch the children digging in the sandpit; they seemed like such a happy little family.

'Let's order. I've got a couple of hours before I have to go.' Ellie shrugged. 'It's been a bit of a complicated week.'

'Want to talk about it?' Gina put her hand on Ellie's arm. 'I'm a good listener.'

And she was a good listener. As they ate, Ellie found herself opening up to this woman she had only just met. Just family stuff, and how she missed her sisters; nothing about her fears.

Binny and Andrew squabbled around them as the two women ate their lunch. Ellie stretched her feet out on the comfortable day bed and yawned as she handed her empty plate to one of the bar staff.

'It's going to be a long drive to Darwin.'

'Do you have to go?' Gina leaned back on her chair.

'No, but I want to.'

'Anything to do with that good-looking guy I saw you with in the bistro last night?'

Ellie sat up. 'I didn't see you there.'

Gina laughed and warmth ran up into Ellie's cheeks. 'From what I saw when we left, you weren't seeing much past the guy who was with you. Boyfriend?'

Ellie shook her head. 'Just one of the guys from work.'

'Hmm.' Gina's voice was soft. 'He'd like to be. You should have seen the way he was looking at you.'

Ellie's face burned as a small tendril of hope unfurled in her chest. 'We're just friends.'

Gina had a pretty laugh 'That's what I used to say when I first met David.'

'Seriously, I'm not going to get involved with anyone.' Gina grinned at her. 'Can I give you a piece of advice?

When you meet someone and you have that instant attraction, don't let go of it. Life's too short.'

'I've only known him a week.'

'I knew David was the man for me an hour after I met him.' Gina leaned forward. 'Don't make the same mistake I did. Don't fight it, Ellie.'

Ellie squared her jaw. 'I'm not strong enough to get involved with anyone, Gina. I don't think I could stand the pain of losing them.'

Gina reached over and took her hand and Ellie stared down at their joined hands. Gina's were soft and nicely manicured, very different to her square-cut unpainted nails.

'You've lost somebody in your life?'

'My father. I don't want to risk that grief again.'

Gina look up, and her eyes were sad. 'Life is one big risk, but if you don't take that risk, Ellie, it's not living.'

# Chapter 19

*Wednesday night*
*Darwin Hospital*

'I'm very sorry. I don't think she will survive the night, Mr McLaren. Her body is too weak from the cancer and she had another myocardial infarction in the ambulance.' The doctor's eyes had been kind, but resigned, as though this conversation was one he was well used to. 'If there is anyone else to call, you should call them now.' The doctor nodded and left the room.

Cancer.

Kane leaned forward in the hard plastic hospital chair beside his mother's bed as shock coursed through his body. Her eyes were closed and she was breathing easier now that she was on oxygen. He looked at her hands on the white cotton blanket.

Thin and dry-skinned, her fingers plucked restlessly at the thick hem of the blanket as her chest rose and fell softly.

Earlier that morning, he had driven to the farm at breakneck speed after getting a distressed call from his mother saying she couldn't breathe. He had heard her rasping breath and her short choppy words, and had immediately hung up and called an ambulance. He'd felt absolutely bloody useless when he'd got her back on the line, but he'd kept talking, reassuring her, keeping her calm as he'd run to his Jeep. By the time he'd arrived at the farm, the ambulance had left. He called the Jabiru Medical Centre but they told him the paramedics had stabilised her and she was en route to Darwin hospital. Kane had collected some clothes and toiletries and picked up his mother's phone before he'd locked up the house.

But she wouldn't need any of them if what the doctor had said was right.

'Kane?' Her voice was soft but at least the wheezing had eased.

He stood and looked down at her. 'Mum. Are you comfortable?'

'Yes. I'm better now, darling.' Susan reached out, took Kane's hands between hers and squeezed them but the pressure barely made an impression on his skin.

'Come closer.' She took a deep shuddering breath and coughed.

'Do you want me to call the nurse?' Kane helped her sit up and waited until she had stopped coughing.

'What about Panos? Did the hospital call him?'

'I don't know.' He tried to keep the disgust from his voice. He was going to have harsh words with his stepfather after –

But now was neither the time nor the place. 'Call his mobile. His number's in my phone.'

'I'll do it now.'

Kane fought the pricking at the back of his eyelids as his mother leaned back against his arm. Her breath juddered and stopped, and she coughed. The rattle of her breathing was the same as he'd heard many times in the desert.

He pulled out her phone, found the contact for Panos and pressed the shortcut. But the call went straight to message bank. 'Do you have another number for him?'

She shook her head. 'Try again later. Talk to me for a

while first. Just talk to me. Tell me about some of the good times we had together.'

Oh, fuck. Kane knew what that request meant, but somehow he managed. He spoke softly and soothingly as his mother fought for breath, keeping his voice steady.

'Remember when I was little and you let me have that cat? I wanted a kitten, and I found that mangy, scabby cat in the bush.' He let the first tear roll down his cheek. 'We had Christmas at Aunty Val's in Brisbane that year. Remember? The last one with Dad? We all went to Redcliffe for a picnic and you let me take the cat on a lead.'

Kane let all the memories fall softly around his mother. Recollections that he hadn't thought of for years poured from him. In his mind, his mother stood strong and caring in front of him. His father stood beside her. Dad had been killed in a car accident the year before Kane had started school, but Mum had always done her best to be there for him.

She'd always laughed a lot and he realised now how sad she'd been over the past few years – on the few occasions he'd made the time to visit her, even before she'd remarried. He had failed her as a son. Just like he'd failed everyone else. Now the breathing of this shell, of his once-strong mother eased, and she turned to him with a sigh.

'We had a good life.' Her voice was soft. 'I missed your father so much when he died. But I had you.'

'Yes, Mum, we had each other.' Kane moved his arm and she leaned back into the pillow. He rested his head gently on his mother's shoulder and a memory came to him, sharp and clear, of resting his head on that same thin collarbone when he was a small boy, sneaking in for a cuddle in the middle of the night. 'I'm sorry I went away, Mum. I'm sorry I wasn't there for you.'

'Hush. It's all right. Panos looked after me.' Her voice was a little stronger and her fingers smoothed the back of his head. Kane lay quietly as she began to speak. 'As best he could. I need to tell you something. I know it's going to confirm what you always thought of him, but Panos is a good man. He's just weak where money is concerned. He was always looking for more.' She raised her hand to her mouth and took a deep breath. Kane could hear the crackling in her chest. 'More than I could ever give him. When Ellie came to see me on Monday, it all came back. I'd tried to forget about it – to put it behind me – but I know that was the wrong thing to do. She told me how her mother is still suffering, and I realise now I should have done more to help them.'

'Help who, Mum?' Kane was confused and he lifted his head. Susan stared at him, her eyes clouding over. Whether it was from her state of mind or the medication that was pumping into her veins, he didn't know.

'Ellie's mother.'

'What happened?'

'It was before we were married. Panos got tangled up with some man in Darwin who had a lot of different interests. He only made friends with Peter Porter so he could be the intermediary for this man who wanted the land.' A bitter laugh escaped her lips and she coughed again. 'He offered him a fortune for it but Panos never knew why he wanted it. He was going to be paid a big commission. He gambles, Kane. Anything. Horses, football, anything he can bet on. It's an addiction.'

Kane fought showing the disgust that filled him. Susan shook her head from side to side, trying to sit up. Kane put his arms gently on her shoulders and held her steady.

'Panos was determined to secure the sale, but Peter wouldn't accept the offers.' Her fingers gripped his arm and her sudden strength surprised Kane. 'What disgusted me most was that after . . . after Peter was gone, Panos came in like the saviour and Sandra was so grateful to take the money from him so she could get away from the memories. She was distraught with grief.' She leaned forward and coughed. 'I was disgusted with Panos.'

'So Panos bought it in the end, not this other person?'

'I don't know. He told me he bought it, but I've always wondered where he got the money. It's in his name. I've seen the papers.'

'How did her father . . . die?' Kane held his mother's gaze; her eyes were so sad.

'He hung himself. Sandra found him in his packing shed. No wonder she's still a mess.' The tears rolled down her cheeks, and Susan reached up and held Kane's chin, turning his head slowly until his eyes were close to hers. 'I've always felt guilty that Peter died. I've always suspected that Peter killing himself had something to do with that man wanting to buy the farm.'

'What was his name?'

'Russell Fairweather. Panos used to go to the races with him.' Her breath came in short hitches and Kane filed that name away as he laid her back gently on the pillows. I'll go and try Panos again, Mum. He needs to be here with you, too.'

He kissed his mother's brow gently, and picked up his

phone and headed for the door.

***

The hospital had a sharp antiseptic smell and Ellie shivered as she crossed the highly polished lino floor to the front desk at the entrance. She'd always hated hospitals – especially this one. Her father's parents had both been in here when she was a child, and they had visited them every weekend for a month. Neither had come home again, and this place held only memories of sadness and death. Even when she drove past, a shiver of sadness always crawled down Ellie's spine.

'Yes?' The receptionist on the front counter smiled at her. 'I'm looking for a Mrs Sordina. Susan Sordina.'

The woman tapped the keyboard and pointed to the bank of elevators to the left of the large foyer. 'Fourth floor. Ward 3A. Mrs Sordina is in a private room. Report to the desk and they'll tell you if you can see her.'

The lift was empty. Ellie stabbed at the button for the fourth floor, regretting her mad dash down to Darwin more as each second passed. It had been a compulsion that she hadn't been able to ignore – a feeling that had pushed her to drive for almost three hours along the Arnhem Highway. Heather had looked at her strangely when she'd met her in the front car park and told her she was taking an unexpected trip to Darwin.

'Why?'

'I'm going to visit Kane's mother in hospital.' She wondered at the relief that crossed Heather's face.

Maybe it wasn't appropriate. Maybe she should have gotten Kane's number from Jock and called him. Maybe there'd be more family here to support them both. Although if there was more family, surely they wouldn't have left Susan alone at the farm? She reminded herself that Susan had asked her to be Kane's friend. That's all it was about, nothing to do with this strange feeling that flowed through her when she was near him.

She was here now; she'd visit Susan, see if Kane was okay and then spend the night in Darwin. She'd have a leisurely breakfast by the harbour in the morning and get back to the lodge with plenty of time to spare for her afternoon shift. It would give her some time to gather her thoughts and look at the email that Emma had sent. Her laptop was in the boot of her car; after two break-ins, she hadn't been confident about leaving it in her apartment.

The doors slid open silently as the lift reached the fourth floor. The desk was unmanned and there was no sign of any staff. The clinical smell was even stronger up here in the wards, and Ellie shivered again. It was quiet and the curtains were drawn, the last shard of afternoon sun peeking through the space between them. She hesitated, uncertain of what to do. As she turned back to wait by the desk, her heart jumped. Kane was sitting in a plastic chair further down the corridor, his head back against the wall, his eyes closed.

Ellie walked slowly towards him, her flat-soled leather sandals making no sound on the shiny lino floor. There were deep lines etched beside his mouth and dark shadows circled his eyes. She stood there for a moment looking down at him before reaching out and placing her hand gently on his shoulders. He lunged forward. His hand grabbed hers tightly as his eyes opened. The pressure of his fingers made Ellie wince and she pulled her hand back.

Confusion crossed his face and Kane put the other hand up to his forehead. 'Ellie! What are you doing here?'

'I thought you might like some company.' She spoke softly. 'I hope it's okay? Jock told me your mum's pretty sick.'

Ellie dropped to a crouch in front of him and took his hands in hers. 'How is she now?' she asked softly.

Kane shook his head. 'Not good.' The doctor is in there with her. She had another turn when she was talking to me.' His voice was clipped as though he was trying to say it in few words. 'They're giving her morphine to ease . . . to ease her last hours.' Ellie's throat closed as Kane continued and his voice shook. 'I've said my goodbyes.'

'Oh, Kane. I'm so sorry.' She brushed her eyes with the back of her hand as the tears filled her eyes. 'What about Panos? Is he in there with her now?'

'We've tried everything. Called his mobile, the office, parliament house, but we can't locate him.' He nodded towards the nurses' station. 'They've been great. They've left messages everywhere and they're trying his mobile every ten minutes or so.'

'Oh, that's not . . . good.'

'Why did you come?' Kane's voice was soft.

Ellie held his gaze steadily. 'I thought you might need a friend.' Kane dropped his head and leaned his forehead against hers.

'Thank you.'

Ellie pushed to her feet and stood beside him. His arms went around her waist and sympathy overwhelmed her as he leaned against her. She knew the grief that had overtaken her when Dad had died. She put her hand on his shoulder and he turned his head slowly to look up at her. The warmth of his skin seeped through the cotton of his black T-shirt and ran up her arm with a jolt.

He held her gaze and something passed between them. A look that reaffirmed their connection. Whether it was friendship or something more, Ellie wasn't sure. She hugged the feeling to herself for a moment and then put it away safely to examine later. Maybe Gina's advice was worth considering.

'Well, I am here. And I'm going to stay.'

She stepped to the side and reached for another plastic chair. Kane was still regarding her steadily, but his face had softened and all she could see was a man who was uncertain and alone, as his mother lay dying in the room across the corridor.

'You don't have to talk to me. I can get you a coffee.' Ellie kept her voice soft.

'Thank you.' Kane reached for her hand and held it loosely. They sat there without speaking until the door opened. The doctor stepped out and walked across to them.

'She's asleep and resting as comfortably as we can make her. Perhaps you'd like to sit with her.' He glanced across at Ellie. 'You can both go in if you would like to. At this stage . . . we don't worry about the rules.' He turned to Kane. 'Did you manage to contact her husband yet? I'm sorry, it won't be long now.'

Kane stood and kept Ellie's hand tightly in his. She swallowed down as hard as she could. The ache in her throat burned as she tried to hold the tears back.

'Thank you. I'll go in,' Kane said. The doctor nodded

and touched him briefly on the shoulder before he walked away.

'I don't expect you to come in.' His mouth turned up in a ghost of a smile. 'Maybe you could get me a coffee from downstairs? I think the coffee shop stays open till late.'

'Sure. If not, there's sure to be a coffee machine.' It would be good to help out in a tangible way. Ellie turned to go, but Kane's hand on her shoulder stayed her. He pulled her gently into his arms and she slipped her arms around his waist. He rested his chin on the top of her head and Ellie rubbed his back, trying to soothe his tight muscles. They stood together without speaking for a minute, before Kane stepped back.

'Thank you. Later . . . after . . . we need to talk.'

'Okay.' She turned away towards the lift, conscious of Kane's gaze on her. But when she reached the lift and looked back he had gone. Ellie gave in to the ache in her throat and the tears rolled down her cheeks.

# Chapter 20

*Wednesday night*
*Parliament House, Darwin*

David slipped his finger into his collar and pulled it away from his neck. Despite the air conditioning, the room was stuffy and his shirt was sticking to him. For the first time since he'd entered public service he'd begun to question whether it was worth it. Loosening his tie, he closed his eyes, wishing he was at Makowa Lodge with Gina and the kids, relaxing by the pool with nothing to worry about.

Now the sterile smell of a conference room surrounded him. And a critical vote loomed ahead. As long as Gina and the kids stayed safe he could handle it; but two weeks was a long time to be away from them and the new baby's birth was getting closer. Once the two decisions were made, he'd be talking to security. The votes would be cast and Fairweather would no longer have a hold over him.

The outcome of tonight's committee meeting was crucial. If the vote approved the change to the national park boundary, the meeting on Monday to vote on the exploration licence would be critical. The future – or even the survival – of Kakadu National Park swung in the balance, dependent on the outcome of these two committee votes. But if tonight's vote rejected the boundary change, it was highly unlikely that the exploration licence would be approved – Fairweather's plans would be dead in the water.

David glanced up as Bill Jarragah hurried into the conference room, only a minute or so before the meeting was due to start. His arm was in a sling and his clothes were rumpled. He pointed to the sling with a shrug of his good shoulder.

'Silly accident,' he said, but despite the good-natured teasing that followed he would not be drawn on what had happened. David watched as Bill took a seat across from him. He and Bill were the only representatives who were on both the committees. The chair called the meeting to order and David focused his attention on the proceedings.

The Honourable Member for Berry read the minutes of the last General Purpose Standing Committee, his speech punctuated by the occasional clink of crockery as members made their way to the corner of the room to replenish their coffee.

When he finished he put the minutes down and looked around the table. 'It needs to be made quite clear that the outcome of this vote today will impact another one next week.' David tipped his head to the side and listened carefully; they were getting to the critical part of the discussion that had been raised briefly at the last meeting.

'It is most unusual for a boundary to be reduced rather than resuming other land to add to the National Park.' The member's voice was flat and David wondered whether he was only going through the motions. Maybe his tone indicated the way he would vote. Hopefully the point he raised showed he was against it.

David looked around the room at the other committee members and caught the eye of Bill Jarragah. Bill lowered his gaze. He knew that Bill would vote against this. He could always count on the Aboriginal vote to protect the water and environment of the Territory; David was as sure of that as he was the sun would rise in the morning. His gaze settled on each of the committee members in turn and he began to perspire.

Were Fairweather's threatening words just posturing? Would he really go after Gia and the kids? Again, David reached up and ran his fingers between his collar and his neck, before he reached for his water glass.

One of the other members held up his hand. 'Are we discussing the specific property here or are we still in general discussion?'

The member for Berry looked at him over his glasses, as though it was a question where the answer was obvious. David didn't mind, the more dissension there was, the less chance that the vote would be in the affirmative.

'Yes, I am sure everyone on both committees has been made aware that it is the South Alligator River property where Black Coal Holdings is seeking to drill for the purposes of exploration.'

'So if the boundary change is approved, it is more likely that the exploration licence will be approved?' Bill spoke quietly. 'That is correct.'

Frowns creased a few foreheads and a couple of the members made notations on the copy of their minutes in front of them.

The member for Arnhem Land raised his hand, and the chairman nodded for him to go ahead.

'For exploration to occur I believe an access agreement with the owner is required under section 28B? Is that correct? And the owner of the land in question will change if the boundary change is approved?'

The chairman nodded and the member's voice rose as he spoke against the vote. 'Isn't it most unusual to recommend a boundary change to a federally administered National Park?'

Good, David thought, another one who's against it.

The discussion moved naturally to the economic viability of coal seam gas mining in the Territory.

He waited, hoping someone else would raise what was at the forefront of his mind. He didn't want to be the one to introduce the issue. It was the elephant in the room; everyone was aware of it, but he wanted to hear it, and see it recorded in the minutes of this meeting. It wasn't long before the words he waited for were spoken.

'Yes, the difficulty lies in the fact that the property in question is owned by Panos Sordina.'

The chairman nodded. 'The members will of course not take that into account when voting, but it must be made very clear that Mr Sordina has declared his pecuniary interest and that he is willing to sell off the affected portion of his property if the approval goes ahead.'

A stifled laugh from one end of the table was quickly turned into a cough. 'Hah, of course he is,' someone muttered.

The member for Berry looked over his glasses at the offending member. 'Order please. To be fair to Mr Sordina, he has owned this property for five years, and the possibility of mineral wealth in the South Alligator region has only come to light in the last eighteen months.'

Bill's voice was soft as he entered the discussion. 'The environmental study is complete and the boundaries of the National Park can be adjusted without significant impact on the northern section of the park if necessary. The land in question is not culturally sensitive.'

Several members tried to speak at once. David looked across to Bill and he again dropped his gaze. An uneasy feeling snaked through his stomach when he saw the perspiration on Bill's brow.

'Order please.'

Papers shuffled as the committee prepared to vote. David took a deep breath. He hoped that his prediction of the outcome was right. He had spoken to the members over the previous weeks and they were evenly split. He had had a long phone conversation with Bill Jarragah last week and he knew that together their votes would defeat the motion. Even so, David's stomach clenched as the vote was called. Bill stared straight ahead, perspiration running down the sides of his cheeks; he looked distinctly unwell.

David gripped his hands in his lap and held his breath. He watched as the three of the four hands he expected rose slowly. 'So are we done?' The chairman's hand was already up, as David had expected.

Disbelief jarred through him as another hand rose. The member for Berry stared down at the table as his hand too, rose. He was the most conservative member of the committee and had been vocal in his opposition to shale gas exploration for many months.

Five up and five down. It was now up to David to choose between his beliefs or his family. A negative vote would put his wife and children in jeopardy, but he couldn't, in good conscience, support the proposal. He clenched his hands more tightly as he opened his mouth to confirm his negative vote. If necessary he would put a round the clock guard on the children.

But before he could declare his negative vote, Bill jutted his chin out and put his hand up.

The chairman looked around the room and counted the show of hands. 'The measure is passed in the affirmative. Six votes to four in favour of the boundary change.' He nodded 'I am pleased, personally and on behalf of my constituents, to see that common sense has prevailed. Hopefully this decision indicates that the exploration application will be looked at favourably next week. It is in the best economic interests of the Territory.'

David's throat closed with disappointment but he kept his expression bland as the chairman called the meeting to a close. David had voted against it; he would not succumb to threats. Fairweather had got to others in this room – maybe more than one. David looked around, but not one member would meet his eye. Bill Jarragah's eyes were closed and perspiration ran down his face.

David closed his office door and collapsed at his desk, staring at the picture of Gina and the children next to his computer. Uncertainty rippled through him. Had he made a mistake sending them away? Should he have kept them close where he could look out for them?

The dropped gazes and the outcome of the vote had convinced him that Fairweather's reach was great. They were solid men of integrity in that committee and more than one of them had obviously been bought. He couldn't believe that Bill Jarragah had voted for the boundary change; but if Bill had sold out for money, he would be very surprised. His passion for his land and love of country had made Bill a valuable member of the environmental committees for which he'd represented the clans since before David had been in parliament. There must be another reason for his decision. He was counting on Bill to speak strongly against the exploration licence.

Pressing his thumbs onto his eyelids, David tried to ease the band of stress that was beginning to tighten on his temple. The last thing he needed was a stress migraine.

And no Gina at home tonight to massage my neck. David glanced down at his watch before taking a swig of water from the bottle of his desk.

He pressed the speed dial on his mobile and stared out the window as he waited for her to pick up. The square below was empty and leaves whirled around in the strong wind. He knew she'd be waiting for his call.

'Hi, darling.' Her voice soothed him even from afar. 'Sorry, it took me a while. I forgot to get my phone out of my bag before I got into bed. It's full of rubbish.'

'For a change,' he said. He had never known anyone to carry as much in a handbag as Gina did.

'I need a new one.'

'A new handbag?' David smiled to himself. He knew what was coming next.

'Yes, I think a trip to Florence is called for.' He could hear the laughter in her voice and then it disappeared. 'Is everything okay there, darling? How did the meeting go?'

David ran his hand through his hair. 'The boundary change was approved.'

Gina was silent.

He cleared his throat and injected a smile into his tone. 'Having a good rest?'

'Yes. I had lunch with Ellie today.'

'Good, I must thank her for catching up with you. How are the kids?'

'They miss you, David. I've booked them into the crèche tomorrow afternoon. I'm going to have another facial.' Gina's voice faded out for a moment.

'You there, Gina?'

'Sorry, I thought I heard one of the kids, but it was just the wind. It's really blown up here tonight.'

Premonition crawled along David's spine. 'You've locked the doors? And the windows are shut?' There was no way Fairweather would know he had voted against the exploration. Surely not.

'Yes, David. I listen to you.'

'It's windy here too. I have to go now, *bella*. I just called to tell you how much I love you.'

'*Mi manchi,* David.'

'I miss you too. All three of you.' David made a snap decision as he stared into the night. 'Gina? How would you like to take a trip back to Tuscany for Christmas? I am sure your mother would love to see our new little one.'

The squeal that came through the phone brought the smile back to his face.

'Really? Oh David, that would be wonderful.'

'We'll start planning it when you're all back home next week.'

'Mwah. Have I told you today I love you?' David smiled as the sound of kisses came over the phone.

'Yes, but you can tell me as much as you like.' The phone on David's desk buzzed. 'Bella, I have to go. Say hello to Ellie for me when you see her next . . . and Gina. Take care, okay?'

'We will. Love you, darling.'

David disconnected and slipped his phone into his pocket, and reached for this desk phone.

'Yes?'

'David.'

His stomach clenched and a metallic taste filled his mouth. 'Russell. I didn't think I had given you my direct line.' The chuckle that came over the phone sent a shiver down David's spine.

'No, I don't believe you did, David.'

'What can I do for you? I was about to leave for an appointment.'

'Yes, I believe you do. The member for Berry, I believe? A good man.'

Jesus Christ. Did the man have the whole fucking committee in his pocket?

'I wasn't aware that my schedule was public knowledge.'

'Don't toy with me, David. You won't be happy with the consequences.'

'Listen to me, Russell.' David bit out the words. 'You will not tell me what to do. Is that clear?'

'No, David. You listen to me. I'm very unhappy with the way you voted in the meeting earlier. I thought we had an agreement.' Fairweather's voice was like steel.

'We had a discussion, there was no agreement.'

'And I told you what might happen if you didn't understand my side of the discussion. Perhaps I wasn't clear enough.'

'Oh, yes. You were mighty clear.' David held the phone so tightly he could feel his fingers going numb.

'I know you have hidden your little family away, but don't underestimate me, David.'

'That is one thing I will never do, Russell.' David kept his voice firm and strong, despite the cold chill that was running down his limbs. 'I'm only going to tell you this once: Leave my family alone. And don't underestimate my integrity. I will always do what is best for the Territory.' There was stony silence at the other end of the phone. 'Now as I said, I have a meeting. Good night.' David dropped the phone and it hit his desk with a clatter.

***

Russell Fairweather slipped the phone into his tailor-made jacket and brushed an invisible piece of lint off his trouser leg before turning to his driver. 'I am very pleased you brought the Mercedes tonight, Mick.'

'My favourite, Mr Fairweather.'

'And your helicopter flight went well this morning? I have another couple of little jobs for you down in Kakadu.'

'It was very satisfactory. When you need me to follow through I have a plan in place.' For the first time Mick smiled. 'Those R44s would be very easy to fall out of.'

'Good. You'll need to take an off-road vehicle down there tomorrow. I'll let you know the details later.'

'My pleasure.' Mick's expression was bland again.

'Did you keep the little souvenir you retrieved from Bill Jarragah last night?'

A single nod. 'It's in the cooler on the back seat.'

'Well done.'

Russell pulled his phone from his pocket. There was one more loose end to tie up.

It was opportune that David had secreted his little family down at Makowa Lodge. And such a happy coincidence that Ellie Porter was working there too. Now to ensure that Bill Jarragah would jump to his bidding a second time.

# Chapter 21

*Thursday night*
*Darwin Hospital*

Susan Sordina held on for another day. She passed away just after eight o'clock the following night, Kane by her side as the final rattling breaths struggled from her frail chest. He remained with her for a long time before he let go of her cold hand and called for the nurse. Panos had not been located. They'd even sent the police to his office but his secretary said he'd gone out and not told her where he was going.

Ellie was sitting outside in the chair where she'd been all day, a cold cup of coffee on the floor beside her. She had supported him, talked to him, held his hand and been there with coffee each time he'd come out for a break. Her legs were curled up beneath her, and her head tipped back on the hard plastic chair.

Kane stood at the door, took a deep breath and composed himself. He clenched his jaw and swallowed. Later he would give in to the grief of losing his mother, but first he had to find Sordina, the gambling lowlife, and tell him his wife was dead.

Rather than driving back to Kakadu that night, Ellie talked him into letting her book two rooms at a hotel down on the harbour front. It made sense; he had to notify his stepfather, and when he had done that, there were more arrangements to make in the morning. Jock wasn't expecting them – she'd phoned earlier and explained the situation – and as Ellie pointed out, he was tired and it wouldn't be safe being on the highway.

'You need to eat something.' She tipped her head to the side and observed him as they took the lift down to the car park.

Kane grasped the small bag of his mother's belongings the nurse had handed him as they'd left the ward. All he wanted now was to get through the next few hours without a panic attack. He was deathly tired, his emotions were in a mess, and there was a constant prickling in his scalp. He was doing the best he could to cope. He turned to Ellie when he realised she'd asked him a question. 'Sorry?'

'Do you want me to pick up some Maccas on the way to the harbour?'

'No thanks.' The thought of food made his stomach churn. A feeling of detachment from the real world precluded any normal activities like eating or sleeping. Even talking was difficult. Kane's feelings were heading in a downward spiral but he made the effort to look at Ellie and answer her. 'Coffee will be fine.'

They stepped through the sliding doors onto the kerb. The bright light shining over the hospital entrance bathed the building in a surreal glow and sharpened the corners of the building. An ambulance was backing into the emergency bay with its lights flashing and the blue light made macabre shadows on Ellie's face.

Kane took a deep breath and held Ellie's arm as they crossed the road towards the car park. 'Come on. Let's get out of this place.'

He drove behind Ellie in his Jeep and followed her towards the city. She took the last turn before the city precinct and turned into Tiger Brennan Drive. The motel was down on the harbour – not the exclusive side of Cullen Bay, but down towards the semi-industrial area where there was a push to make it more attractive to tourists. As Kane followed her small car through the deserted streets, he came to a decision. After they reached the motel and he had seen Ellie safely inside, he was going to find Panos.

Now. Tonight. Kane didn't care if it was the middle of the night. The death of your wife was not the sort of news anyone deserved to hear over the phone.

Ellie swung her little sedan through a wide archway one street back from the waterfront. Kane parked on the road and walked into the small car park at the side of the motel. The receptionist had promised the keys would be left in the door of their rooms. He pulled his phone out and scrolled down to Sordina's number as he walked across the road.

This time Sordina picked up after a couple of rings.

Finally.

'Panos, it's Kane. Where have you been? I've been leaving messages for you for the last twenty-four hours.'

'Wha . . . who?' The voice was slurred and Kane clamped his lips together in anger. It was obvious now. His wife had died while he was out on a binge. Not only a gambler, it seemed Sordina had a drinking problem as well.

'It's Kane. Are you in the city? I need to see you.' Kane kept his voice calm holding back the harsh words that were on his tongue. He glanced across at Ellie. She stood silhouetted in the doorway of one of the rooms.

'Iss the fuckin' middle of the night.' Panos sounded like a petulant child.

'I need to see you now,' Kane repeated. 'Where are

you?'

'My office. I was asleep.'

'Meet me at the 24-hour McDonald's at the harbour end of McMinn Street.' There was no way he was going to his office to meet his stepfather, he'd end up fucking killing him. But the McDonald's was around the corner. He'd met his mother there a couple of years ago on his final deployment. Kane's voice was icy and calm. 'I'll be there in ten minutes. And Panos? Walk there. You don't sound as though you are in any fit state to drive.'

'Wass it for?'

'Be there. Ten minutes.' Kane slipped his phone back into his pocket and walked over to the motel room where Ellie had stood in the doorway. The door was still open but he couldn't see her. He poked his head inside. 'Ellie?'

She looked up from the small kitchenette on the other side of the room.

'I'll be back in half an hour. I'm going to tell Sordina that –' Kane cut his words off. He couldn't bring himself to say them. Mum was gone, but he yet couldn't put it into words.

'So you found him? Do you want me to come?'

'No. I need to do this on my own.'

She gave him a sad smile and walked over to the door with him. 'I'll wait up for you till you get back.'

'You don't have to.'

'I want to.'

Kane looked down at her. He wondered if she knew how much it meant to him, having her there with him tonight – or rather this morning. 'Thank you.'

***

Panos Sordina landed on his knees as he missed the single step from his office to the street and his iPhone flew from his hands, skittering into the gutter in front of the wheels of a dark car parked at the kerb. 'Bugger.' As he scrabbled around for the phone, the vehicle's headlights came on, almost blinding him. He put a hand up to shield his eyes and shook his fist at the driver.

'Bloody wanker!'

He spotted the phone in the gutter and bent down to pick it up. His head swam. Taking a deep breath, he made a conscious effort to clear his mind, but that last mouthful of whisky he'd drunk before passing out at his desk had been one too many. He leaned across the gutter and retched. The whisky burned his throat as it came up, the sour smell of his own vomit disgusting him.

What the fuck did his stupid stepson want this late at night anyway? He slipped his work phone into the pocket of his trousers. He'd expected the call to be from Fairweather, but the other phone had been silent for two full days. Panos reached into his shirt pocket and pulled it out. He needed to beg; he didn't want out – that had been a stupid thing to say. He needed the money.

Panos stumbled along the footpath as the car took off quietly ahead of him. He pressed the shortcut for Russell and then noticed the time on the screen: two o'clock. It wasn't night, it was the middle of the fucking morning. What the hell did Susan's son want him for?

Kane McLaren, bloody war hero, had made it very clear

from their first meeting that he didn't think he was good enough for his mother. At the time, he'd just moved into her house in Cullen Bay. Now Susan was at the farm, living in that bloody falling-down house where it had all begun. It was probably what Kane wanted to front him about, but for God's sake why at this time of the morning?

'What do you want, Panos?' Fairweather didn't sound as though he'd been woken. Maybe he never slept.

'I'm sorry. I was out of line the other day.' He pulled himself straight and forced a worried tone into his voice. 'I hear the vote went our way.'

'Our way? We're finished. Remember?' Fairweather's chuckle was almost friendly.

'No, no. I'll help you. I'll do whatever you say. I've been a loyal friend to you, Russell.'

'You had your chance. It's too late now.'

'I'll come and see you. Tomorrow.' Panos knew he couldn't do what Russell wanted but he could bluff his way through. 'I'm sorry, I was wrong.'

'Panos? I'm sorry too.' With that enigmatic comment, the call disconnected.

Shoving the phone into his trouser pocket with the other one, Panos brushed his hands down the front of his shirt and then wiped his mouth.

The salt-laden air from the harbour hit him full in the face as he rounded the corner and he sobered a little more. The garishly lit McDonald's on the corner of McMinn Street was empty. No sign of Kane. He'd better bloody turn up.

First thing tomorrow, he'd call Russell again.

He crossed the road to the small park at the edge of the

harbour. He often sat there when he got sick of being in his office, and he knew there was a tap down the steps near the boat ramp. He'd get himself a bit presentable and watch this bloody awful taste out of his mouth.

A vehicle cruised along the street behind him and pulled to a halt as he hurried across the grass. As he sluiced cold water over his face, Panos shivered. The row of industrial buildings was in darkness and all was silent. The garish blue light of the Fishermen's Co-op lit the far end of the street as it flashed every few seconds but its customers were long gone.

He straightened up and stared over the inky black water. The lights of distant fishing boats twinkled silently back at him. To the north, just beyond the horizon, were the Tiwi Islands. If Russell wouldn't listen to him, maybe he could get on a boat and disappear there. Or into Arnhem Land. He had some cash in the office.

But there was Susan to consider.

The door of a vehicle swung open with an ominous squeak. He looked up. A tall man stood on the footpath above him, clad in black. The light was behind him and his features were hidden beneath a dark cap pulled down over his hair and covering his face. The man pulled a torch from his pocket and shone it into his eyes.

Now he couldn't see a damn thing. 'Kane?

Panos took a step towards the man. A slither of movement moved the air as the man jumped over the rocks in a swift panther-like movement. Suddenly his hands were held tightly behind his back and he had been twisted around to face the water again. Tears sprang to his eyes as the man grabbed his hair, pulling his head back almost at right angles to his spine.

He tried to make out his attacker's face but all he could see were dark eyes staring down at him impassively in the dim light.

Guttural sounds came from his throat as he tried to protest. 'It's a long time since I've killed anyone like this.' The words were delivered in a harsh whisper.

The assailant kicked the back of his knees and let go of him at the same time. Panos fell forwards, his forehead hitting a rock at the base of the low rise to the footpath. With a soft grunt he lay on his stomach. Terror filled him as the man above him spoke again.

'The crocs are going to enjoy their breakfast today.'

'Kane? Is that you? Please, I'm sorry.' But there was no response.

Before he could move, strong arms looped behind his elbows and he was dragged across the small car park, his legs flailing uselessly on the rough bitumen. The assailant paused for a moment to unhook the chain across the boat ramp, and Panos looked around desperately. A single vehicle with an empty boat trailer was parked beside the concrete ramp. A wild hope surged through him.

'Help me,' he croaked. He looked out to the harbour, but the lights of the fishing boats were far from the shore.

'Stand up.'

The man yanked him to his feet and his head spun. Vomit filled his throat again and he gagged.

'You filthy bastard.' The voice was louder this time and Panos closed his eyes as fear took over.

The man in black looked away at the water swirling onto

the concrete ramp. Panos could hear the incoming tide lapping against the rocks; it was almost to the top of the boat ramp and the night feeders were stirring with the influx of fish.

The man pulled a knife from the harness on his ankle and smiled. Panos' bladder let go as the pale moonlight glinted on the long blade. The strong smell of urine surrounded them.

'You fucking coward.'

As he waited, expecting to feel the cold blade of the knife, a couple of pebbles rattled down the ramp behind them. The man turned swiftly, dropping into combat position, the knife poised to attack. His head swivelled quickly from side to side as he scanned the car park above them. Panos' last hope dissolved as a scrawny cat slunk away and disappeared into the dark gap between the two buildings on the far side of the car park.

'Enough.' The man spun around on his haunches.

After one long swipe across Panos' neck, the man stepped to the side to miss the spray of his blood. With a wet gurgle, a bubbling choke and a final expulsion of air from his lungs, his life was over. His vision faded and he welcomed the blessed darkness.

# Chapter 22

*4.00 am Friday morning*
*Harbour Side Motel, Darwin*

Ellie paced the sparse motel room, wondering when Kane would be back. She couldn't sleep; like him, she was wired – the two cups of coffee she had while waiting added to that. She briefly considered using her phone to read the attachments on Emma's email, but knew her concentration wouldn't be good enough to focus. Her mind was full of sadness for Susan and sympathy for Kane. A muscle had been pulsing in his cheek ever since she'd arrived at the hospital and she knew he was putting up a strong front. She was glad she'd made the effort to drive to Darwin. There'd been no one else there for him; he was a loner.

She flicked through the dozens of cable TV stations for a while before leaving the television tuned into an old black and white movie, more for company than an interest in the movie. She must have drifted off to sleep despite the caffeine because a light tap on the door and Kane's voice roused her a while later. Ellie opened the door and he walked in slowly. His face was pale and his eyes were dark.

'Hey, come on in.' She kept her voice soft. 'I'll make you a coffee.'

Kane put his keys down on the small table next to the sofa where Ellie had been curled up. He sat down and leaned forward, staring down at the floor. 'Thanks.'

She didn't want to pry so she left him sitting there and went into the small kitchenette. What Sordina had said, how he had reacted to Susan's death, was none of her business. She glanced across at her iPhone sitting on the bench; it was just before four o'clock. All was quiet as she waited for the water to boil. By the time she returned to the small sofa with two cups of coffee, Kane had rested his head back on the sofa and his eyes were closed. She put the mugs on the small coffee table and sat beside him. His dark lashes fanned his cheeks and Ellie let her gaze travel over his face. The hollows in his cheeks appeared gaunt tonight and a rush of feeling ran through her. She wanted to put her hand to his brow and smooth his hair back and tell him everything would be okay.

But it wouldn't. His mother had died and he had to work through the grief. She thought back to what Susan had said about Kane needing a friend. She could be that; she would be there for him. Apart from her friendship with Heather, Ellie kept distant from most people. Even her relationships with her sisters were distant most of the time. This feeling of wanting to comfort Kane, and be here with him was very unfamiliar.

Ellie's eyes were heavy and her eyelids slowly closed as she let Kane rest.

The ringing of a phone on the floor beside them roused her a short time later. Kane jumped to his feet and looked around the room, a frown wrinkling his forehead and his shoulders tense.

'Your phone?' he said.

Ellie shook her head as she reached up and pulled her hair back from her face. 'No, it's not mine. Mine's in the kitchen.' She looked down at the plastic bag on the floor and frowned. 'It's in with . . . with your Mum's stuff.'

Kane reached into the bag and pulled out a small dark

red phone. He looked at it for a moment before flipping it open and putting it to his ear.

***

'Hello? Who is this?' He didn't recognise the number. Who the hell would be ringing his mother at this hour of the morning? It certainly wouldn't be Panos, would it?

'Is that Mrs Susan Sordina's phone?' It was a man's voice, deep and authoritative.

'Yes. Who is this?'

'To whom am I speaking?'

'Who wants to know?' Kane wasn't telling anyone who he was until they identified themselves first. He knew he was being rude but he couldn't give a shit. Not after the night he'd had.

'My name is Detective Sergeant Garrett from the Darwin Metropolitan Command. I need to speak to Mrs Sordina as a matter of urgency. Is she there please?'

Kane dropped to the sofa beside Ellie, conscious of her gaze on him.

'This is Kane McLaren – her son. And no, she's not here.' He couldn't bring himself to elaborate, not yet. 'What's this about?'

'I need to speak to Mrs Sordina personally.'

'I'm sorry, you can't.'

'I have to. It's an urgent matter.'

'She's not . . . here.

'Can you tell me where I could locate her please? As I said it is a matter of urgency.' The man's voice was firm.

'Where are you?' Kane ran a hand over his eyes.

'I'm at police headquarters in Smith St.'

'Look, I'm in Darwin, I'll come in to see you, okay? I can't . . .I can't talk now.'

'Very well. I'm on the sixth floor of the NAB building. Say about nine?'

'Fine.' Kane disconnected and put his mother's phone on the table. He leaned back and the tired sofa sagged beneath his weight.

'Is everything okay?' Ellie shook her head. 'Sorry, stupid question. I know it's not.'

'That was the police. They wanted to talk to Mum.' Kane shook his head and looked away. 'What now?'

Ellie put her hand out and her warm fingers held his arm gently. Kane looked down at her hand against his skin, uncertain of this feeling that was rising in him. Something about Ellie touched him, bolstered his confidence. He relaxed his shoulders as the warmth of her fingers travelled up his arm and eased the tension. His gaze swept over her and he was surprised when the warmth turned into the unexpected flaring heat of desire. Her eyes were wide as she looked at him, and tinged with dark shadows.

'Thanks for being here, Ellie.' Kane dropped his head slowly and rested his forehead against hers. 'You didn't have to come, but I am really glad you're here with me.'

Ellie leaned into him and he spoke honestly. 'I'm shattered. If I don't get some sleep, I'm going to be an absolute cranky bastard and there's so much to do tomorrow . . . I mean today.'

'I probably should get some sleep too. It was good of Jock to give me the extra day off. I'll need to leave at noon to head back to work.'

Kane brushed his thumb across her cheek and let it linger on the soft skin. 'You probably didn't need to book two rooms. I could have bunked here on the sofa.' He pushed himself to his feet and looked down at her. 'But it's been good having you here with me.'

Ellie stood and slipped her hand into his. 'Stay.' A smile glimmered in her eyes and her mouth tipped up on one side. 'Don't take this the wrong way, but I don't mind if you want to lie down here with me. It's crazy to go next door.'

Rational thought fled and Kane's heart kicked in his chest. This was dangerous territory. Her hand trembled in his and the intensity in her expression hit him low in his belly.

'I'd appreciate that. Being alone is not too appealing this morning.'

Ellie led him into the bedroom and pulled back the cover on the large bed. The air conditioning was humming in the space next to the window. She kicked off her sandals and lay on her side and he stood looking down at her for a moment, before he sat on the side of the bed and took his shoes off.

Ellie snuggled into him and he put his arms around her. The need rocking through him was muted by the exhaustion that overwhelmed him. Kane closed his eyes and let sleep overtake him as Ellie's hair tickled his face.

It seemed only a short time later that Kane woke with the sun shining through the thin curtains and hitting him squarely on the face. He lay there for a moment, trying to gather his thoughts. Ellie still lay beside him, her soft curves pressed hard against his chest. He closed his eyes again and took comfort from her closeness; fighting the urge to run his hands down her sides and trace the curve of her breast with his finger. She moved beside him and when he opened his eyes again, Ellie was watching him; her pale blue eyes intense and fixed on his face. He returned her gaze steadily. There was no need for words. She lifted her hand and brushed the hair back from his forehead. Kane reached up and snared her fingers in his, holding her close so she couldn't move away. Desire and uncertainty ran parallel inside him.

'How do you feel this morning?' Her voice was a whisper, and she too, seemed a little unsure of herself.

'I'm okay.'

As they stared at each other, something shifted between them.

Kane lowered his head and took her lips gently. When her lips opened beneath his, he reached around and cradled her head in both palms. He could feel the slow heavy beat of her heart against his chest, and he held back, willing to take whatever path she chose. Ellie's soft sigh puffed against his mouth. Slowly Kane lowered his lips to her neck and her breath quickened as he trailed his mouth to the indent at the base of her throat.

Lower. She arched against him with a soft cry as he closed his hand around her breast.

He was lost.

'Please.' He had no idea if the words came from his mouth or if they were just in his head but he tensed when Ellie pulled away. Regret surged through him. He'd moved too fast.

I shouldn't have kissed her.

He shivered as she reached out and slipped her fingers

beneath the bottom of his shirt. Her lips curved in a smile as her hands slid up over his chest. She softly traced his skin, holding his gaze steadily with those pale blue eyes.

He grabbed both of her hands and rolled over onto his side, and then reefed his own shirt off before he pulled her close. Skin on skin, face to face, their bodies pressed close together. A shudder ran through Kane's body and he groaned and then lowered his mouth to hers again. This time the kiss was not gentle, and he took pleasure in the way she responded to his kiss, to his touch.

'Ellie?' He lifted his head and looked up at her.

'Yes.' The single word sent a spark of healing joy rushing through him

# Chapter 23

*8.00 am Friday morning*
*Harbour Side Motel, Darwin*

Ellie lay in the bed, listening to the shower run in the ensuite bathroom. She stretched, feeling the unfamiliar tingling and pleasant ache deep in her body. Being with Kane this morning had been different to the first night they'd slept together. As well as the physical pleasure given and taken, this time there here had been an emotional connection. It was a tentative beginning that Ellie didn't want to resist this time. A new and unspoken level of trust had been reached.

But was she ready for it? She rolled over and stared the ceiling as the shower switched off. She'd long vowed to be independent. If she let herself fall for him, could she trust Kane not to leave her?

Kane wandered out from the bathroom, droplets of water caught in the smattering of hair on his bare chest. A ripple of pleasure whipped down Ellie's skin and settled in her lower belly. The white motel towel barely made it around his hips.

He sat on the bed and smiled down at her. 'Okay?'

Ellie nodded but he must have seen the expression that flitted across her face.

'I want you to know that what we've shared is very special for me. I haven't been close to anyone for a very long time.' He held his head proud as he stared at her; aquiline nose, his forehead wide and high. A rush of need raced through Ellie.

She pushed herself up in the bed and pulled the sheet up

over her bare breasts as she spoke softly. 'I'm pleased I could be here for you.'

'Don't sell yourself short, Ellie. You pushed my buttons since the first minute you strode across that hangar and tried to boss me around.' His lips tilted in a boyish grin and the crinkles beside his eyes deepened. But his eyes were still full of sadness; she knew that it was more than the death of his mother that he carried with him.

Kane reached down and took one of her hands. Ellie hadn't realised that she'd been playing with the frayed edge of the cotton sheet.

'I know we haven't got much time this morning but I want you to know why I'm the way I am. Why I can be so bloody moody.'

'It's okay.' She shook her head. 'You don't have to explain yourself to me. I'm not the easiest person to get on with at the best of times either.'

He ignored her words. 'I know Mum told you I was a hero. She was proud of me.' His voice was bitter. 'But she had nothing to be proud of.'

Kane looked down at their hands still joined together on the white sheet, and then his attention moved back up to her face.

'My entire crew died and it was my fault.' His voice was flat and expressionless. 'Ellie, I made one simple error of judgement. I flew in too close to the insurgents and we got shot up. I crashed my bird. One of my crew . . . Hawk.' His voice shook for the first time. 'You remind me of her.'

Ellie listened as he told her about the crash. The death of his crew, and the hopelessness that filled him as he'd trudged through the desert carrying the woman, knowing she was dead, but not being able to leave her at the crash site.

'The official line was that it was a mechanical fault but it was my fault, I listened to the guys and I flew too close. The first round shattered the cockpit and then –'

Ellie lifted her hand and cupped his cheek. His eyes were flat and his mouth was set in a straight line. All she wanted to do was move his thoughts away from where they were. The haunted expression in his eyes chilled her to the depths of her soul.

'You've had a lot to deal with.'

'I can't seem to let go. The day you took me to that billabong, I relived the whole fucking crash. It's like being there all over again. Flying back to Darwin was hell.' He put his hand over hers on his cheek. 'And then when I went up with you that first day, I thought I was going to lose it.'

'You need to see someone to work through it.'

Immediately Ellie sensed his withdrawal and regretted her words. It wasn't up to her to tell him what to do. 'Just one step at a time.' She smoothed her hand over his short hair and he relaxed against her again. 'Dealing with the grief for your mum is the most important thing for now.'

An ache filled Ellie's throat as her hand brushed against Kane's face, damp with tears.

'How . . . how was Panos when you told him last night?' Ellie had been wondering why Kane was so quiet when he'd come back in.

He lifted his head and his eyes were cold and hard. 'I didn't see him. I waited on the corner but the bastard didn't show. He still doesn't know Mum's gone.' Kane's eyes narrowed. 'He's such a money-grubbing lowlife nothing would surprise me about him.'

'You know, I always thought he was helping out when he bought the farm from Mum. But he was no friend to Dad. It's been in front of me the whole time. He was after the farm all along.'

'Don't worry. I'll get the truth from him. The truth about selling Mum's home, and his involvement with your family's farm.' Kane's tone was cynical. 'How long had your Dad known him?'

'Only a few months, but they'd spent a lot of time together in the last few weeks before Dad died.'

In those last weeks, the mango trees had been left to fend for themselves – not that that was really anything different, but Dad had spent more time in the paddocks before Panos had arrived on the scene.

And then, it was only a few weeks later that Mum found Dad hanging in the shed.

Dru had come home from school that fateful afternoon and seen the police cars and the ambulance at the house. Ellie could still hear Mum's guttural sobs in the background when Dru had called her.

'Ellie?' Kane's hands slid down her shoulders and gripped her arms. 'Ellie, listen to me. Mum told me something that makes me believe there might be someone else behind Panos. Have you ever heard of a man called Russell Fairweather?' His deep voice against her hair was soothing.

'No. Should I have?'

'I'll make some calls and we'll look into it when I get back tomorrow. Okay?'

She lifted her head as she thought about his words. If there was someone trying to get this approval through, what else were they capable of. She fought down her rising apprehension. They'd hurt Bill for some reason. They could do it again.

'You really think Panos was acting for someone else?'

'I'm sure of it. He hasn't got the ability to be in something this big himself. And he wouldn't have the balls to hurt someone.' His voice filled with disgust. 'Just enough to dump his dying wife down where she's out of his way.'

Ellie reached up with both hands and held Kane's face. 'There has to be a way to deal with this. Surely we can report it. But stay calm, don't let your grief feed your reaction when you see him. Don't do anything rash. Okay?'

Kane dropped his forehead to touch hers. 'That's the story of my life. You really don't want to get mixed up with me.'

Getting him to face his anger about what had happened in Afghanistan and his mother's death would be something to tackle together after they dealt with the funeral and what was happening at the farm. She knew more than anyone what he was going through. Dad's death had shaped the adult she'd become.

'I'm still here, Kane.'

He ran his fingers through her loose hair and she smiled up at him.

'Thank you. So what are we going to do?' he said.

'Are you coming back to Makowa to stay after . . . after you organise things?' Now that his mother had passed away, Ellie wondered if he really had any reason to be there.

'Yes. I'm going to stay here. For a while anyway. I've been happier here –' he reached up and covered her hand with his '– even with Mum being ill, I've felt like I belong somewhere for the first time since –'

Ellie put her fingers against his mouth and shook her head. 'That's all I need to know – that you're going to be around for a while.'

'And we'll work together.' A great sense of relief filled Ellie. To know that she could share the burden of what was happening at the farm, but still a little trepidation stayed with her.

'Sordina knows I've been down the back and seen the fracking. I fronted him about it on the phone the other day.'

'Shit. Did you really?' Admiration crossed Kane's face and he reached out for her. 'You are certainly one feisty little lady, aren't you? Panos may be dishonest but like I said, he's a coward. Christ, he wouldn't even meet with me.' He stared past her shoulder, his eyes fixed on the wall above her head. 'Now I'm not so sure. It depends who he's working for. Trust me, there'll be money involved.'

'He said he'd see me this weekend when he came down to the farm. I doubt if he will now.'

'Probably not. But don't worry, I'll get what I can out of him today.'

Slowly Kane's arms tightened around her and Ellie let herself rest against the hard angles of his chest. She loved him holding her and the comfort brought tears to her eyes.

'But I still can't believe Panos is involved. He can't be. He's in parliament.'

'That doesn't mean he's honest. Maybe he doesn't

know what's going on down there, but I doubt it very much.' Kane frowned.

'He knows. He lied to me. He told me that there was a new dam being built.'

Deep furrows lined Kane's brow as his frown deepened. She reached up and smoothed her hand over his forehead. He caught her fingers in his and stared at her, his eyes shadowed as he faced into the night.

Slowly he lowered his head and his lips were firm and cool against Ellie's mouth.

She put her arms around his neck and held him there as she spoke against his lips. 'Thank you.'

He leaned back a little but his breath still warmed Ellie's lips as he spoke.

'For what?'

# Chapter 24

*9.00 am Friday*
*Makowa Lodge*

Gina tried David's number for the fourth time that morning. She'd given up on sending texts after she'd filled her iPhone screen with texts that he didn't answer.

'Miss U.'

'Love U.'

'Where ARE U?' He must be in committee or he'd forgotten to take his phone off mute – again.

'David pls TXT me.'

She hadn't spoken to him since he'd left them last night, and she wanted to check he was home safely. Not only that, it was unlike David not to call her here before he left for work, no matter how early it was. There'd been no sign of Ellie since they'd had lunch together on Wednesday. Gina tucked her phone into her bag, hoping David would get back to her soon. A persistent ache had dragged at her lower back since she'd lifted Binny up this morning and she was worried that she'd pulled a muscle.

Gina held the children's hands as she waddled over to the crèche at the back of the office building. Yes – waddled. She was getting bigger and more ungainly by the day. One of the women around the pool had even asked her yesterday if she was having twins.

Heather, the pretty Aboriginal girl who had been on reception the day she'd checked them in, welcomed them. She had dark shadows under her eyes.

'Hi Ms Perini. Hi kids. Have you come to play?' She came over to the gate and crouched down to greet the children.

'My day spa appointment has been changed.' Gina glanced down at her watch. 'Can the children stay here this morning instead of this afternoon?'

'Of course. The day spa is closing at noon today.' Heather stared at her before she turned to the children. 'Come on, kidlets. Come and play with Heather.'

Binny and Andrew ran inside to the play dough table.

'I'll come back and collect them as soon as I'm finished.' Gina blew a kiss to the children. As much as the time here was restful, she was beginning to wish they could just go home to normality. She hated the days here without David. It was as though they were waiting for something to happen.

The technician showed her into the treatment room and before Gina slipped her clothes off and stepped into the pale pink, fluffy robe, she grabbed her phone from her bag in case David called.

'Is this the biggest size you have?' she asked with a smile.

The tie only just went around her pregnant bump.

Gina lowered herself carefully into the soft leather chair and fought the usual vertigo as it tipped back. The girl positioned the chair so she could sit behind Gina and begin her facial. She grabbed for her phone as it slipped off Gina's lap and threatened to slide to the floor.

'I'll just put your phone over here, okay? Snazzy case.'

'Thank you.' Gina nodded and closed her eyes. The soothing music played soft and low and she let her thoughts drift as the technician's skilful fingers moved gently over her skin. Warm cloths alternated with cool liquid, and then her face was covered with soft gauze. The light was muted to a hazy grey through the gauze pads that pressed lightly on her eyelids. The sharp smell of a fruity cream drifted up as the girl worked her magic.

'I'll leave you to rest for fifteen minutes. All okay?'

Gina heard the sound of the door closing gently. For five minutes, she lay there alone and dozed lightly, aware of the low hum of voices in the next room. The music turned up louder as the door opened. Gina's chair tipped back a little more as someone adjusted it. A muffled conversation buzzed around her. 'Needed in the office . . . I'll finish off here '

She frowned. It sounded like Heather's voice. 'Okay, thanks. Just the facial to come off.'

'Is everything okay with the children?' she asked but there was no reply.

The door closed with a soft click. There was the sound of someone moving quietly around the room and Gina tried to open her eyes, but the gauze was stuck to her eyelashes. She tried to sit up but firm hands pushed her shoulders back gently.

'Just relax. Everything's fine.'

Dread filled Gina as a sharp sting pricked the skin of her inner wrist. Grabbing for her arm with her other hand, she ran her fingers over the spot as an icy cold travelled up her arm.

'What was . . . –' Gina opened her mouth to protest but a wave of nausea and giddiness overwhelmed her. Cold sweat ran down her neck and her mouth suddenly felt as though it was full of cotton wool. Her panic increased and her heart began to race as a strong cramp seized her belly. She wrapped her arms around her chest and shivered as weakness stole through her limbs.

'I'm sorry.' The woman sounded as though she was crying. 'So, so sorry. But it'll all be okay . . . I'm so sorry.'

Gina tried to call for help but no sound would come out. David was right. Someone was trying to hurt her. This was what he had warned her about. Oh God, will I ever see him again?

And my babies. She lifted one arm and managed to reach out; silver lights were clouding her vision.

Her hand was lifted gently between smooth, soft fingers as the husky voice faded in and out. 'It won't be for long and I promise I'll take good care of Binny and Andrew.'

Gina shook as a final shiver wracked her and the soft grey light turned to black.

## *Parliament House - Darwin*

David glanced down at his phone: four missed calls from Gina as well as a string of texts. He pressed her number on speed dial and held the phone to his ear, waiting for her to pick up as he flicked through the emails on his computer.

Gina's phone switched to voicemail but he hung up without leaving a message. Knowing his wife, she would call back shortly. A day didn't pass without them having at least one conversation – often three or more. Last night had been horrendous, back-to-back meetings until midnight. He'd intended calling Gina after they'd finished but it had been too late when he'd got back to his office and he knew she'd be asleep. He missed them so much; the house was as quiet as a morgue. David crossed the room and leaned on the doorframe, looking out into the adjacent office to where his media advisor usually sat. His desk was clear and his computer was switched off. He needed him now; they had a lot of work to do before Monday's meeting.

'Helen?'

His secretary looked up from her computer screen. 'Yes, David?'

'Do you know where Sean is?'

'He's been doing some work over in the technology unit.'

'Can you get hold of him for me, please?'

'Sure.' Helen nodded and picked up the phone and David flashed her a brief smile and went back into his office. The media release prior to Monday's meeting was going to be a key factor in ensuring that the right outcome was achieved.

But it would all be a waste if Fairweather had gotten to any- one else on this committee. Some of his colleagues were acting strangely; eyes downcast and unwilling to stop for a friendly chat as they passed on the corridors. If only he could get someone to confirm it, he'd have Fairweather up before a corruption hearing as soon as the vote was over. But he was too careful to take him on without hard proof. A throwaway line to him with no witnesses was not going to stand up in a court of law.

David crossed to the window and stared across the expanse of water in front of him. A breeze had whipped the waves into white caps on the harbour. The flag at the front of Government House snapped in the stiff breeze. The white gables reflected the strong morning sun and tourists were wandering along the path that skirted the harbour. They didn't have a worry in the world.

His shoulders sagged for a moment; it had all became too hard. The more time he spent fighting for what he believed was best, the more he became disillusioned by the power of people like Fairweather. No longer was it for the good of the Territory or Territorians. A parliament free of political corruption, where decisions could be made based on integrity and a balanced consideration of the risk for the environment, was never going to be the reality. He'd been idealistic and naive.

To the detriment of my family, and my life.

Despite his uncertainty, David had still prepared thoroughly for the meeting on Monday. He hoped Russell Fairweather would be very disappointed with the outcome of the vote.

There was a light tap on the door, and the door opened before he could speak. His media advisor strode in, a smile plastered on his face.

'Dave. The dragon lady –' he inclined his head towards the outer office '– told me to get my butt in here.' He turned the chair at the other side of David's desk around and straddled it. 'We've got some work to do, Sean. Thanks for coming over.

I need your expertise.'

Before Sean could respond, the door opened and Helen walked in slowly. Her face was ashen and her hands shook as she put them up to her face.

David stood and hurried across the room. In the four years, he had worked with Helen, he had never seen her show any emotion. By the time he reached her, tears were running down her face. Cold fingers of premonition settled in David's gut.

'What is it? Helen, what's wrong?' She was shaking and turning her head from side to side. 'Is it Gina?'

'Oh David, I'm so sorry. It's dreadful, dreadful news.'

# Chapter 25

*9.15 am Friday*
*Police Headquarters, Darwin*

'Dead? How can he be dead?'

Kane stopped chewing his gum and clenched his jaw. He stared at the policeman across the other side of the large desk. The room was bare, a couple of filing cabinets were against the side wall, and the desk in front of them was clear. Apart from the low hum of the air conditioning pushing out frigid air, the room was silent. Ellie shivered beside him and he reached across and put his arm around her shoulders.

When they'd driven along the waterfront from the motel, they'd seen the blocked off street and the police vehicles. But they'd not suspected the connection between the crime scene and the reason for their visit to the police station. Not until they were informed that Panos Sordina's body had been found beside the boat ramp by a couple of early morning joggers.

'We're trying to get in touch with Mrs Sordina. Do you know where we can find her?'

The colour drained from Kane's face. Ellie squeezed his hand tightly and answered for him. 'His mother died last night. In the hospital.'

'I'm sorry to hear of your loss.' But the detective's voice was formal and he continued without a pause. 'So, Mr McLaren. According to Mr Sordina's phone records, you had been trying to call him for most of the night. One call registered as being answered. Did you actually speak to him?'

Kane nodded. 'Yes. I did.'

'What time was that?'

'I'm not sure. It had to be well after midnight. My mother had just passed away. I wasn't taking much notice of the time.'

Ellie squeezed his fingers again and he rubbed his thumb absently across her skin.

'Mr Sordina's phone registered a forty second call from you at twelve minutes past one. Just before two o'clock, we have CCTV footage of you standing outside the door of the building where his office is located.'

'That's correct.'

'A strange time to organise a meeting?'

'I already told you. We had agreed to meet on McMinn Street. He didn't turn up so I went looking for him.' Kane kept his voice steady. 'He wouldn't answer his phone all night. Christ, man, I had to tell him his wife was dead.'

'Again, I'm very sorry to hear of your mother's death, Mr McLaren.'

Kane nodded tersely.

'So when was the last time you saw Mr Sordina?'

'I've only met him on a handful of occasions. I haven't seen him for at least two years but I had a big problem with the way he treated my mother, and I was going to speak to him about it. For all I know he fell in the harbour and drowned on his way to meeting me.' Kane shook his head. 'Christ knows, he sounded drunk enough on the phone.'

Detective Sergeant Garrett steepled his fingers on the desk in front of him. 'Actually it's interesting that you mention the harbour. That's where he was. In the harbour before the tide washed him in.' He stopped speaking and held Kane's gaze for a full minute. Kane clenched his jaw. 'However, he didn't drown, Mr McLaren. The initial observation by the forensic pathologist indicates that Mr Sordina's throat was cut. Your stepfather's death was no accident. This is a murder investigation.'

Ellie's fingers tensed in Kane's hand as she expelled a soft gasp. Kane glanced at her; her face was white.

'I have my mother's funeral to organise and then I have to get back to work. If you want me, you have my number.' He turned to Ellie and held out his hand. Relief filled him when she took it. 'I know nothing more than I've told you.'

'Thank you, Mr McLaren.' Garrett nodded at Ellie before turning back to Kane. 'Once again, I'm sorry to hear of your mother's death. It's been a very difficult night for you and I do appreciate you coming in.'

'You can find me at Makowa Lodge in Kakadu. I have a job to go back to.'

Kane strode from the building. Ellie's hand was still in his and she kept up the pace he set. They stepped out into the street and the noise of the morning traffic was a welcome distraction to the jumble of his thoughts. Kane stopped and looked down at her.

'Bloody hell. What's going on?'

'Are you okay? I know you didn't get on with Panos, but it's still a shock.'

Kane shook his head. 'It might sound hard, but Panos' death has had no impact on me at all. I'm just grateful that Mum was gone and she didn't have to deal with it.'

Ellie slipped her arms around his waist and leaned into

his chest. Kane dropped his chin to rest on the top of her head and took comfort in her warmth. They stood silently for a moment outside the office block as the busy crowd pushed past them.

'I'm going to have to leave for Makowa soon. Will you be okay?' Ellie lifted her head and Kane stared into her clear, blue eyes. He wondered if she knew how much her support had helped him through those early hours this morning.

'Kane. Stop looking at me like that.'

'Like what?'

'Like you're wondering if I believe you. Don't even go there. That man was so rude asking you those questions.' Her hands tightened on his back. 'You should put in a complaint.'

Kane shook his head with a rueful laugh. 'He was only doing his job. I understand where he's coming from. The timing sucks but he has to find out what's going on.' He put his hands on Ellie's shoulders. 'And the reality is that Panos was murdered. It was no drunken accident. When it hits the news, it's going to be big.'

'Kane?' The tremble in Ellie's voice sent a surge of protective warmth spiralling through him. He'd failed before and he wasn't going to fail again. The thought of sending her back to the lodge alone bothered him. He suspected – no, he knew – that Sordina's death was not a random killing. It was somehow tied up with what was happening at the farm. His mother had said enough to make him certain of that.

Ellie's next words echoed his thoughts. 'It's too much of a coincidence isn't it? The fracking, Bill's accident. Panos' death.' Tears filled her eyes as she looked up at him. 'There's someone behind all this. What are they trying to achieve?'

'I don't know, Ellie.' He rubbed his thumb gently along her full bottom lip. 'But I'm going to find out.'

'Should we go back and tell that detective what we suspect?' Ellie stood on her toes and brushed her lips across his. Her hair brushed against his face and he was filled with need. Kane wasn't used to that feeling and a warning rippled through him as he held her.

What the hell are you doing? He was leaving himself too open. Slowly he dropped his hands and the expression on his face must have mirrored his thoughts.

'Not yet.'

Ellie lowered her gaze and stepped away. 'You'd better take me back to the motel, so I can collect my car.' She glanced down at her watch. 'I'll be cutting it fine as it is.'

'I'm only going to do the essentials with the funeral home. I'll get back as soon as I can. I want you to be very careful. Make sure you're not alone at all. Stay around the rest of the staff till I get back. Don't even go to your apartment. Okay?' Kane tilted her chin up with his fingers. He couldn't help himself. He leaned down and took her lips with his in a brief kiss. 'Drive carefully. Okay?'

'I will.' Ellie held his gaze, her blue eyes steady.

Full of trust. The cold feeling began at the base of Kane's neck as Ellie's eyes changed to the dark brown of Hawk's. He took a deep breath and pushed away the growing panic before it could take hold of him.

# Chapter 26

*2.00 pm Friday*
*Makowa Lodge*

Ellie had plenty of time to think on the way back to the lodge. So much had happened in the short time since she'd driven down this highway. There'd been no mistaking the feelings that had consumed her when she'd been with Kane in the early hours of the morning. Not just when he'd held her. The intensity of his gaze in the motel bed had made her stomach swoop like it did when she put her helicopter into a steep dive. He'd let her into his head, into his heart and she suspected that giving himself to her had been a huge step for him; as big a step as it had been for her.

Meeting Kane had set her on the right path towards her own healing. Once they'd investigated this stuff at the farm, she would decide whether she could let the past go and focus on her future. It would take some time to figure out what that future held, and whether Kane would be a part of it.

Slowly, slowly. A frown wrinkled her forehead as her father's words echoed through her thoughts. He'd taught her patience as they'd raised the trees from seedlings, and as he'd sat with her in the shed, waiting for her chickens to hatch beneath the special lights they'd set up. She hoped that Kane had good memories of his childhood; he was going to need something to look back on to help him grieve for his mother.

She stared straight ahead as she drove past the farm. Time for that later.

The sight of the high phone towers looming ahead at

Jabiru surprised her. Ellie had been so immersed in her thoughts that she'd paid little attention to the traffic. Now the short final leg towards the lodge awaited her. A pall of smoke hung in the still air of the early afternoon, indicating the seasonal burn-off was still going. Ellie slowed down as the smoke thickened, and cursed as she came to a line of traffic stopped ahead of her on the highway just south of the Bowali Cultural Centre. She slipped the car out of gear and pulled the handbrake on, settling back to wait. If the fire had jumped the road – which it looked like it had – she could be in for a long wait.

Ellie put her head back and closed her eyes; she'd not had much sleep in the past twenty-four hours and she knew had at least two flights to take up late this afternoon.

It was a full half hour before the caravan in front of her began to move as the traffic was allowed through. She was just going to get back in time for her shift. The revving of a powerful engine came from behind her car and Ellie glanced in the rear-vision mirror. A black Mercedes SUV was almost nudging her bumper and a memory tugged at her. Mercedes? Where had she seen one of them recently?

Once the traffic was flowing, the Mercedes accelerated with a roar and flew past her. Idiot.

By the time she turned into the lodge and parked near her apartment, there was barely enough time left for her to run in and change into her work clothes. Despite what Kane had said, she had to go there to get changed. Terry was mowing along the edge of the car park but still trepidation filled her as she unlocked the door. She looked around carefully, but the place was as it should be. Changing quickly, she grabbed her work boots and locked the door before sitting outside on the steps and pulling them on. She'd have to run the pre-flight check before the three o'clock flight.

The hangar was hot and the smell of smoke hung in the air. If this burn-off covered a large area, there wasn't going to be much of a view for the tourists. She logged on and checked the weather forecast before stepping out onto the tarmac. A north-easterly change was forecast to arrive through the afternoon, which might clear the smoke. On the other hand, it could make the fires flare up more, and the flight would be a waste of time. Plus a change from the north could bring a thunderstorm, even in the dry season.

Ellie picked up the phone and dialled the office. She tapped her fingers as she waited for Jock to pick up. 'Hey Jock, it's me, Ellie.'

'Where are you?'

'I'm over in the hangar. Did the Cooinda guys come over this morning?'

'Yeah they did. Had another flight booked too but they checked over both choppers before they left. You should find the paperwork over there.'

'Yeah, see it. I just checked the forecast. What do you think?'

'Hmm. I was just about to do the same. Give me a minute.'

She waited as the sound of Jock pounding on the keyboard came down the line.

'How many booked?'

Ellie checked the schedule. 'Looks like we've had a cancellation. Only one left. Henry.' The name was familiar.

There'd been a Henry a few days ago; tourists would often come back for a second flight when they stayed at the lodge.

'Can it. Hang on, I'll see if we can contact them.' More keyboard clicking as he checked the guest register. 'Sorry, no Henry staying here. Must be staying somewhere else. You'll have to wait until he turns up.'

'Okay, will do. Thanks, boss.'

'No worries. I've got a meeting up at the park headquarters.

Sorry but I gotta go, I'm late as it is.'

'See if you can find a spare pilot while you're up there. Okay?'

'I'll do my best.'

Ellie flicked the light switch off and closed the office door. It had become darker; the combination of low cloud and smoke hanging in the air confirming that Jock had made the right call. She turned towards the tarmac to re-lock the gate she'd unlocked when she'd arrived. A shadow moved to her right and Ellie jumped as a man appeared in front of her.

'Holy shit. You scared me.' She took a quick breath.

'My apologies. I thought you were leaving. I've got a flight.' Ugh. The same guy she'd taken up on Wednesday. Henry. Now she remembered him. He was the one who'd wanted to fly the chopper. He'd been more interested in the workings of the helicopter, the seats, the radio and the doors than any of the scenic spots they'd flown over.

'Ready to take me up again, love?' He was a big man, and he invaded her personal space as he leaned close. Ellie took a step back, trying to keep a polite expression on her face.

'Sorry, all flights have been cancelled for the afternoon.' She took another step back and turned to leave the hangar. 'Too much smoke. If you go over to the main office, they'll refund you or give you a voucher for one of the other tours.' The guy shook his head. 'Uh-uh. I want to go up now.'

He looked around. 'Where's your partner?'

Ellie ignored his question and waited for him to come out onto the tarmac with her. He followed her outside slowly and a small shiver ran down her spine. He pulled a cigarette from his top pocket and she shook her head. 'No smoking.' She pointed to the large sign on the side of the building.

He put the cigarette in his mouth but didn't light it. 'So are you going to take me up or not?' His hands fidgeted with the lighter and Ellie looked around. There was no one in sight. She had a feeling this guy was trouble.

He reached out and took her arm but Ellie gritted her teeth and shook his hand off. 'I already told you; flights are cancelled. Walk over to the office with me and I'll sort out your refund myself.'

'Did you hear me?' He grabbed her again and Ellie looked down at the thick fingers holding her hand. 'I've paid and you're taking me up now. The smoke doesn't concern me.'

His fingers pressed hard and Ellie tried to pull her hand away, but he had a firm hold.

She lifted her boot and stood on Henry's foot at the same time as she pulled her arm away. 'Let go of me!'

'You're going to pay for that.' His voice was low but it was the cold smile and the expressionless eyes that raised the hair on her neck.

As Ellie ran away from him, across the tarmac and through the gate, the sound of a mower came from around the nearest building. Relief surged through her as Terry waved. She crossed the lawn towards the ride-on mower.

'What's up?' Terry yelled above the noise of the engine. He reached down and turned it off.

Ellie turned and pointed to the guy who was walking quickly in the other direction. 'It's okay. Just a creep being difficult when his flight was canned.'

'Want me to deal with him?'

Ellie smiled and shook her head. 'He's gone now.'

Terry climbed off the mower and stood beside Ellie as they watched Henry cross to the car park.

'Might be a creep, but he drives a Mercedes.' Terry let out a low whistle of appreciation as the vehicle roared down the road and turned onto the highway with a squeal of tyres. 'More money than brains, that's for sure.'

'A black Mercedes.' Ellie muttered beneath her breath, as she remembered where she'd seen it before. Heather had seen a Mercedes the night that Bill had been hurt. That was the night before she'd gone up with Henry the first time.

Was it the same car?

'You sure you're okay? You're a bit pale.'

Ellie forced a smile onto her face. 'I'm fine, thanks, Terry. It's just been a big couple of days.'


Ellie spent the afternoon in the office over in the main administration building, catching up on paperwork and surrounded by others. She could have done it in the office or over in the hangar, but the encounter with that guy had unsettled her. Maybe her imagination was running wild because of Sordina's murder, but it didn't hurt to be careful. When Kane was back – there was no sign of him yet – she'd go back over there to work in the office in the hangar.

The main office was busy with tourists coming and going, and she helped out when the queue was long, taking several bookings for ground tours and sunset cruises.

Amanda, the afternoon receptionist, thanked her as the last tourist headed off towards the wharf. The two-hour sunset cruise was about to board and the rush for bookings had finished. 'It's been so busy today. I appreciated your help.'

'I thought Heather was supposed to be in the office with you today?'

'No, she and Jenny have shared duties in the crèche and day spa.' Amanda looked up at the clock. 'Although she's probably finished by now. We closed the day spa early because we were short-staffed. How about an early snack at the bar? I think we've earned a break after this busy afternoon. And I hate going home to that small unit in Jabiru.'

'Sounds like a plan. I'll go over and see if she's finished up.' Amanda had only started at the lodge a few weeks before Ellie went across to Queensland. By the sound of things, she was still finding her way in the loneliness of the Territory. 'You should move into one of the staff apartments here. A bit more company for you onsite.'

Ellie opened the door and looked around. Most of the clouds had cleared and the sky was shot with the lingering remnants of smoke from the burn-off. Molten gold edged the pink clouds and rays of soft light filtered down towards the horizon on the other side of the river. She paused and took a deep breath, letting the natural beauty seep into her. Guests were milling around the lawn between the two buildings, cameras at the ready to snap the sunset. With the smoke hanging in the sky tonight it would be a photographer's dream. She looked up as she crossed the manicured lawn. The crocodile-shaped building usually made her smile, but this afternoon, the eyes that that were set in the peak of the roof glinted ominously as the rays of the setting sun flashed off the high glass windows. She glanced over her shoulder as footsteps crunched on the gravel behind her but there was no one there. Just her edginess keeping her company.

Ellie almost ran down the path between the overhanging bougainvillea and pushed open the door of the crèche. Heather was sitting at the desk with her hands over her face.

'Hey. You okay?' Ellie crossed the room and Heather looked up. 'Hi. Yeah, just a bit tired. It's been a long day.'

'Tell me about it. You and me both.' Ellie dropped into the sofa beneath the window and looked up in surprise as a little voice called out to her.

'Ellie!' Andrew ran across holding a plastic, wind-up train. 'Watch this.'

'You know these kids?' A strange expression crossed Heather's face.

'Yeah, I'm an old friend of their dad. I went to school with his –' Ellie stopped as Heather pushed her chair back suddenly and it tipped over with a crash.

'So you know their mother too?' Her voice was strained. 'I've only got to know Gina while they've been staying here.

She's lovely.' Ellie frowned; she'd never seen Heather

so tense.

Heather's hands were crossed against her chest and she looked away.

'Go and get me some tracks and I'll help you build a circle for the train to go around. Okay?' Ellie smiled down at Andrew.

While Andrew was engrossed in pulling out the blue plastic sections of track from the toy box, Ellie stood up and followed Heather over to the window. 'What's wrong? Are you all right? Is your dad still okay?'

Heather nodded but still her eyes wouldn't meet Ellie's. 'Yeah, he's fine. I'm fine. It's all good. I'm just waiting for them to . . . to be collected and then I'm going home.' Her voice was fast and her words ran together. 'I have to go home.'

'I came over to see if you want to have dinner with Amanda and me.'

'No. No, I have to go. Dad's . . . he's left his car for me.' Heather shook her head and her voice was shaky. 'I'm really tired.'

'Are you okay?'

'Yes.' Heather wouldn't meet her eyes.

'I can watch the kids till Gina gets here if you want?'

'That'd be good.'

'Where is she?'

'Don't know, she didn't say where she was going.' Heather's eyes were darting around and her breath was catching as she spoke. 'Just dropped the kids off.'

Ellie put a hand on her arm. 'Are you sure you're okay?'

'Yes. I told you I'm fine.' Heather hissed the answer at her and Ellie took a step back with her hands up.

'All right. All right. No need to get pissy with me again. I thought we'd sorted that.'

'Sorry, I'm cross because she's late. It's been a long day.' Heather's lips trembled 'You know I'd rather work in the office than in the crèche.

'I want Mummy.' Ellie moved her gaze over to the little girl. Binny had her thumb in her mouth and her little eyes were huge.

'Yes, sweetheart.' Ellie crouched down beside her and smoothed her hand over the little girl's hair, conscious of Heather's gaze. 'She shouldn't be too long now.'

'I'll just get my keys.' Heather crossed to the desk. Ellie rose and followed her across the room and she pulled out her keys and closed the drawer with a snap.

'Do you think she might have gone on the sunset cruise?' Ellie glanced across at the two children. Binny was leaning against her brother and as Ellie watched he put his little arm around her and she snuggled in.

Heather shrugged. 'I don't know.'

'The kids look tired. What time did Gina drop them off?'

'They've been here since I opened up.'

Ellie put her hands on her hips. No way. 'All day? Have you tried to call her?'

Heather dropped her eyes. 'Yeah. Not answering.' Ellie pulled out her phone. 'I'll try.'

Heather quickly grabbed her hand. 'No point. I just called her.'

'Are you sure you've got the right number?' Ellie pulled up Gina's details, and read the number as Heather double-checked it on the sheet in front of her.

'Yep, that's right. I've just tried it, twice. It went to voicemail.' Heather stared at her as her words ran together. 'Maybe her phone's flat. Or maybe she did go on the sunset cruise. There's no service up on the billabongs anyway. I have to go. I'm sure she'll be back soon.'

Something wasn't right. Heather was acting strangely. A shaft of unease lodged in Ellie's throat. This all felt wrong.

'Okay, you go then. She must have gone on the sunset cruise and didn't realise how late it came in. That's the only place she could be.'

'Thank you.' Heather picked up her bag and headed quickly for the door.

'Heather?' Ellie was surprised at her friend's haste to get away. 'Will you please swing by the bistro and tell Amanda not to wait for me?'

'All right.' Ellie frowned as the door closed. She crossed to the window; it was almost dark. She watched Heather turn in the opposite direction to the bistro and hurry across to the back of the day spa. Bill's old Landcruiser was backed right up to the staff entrance. Heather opened the driver's door, jumped in, and black smoke billowed from the exhaust as she drove towards the main gate of the lodge. She indicated and turned onto the highway.

Thanks pal, for telling Amanda not to wait. Heather's behaviour was bizarre. Ellie frowned as she walked across to the children. She pulled down a couple of large cushions off the sofa and switched the television on. Once they were engrossed in the children's program, she took out her phone and flicked through until she found Gina's number and pressed call. Like Heather said it went straight to voice mail. She wondered if she should call David to see if he knew where Gina was; it wouldn't hurt. She kept her voice low as she called Call Connect. 'Parliament House, Darwin, please.' Once the call was picked up she asked for the office of the Chief Minister. While she waited for it to be answered, she dropped into the chair at the desk and reached over to the drawer. It was partially open and a piece of bright red paper was caught in the top. 'No fracking for Kakadu' was emblazoned across the top in big letters. A public meeting was happening tomorrow morning at ten o'clock.

*Join us and be part of the fight to keep this ancient land healthy for all of our children, black and white. Hear Bill Jarragah speak about the dangers to our environment.*

She opened the drawer wide to pull out the paper for a closer look, and something shiny caught her attention.

Ellie gasped and put her hand over her mouth, but the children were too engrossed in the television to hear her. She reached in and pulled out a crystal-encrusted phone case. There was an iPhone loose in the drawer beside it.

# Chapter 27

*5.00 pm Friday*
*Parliament House, Darwin*

'You bastard.' David closed his eyes and grasped the handset tightly as the chilling laugh came through the line. 'Where is she? Where are my children?'

'David, David. Calm down. There's no need to be like that. She's in good hands.'

Fairweather's voice sent ice through David's veins. He'd been trying to reach Gina ever since the news had broken of Panos Sordina's murder that morning. After several attempts, he'd given up on her mobile and called the main number of Makowa Lodge, but there'd been no answer when they'd put the call through to the room. He'd tried to convince himself that she'd let the battery run flat, or she'd gone out and left the phone in the room, but deep down, his conviction that something was very wrong jelled into certainty as the hours had passed: Fairweather had her. The confirmation turned his stomach to liquid.

'Your wife is fine.' His voice was friendly as though they were having a social conversation. 'But you know what you have to do, don't you, to make sure she stays fine?'

'Why? Why now?'

'You let me down with the boundary change vote, David. So I thought you needed a little prompting to make sure you vote the right way this time.' Fairweather sighed. 'I really thought I had made the consequences clear to you.'

David clenched his hand around the phone. He had no

choice but to submit. 'I will vote for your drilling licence. You have my word. But so help me, if you harm one hair on Gina's head . . .' He kept his voice level and strong.

'Now, now, David. You don't want to get me cross.' Fair- weather's voice hardened. 'One of your colleagues made me cross yesterday. And I heard on the radio he had a very unfortunate accident last night.'

David eased himself down into his chair as Fairweather's meaning registered. 'Sordina?' His voice was hoarse and he struggled to take a deep breath. The air was thick and hot, and a trickle of sweat ran down the side of his face. 'Where are my children, Russell?'

Fairweather laughed. 'I really don't know. I'll be in touch soon, David.'

David stared at his mobile as the call disconnected at the other end. His hand was shaking as he put it down on the desk and searched frantically for his car keys. Everything was moving in slow motion and his ears buzzed as though a thousand cicadas were in his head.

Oh God, where are Andrew and Binny? Surely they hadn't been left alone in the apartment.

He'd try Gina's phone one more time before he jumped in the car and flew down the Arnhem Highway. Maybe she still had it on her. Maybe she'd hidden it, or switched it off.

His fingers were shaking as he pressed speed dial. David stared straight ahead willing her to pick up. Again it went straight to voicemail. As he threw it to the desk in frustration, the land line on his desk buzzed and he grabbed the phone. 'David Johnson. Who's calling?'

'A call for you, David.' Helen's voice was hesitant. 'She

wouldn't say who it was, just that it was important. Do you want to take it?'

'Yes. Please.'

The call clicked across. 'Who is this?'

'It's Ellie. David, is that you? Look, I've got Gina's phone and I'm a little bit concerned.'

Ellie? Why does she have Gina's phone?

'Ellie. Listen to me.' His voice was shaking as he rushed the words out. 'Do you know where Gina and the children are?'

'Andrew and Binny are right here with me.'

Thank God. 'Are they okay?'

'Yes. They're fine. We're in the crèche. Gina dropped the kids off here this morning, but David –' He could hear the hesitation in Ellie's voice '– she's very late coming back. I was wondering if she mentioned going on a tour or anything.'

Relief that Andrew and Binny were safe was overlaid by his desperate fear for Gina's safety. 'Ellie, listen to me. Listen very carefully. Hang up the phone and wait. I'll call you back from another line.' David was sure that Fairweather had his phone tapped, somehow, and he didn't want him to know what he was planning. The man's reach seemed to spread everywhere.

David threw the phone onto the desk and ran for the door, his car keys in his hand.

***

Ellie locked the door and drew the blinds while she waited for David to call back. For extra security she pulled a large box of toys against the door. David's voice had sent a shiver down her spine. Something was very wrong. It was only a few minutes until the phone rang and Ellie snatched it up.

'David?'

'Listen carefully, Ellie. I want you to do everything I say.

Where do you live?'

'In a staff apartment at the back of the lodge.'

'Look, I know it's a big ask, but I'm on my way to the lodge now. Can you get the kids over there and lock the door until I get there? And don't tell a soul.'

'I can do that. David, what's going on?'

'I'll explain when I arrive. You said you've got Gina's phone.

How much charge has it got?'

'It's switched off. Wait a minute.

She powered it up and waited. The battery icon showed about eighty per cent. 'Plenty.'

'Good. I'll call you on it when I get there.' David's voice dropped and Ellie sensed he was trying to hold it together. 'Are you sure the kids are okay?'

Ellie looked over to the corner. Binny had fallen asleep against her brother and Andrew's eyes were heavy. 'Yes. Yes, they're fine. Ready for their dinner, I guess, but I'll feed them.'

'Keep them safe. Lock the door and don't let anyone in. Not even anyone you know. Not even anyone you trust. No one.

And Ellie, thank you. I owe you.' David's voice cracked as the call disconnected.

Ellie carried Binny on her hip, and she locked her little arms around Ellie's neck as they walked the path to the back of the lodge. Binny's soft lashes brushed Ellie's face in a butterfly kiss as her eyes closed. Ellie inhaled the sweet smell of the little girl's hair and took a deep breath. She wondered where Gina was. And worried why Kane was so late getting back.

'It's nearly dark. Binny doesn't like the dark.' Andrew clung tightly to her hand and he yawned. 'And I'm hungry. Have you got chips at your house?'

Ellie glanced over at the bistro. One of the lodge buses had just dropped off a large group of tourists from the sunset cruise and they were heading for the restaurant. God knows, she'd be lucky to find a lettuce leaf in her fridge and there was no kid food in her tiny pantry. She considered a detour, but David had been quite clear about keeping the kids out of sight. No, she'd call the bar and get some food sent over once they were safely in her apartment.

A large dark car cruised slowly down the road towards them and Ellie's heart rate picked up. Henry again? She stepped out off the path into the shadows at the side of the building, pulling Andrew in with her.

She leaned down and whispered urgently as Binny snuggled further into her shoulder. 'Do you know how to play hide and seek?'

Andrew nodded.

'We are going to hide and be very, very quiet. Okay?'

The car cruised past with its lights dipped low and Ellie let out a sigh of relief when she saw the Jeep insignia on the back door.

Kane was back.

David's words filled her head as they pressed back into

the shrubbery.

    Not even anyone you trust.

# Chapter 28

*8.00 pm Friday*
*Black Jungle Springs*

Gina rolled over from her side to her back and bit her lip, stifling the cry that threatened as her elbow scraped on the rough timber wall beside the bed. Her hands had been bound together in front of her; the tie from the day spa bathrobe secured them tightly in front of her pregnant belly.

The first time she had regained consciousness, she'd been on a soft bed in a darkened room. As she looked around frantically, trying to work out where she was, another prick in her arm had dropped her back into the blackness that fogged her mind.

'I'm so sorry.' She was sure she heard a husky whisper but the thread of sound faded as the darkness descended again.

Next time, she'd woken enough to lean against the woman who helped her from the bed but Gina had not been strong enough to resist when she'd put her arm around her and quickly walked her to a door. She'd closed her eyes gratefully as she'd been laid down and covered with a soft blanket. The soft fibres tickled her nose as a car door closed quietly but she'd drifted back to sleep.

When she'd woken this time, she'd been lying in a vehicle that bumped and scraped over a winding road. Opening her eyes a crack, she held herself steady as the car swayed from side to side, stifling a cry when the car hit a bump. The roof above her was torn and splattered with drops of what could have been blood. Her stomach roiled and she hitched a breath.

As her eyes became accustomed to the faint light, she tilted her head slowly, but all she could see was the back of the stained seat behind her. When she was sure there was no one watching her, she opened her eyes wider and turned her head to the side. A smell of something putrid reached her nose. It was almost dark, but there was just enough light to make out she was in the back of a large vehicle.

'Are you awake?' The car slowed a little.

It was Heather from the crèche; she'd recognise that husky voice anywhere. What had she done with Andrew and Binny? Were they all right? Bile burned her throat as nausea threatened to overwhelm her.

'Where are we?' Gina's voice broke. 'Where are my children?'

'They're with Ellie.'

'Ellie?' *Dio*, Ellie is involved in this too? And she had made friends with her?

Gina licked her lips. Her mouth was so dry. 'What did you give me?'

'Nothing bad. Don't worry. It was just something to put you to sleep for a while. I'm sorry I had to do this.'

'What are you doing?'

'Please don't be frightened.'

Gina tried to sit up but a cramp seized her lower back.

She lay back and took a deep breath.

'It's going to be all right. Just stay calm.' Heather's voice was firm.

Gina's body slid back a little as the vehicle traversed a steep incline and she closed her eyes again.

Where were they going? Was this man going to be

there?

It had to be the one who had threatened David.

Ellie? What did Ellie have to do with it?

'Are you really sure my children are safe?' Gina's voice cracked; her mouth was dry and she needed water.

'Yes, Ellie will look after them.'

Another few minutes and the car rolled to a stop. She closed her eyes as the car door slammed shut. The door at the back of the wagon opened with a squeak.

Gina didn't resist when Heather held her ankles and gently pulled her along on her back until her legs hung over the back of the car. She pushed herself up on her elbow.

'You're going to have to stand up and walk.'

'I haven't got any shoes.'

'It's all right. It's only a little way on the grass. I'll keep an eye out for snakes.'

Gina shivered but she didn't resist when Heather took her arm gently and pulled her up to a sitting position.

'Where are we?' Heather had turned the headlights off and it was pitch dark. Only the noises of the bush broke the silence. Fear slithered through her, like a cold rush in her blood; no matter what she said, she wasn't sure if Heather was telling the truth. Anyone who would sedate and kidnap someone was not a good person.

Heather took her Gina's tied hands in her own. 'Don't worry. Please, you have to trust me. You're safe and it will keep him happy. When it's all over I'll come and get you and take you back to your children. I promise.'

'Is this where you live?' Gina looked around. It was dark and there were no lights, no sign of any habitation.

'God, no. It's a fishing shack that Dad uses sometimes. I can't take you to our place because then Dad would know what I've done. He'd kill me.' For the first time, a glimmer of humour came onto Heather's voice. 'As soon as he votes, I'll come and take you back. I promise.'

'Votes? But that's not till Monday.' Gina's voice broke.

'I have to go home now. I'll come back tomorrow with something for your dinner.'

Home? Where was home? After she'd regained consciousness, they had been in the car for only a short time but Gina had no idea how long she'd been out to it.

'I can't stay here by myself.' Horror at being left alone set her shaking again. 'Why can't you stay with me?'

'Because I've got Dad's car, and he'll wonder where I am. I'll get you a blanket. There's some biscuits in the fridge and lots of water. You'll be fine.'

'Are you going to untie my hands?' The conversation was almost surreal, but unless she was misreading Heather's intent, there was no malice in her actions.

'Yes, when we get inside. As long as you promise that you won't try anything. I don't want to frighten you, but don't go outside. The shack is close to the river and it's a gathering place for crocodiles . . . and there are snakes around too.

Heather held a small torch that lit their way through the long grass. Holding Gina's arm, she led her up two steps onto a wooden porch before pushing open the door. The musty smell was cloying and Gina gagged again. Heather led her over to a low bed and she sat down as Heather disappeared through a door. Gina's back was aching from being in the back of the car. When Heather returned, she held a bottle of cold water. She put it on the floor beside them and stared at Gina in the torchlight.

'If I untie your hands, will you promise not to try anything?' Her dark eyes were serious as she held Gina's gaze.

Gina stared at her. She would do anything to get away from here, even if it meant driving that car herself. Her intent must have been clear. Heather sighed and turned around. She picked up the water bottle and unscrewed the lid before placing it in Gina's hands.

'Thank you.' The bottle was cold in her hands as she drank and the cold water soothed her throat.

'Lie down, and put your hands on your stomach.' Heather pulled something from her pocket. Gina's blood chilled as she tried to see what was in her hand.

'It's all right. I just have to take your photo and send it to him.'

The door closed and Gina was left alone. The sound of a vehicle driving away was the only sound in the still of the night. She lay on her back and worked at the tie around her wrists until the muscles in her forearms burned with the effort. She wasn't going to risk standing unless she could use her hands to support herself; her head was still woozy from whatever it was Heather had given her. The last thing she wanted to do was fall and injure the baby.

Oh *Dio*, what if the drug has hurt the baby?

She lay still and waited for the baby to kick, but there was no movement. She pressed her hands onto her stomach and waited. In her haziness, she couldn't remember the last time she'd felt it.

'Come on, little one, wake up. Kick your mama. Please.' She pressed again. Tears seeped from her eyes as she held her breath and waited for the familiar strong thrust against the walls of her womb. Waiting for what seemed forever.

But there was nothing.

A sob tore from her throat and Gina gave in and let go of the scream that had been building in her chest. 'Help me, somebody help me.'

The mournful cry of a night bird was the only reply.

# Chapter 29

*Friday night*
*Darwin*

Russell sat back in his leather recliner and sipped a glass of the finest shiraz. The sharp blackberry taste settled on his tongue as he rolled the liquid in his mouth. It had been a satisfying end to a successful day.

David Johnson had hightailed it to Kakadu, and as far as Russell could ascertain from his contact at police headquarters, there had been no report of a kidnapping.

He smiled as he stared down at the picture on his phone. The fear in the woman's eyes and the sight of her bound hands on her stomach sent a surge of power through him. Bill Jarragah's daughter had done everything she'd been told. Nevertheless, Bill Jarragah was still in his sights. No one spoke to Russell Fairweather the way he had and got away without a consequence. He would take the fall for the kidnapping of the Chief Minister's wife.

That stubborn old man had drawn the line at taking Johnson's wife, but another small threat had secured his assurance that he would vote for the drilling. Every other vote was in the bag; there was only David Johnson to keep on track – he was too honest for his own good.

Russell had never understood the ease of manipulating people by threatening those they cared about; love was a foreign concept to him. He sipped his wine and stared into the darkness. The harbour lights flicked on and off sending flashes of green and red through the night.

Six years of careful plotting, six years after the secret report that showed the wealth of coal beneath Kakadu from the Porter farm and south along the river, Russell's plan was about to come to fruition. The boundary change to the National Park was underway and the drilling would go ahead.

He smiled. Officially that is. The preliminary reports from the site were beyond expectations.

Over the years, Russell had learned that the right connections and corrupt behaviour had the potential to deliver hundreds of millions in windfall profits. For the right price, anyone could be bought. With Panos Sordina as his puppet, he had consolidated his position from behind the scenes. Paying off Sordina's gambling debts and allowing him to dig a deeper hole for himself had ensured Fairweather not only influence and access to the Northern Territory Government, but had placed him in a position where he controlled many of the decisions.

After a chance introduction to Bill Jarragah at the races one weekend, he had listened to a conversation between Jarragah and Panos Sordina about mineral exploration on the farm that Jarragah worked on. With his connections it had been an easy matter to get his hands on the map that showed the potential deposit that continued far into the Kakadu National Park. Fair-weather immediately bought the company that had discovered the deposit. He smiled at the memory.

'It will never get through, Russell. The land there is World Heritage-listed. A shame, but it will never be approved.' The CEO of Black Coal Holdings had taken his million dollars without a backward glance.

He took another sip of the shiraz. If only the fool could

see him now.

The doorbell rang and Fairweather put his wine aside, cursing as his hand bumped the edge of the table and a drop of the ruby red liquid splashed on the white cuff of his silk shirt. He frowned and put his finger over the stain as he rose from the chair.

His Gucci shoes made no sound on the marble tiles in the entry foyer and he looked at the image from the security camera on the small screen above the door, nodding with satisfaction as Mick Dawson stared back at him, his eyes as cold as ever. Russell put in the code to release the electronic lock and the door swung open silently.

'Follow me.' They would talk in the study; business and pleasure were not to be mixed in his home.

Fairweather gestured to the chair next to the desk and waited for Dawson to sit.

'You almost failed me last night. Sordina was supposed to be crocodile food. I was not happy when the body was found this morning.' He let Mick squirm for a moment. 'No matter. I have two more little tasks for you. I think you'll enjoy both of these.

'The politician's wife is in a safe place. Take the four-wheel drive and go back to Kakadu. Check that she is secure. I want her alive till Monday.' Fairweather clicked the mouse of his computer and brought up a Google map, highlighted a location and sent it to the laser printer beside the computer. 'After that, you can do what you like with her. But before you go out to Black Jungle Springs, I want you to finish the job on that helicopter.' He reached over and pulled the map from the printer. 'I want it to come down tomorrow. There is no room for error this time.'

# Chapter 30

*8.00 pm*
*Friday Makowa Lodge*

Ellie hurried up the steps with the children just as Kane put the key on the door lock of his apartment.

'Kane,' she called softly.

He turned around, surprise wrinkling his brow as he looked at her with the two children.

'I was just going to throw my bag in and come and find you.' He dropped his bag outside his door and came across to her. 'What's with the kids?'

Ellie's control slipped for the first time and her voice shook. 'We have a problem.' She sagged against Kane as his arms went around her and he rested his head against her forehead.

'What's wrong?'

She gestured to Andrew, who was listening to them. Ellie wasn't used to having children around and watching what she said. Smiling down at the little boy, she ruffled his hair. 'We have to find some chips to feed some hungry children, that's the problem.' When she put Binny down after she opened the door, she mouthed to Kane. 'I'll tell you in a minute.'

She sent Kane off to the bistro while she settled Andrew and Binny in front of the television. A few minutes later he returned with food.

'Thank you.'

The kids demolished the bowl of chips and shared a

milkshake. Leaving them on the couch, Ellie and Kane went outside to the verandah. She left the door slightly ajar so she could see the children. She sat on the hard wooden chair beside the door and rubbed her arms.

Kane leaned on the rail and watched her. 'Now what the hell is going on? Who are these children?'

'It's a long story, but they've been staying here at Makowa with their mother since last weekend. Their father is –' She caught herself, remembering what David had said about keeping their presence a secret. 'Their father is an old friend of mine. Gina – their mum – dropped them off at the crèche this morning. No-one has seen her since.'

Kane's eyes narrowed as he frowned. 'And you think she's missing?'

'I'm sure she is. I think it's tied up with what happened to Bill the other night.'

'How can it be? What's the connection?' Kane stared at her. 'I don't know. I'm hoping David knows what's going on.

He's on his way from Darwin. He asked me to keep an eye out for them until he gets here.'

The moonlight played on the row of pot plants along the rail. Half a dozen pots that were full to bursting with a variety of herbs, added to the small garden she had in the kitchen. She stared down at them; one day when she sorted herself out, she'd get some land and grow stuff properly. She had more of her father in her than she'd realised before.

What was happening to her? Ever since she'd arrived back at the lodge from visiting Emma, Ellie's life had been turned upside down. Her feelings, her safety, her confidence had all been touched by the events of the past couple of weeks.

She stiffened as uncertainty and fear fought for precedence.

'Ellie, it'll be okay.' Kane's soft voice soothed her as he took her in his arms. But the instant comfort she took from his quiet confidence worried her on another level.

'There's something else. There's this guy I took up on a flight this week and he creeped me out. The more I think about it, I'm sure he wasn't just a tourist.' Ellie shivered. 'He was at the lodge this afternoon, hassling me down at the hangar.' She turned to Kane. 'And he had a black Mercedes. He's tall and blond like that guy you saw near my apartment the other day.'

'Shit. I shouldn't have let you come back by yourself.' Kane put his arm around her. 'What happened at the hangar?'

'It doesn't matter. I sorted it.'

They sat on the verandah and waited and the need to be close to him surged through her. She had fallen for Kane McLaren, even though the thought of relying on someone else other than herself was one she was not comfortable with.

'Here he is.' Kane's voice interrupted her brooding.

The headlights of an approaching car arced across the wall behind them, and she made sure it was David before she stepped out into the light. She was jumpy; but there was nothing wrong with being too careful.

David closed the door of the dark SUV quietly and bounded up the steps and took her arm.

'Where are they? Are they okay?'

'They're fine. Both asleep on my sofa.' Although David's face was in the shadows, Ellie could still see the bleakness in his eyes. 'Come inside and tell us what's going on. Do you have any idea where Gina is?' She kept her voice low.

'Us?' David stared at Kane as he stepped from the shadows. 'I told you not to let anyone else into this, Ellie.'

'It's all right. You can trust Kane.' She turned to Kane as he held his hand out to David.

'Kane McLaren.'

'David, Kane is a helicopter engineer here at the lodge, and a . . . a very good friend.' What else could she call him? My lover? My boyfriend? 'I've told him what's happened. A little bit anyway.'

Two men shook hands.

'I think you should both come in,' she said. 'We all need to talk.'

'No. I'm going out to look for Gina. Can the kids stay here with you?'

Ellie put her hand on his arm as he headed towards the stairs. 'Where would you look? You can't go. First, she could be anywhere. Second, it's too dangerous . . . do you want to be taken too? Think of your children.' It was harsh to imply that Gina had been murdered but she had to convince David not to go rushing out on a wild goose chase.

David stared out into the dark, before his shoulders dropped. 'I suppose you're right. I just feel so bloody responsible . . . and useless. I should have taken better care of my family.' His voice was bitter.

The two men stood back and waited for Ellie to go inside ahead of them. David followed her and crossed to the sofa, dropping to his knees, and cupped a hand on each of the children's cheeks before leaning down and kissing each of them in turn. The look of anguish on his face brought tears to

Ellie's eyes. She cleared her throat aware that Kane's eyes were fixed on her.

'Get everything sorted today?' she asked him softly, tearing her gaze away from David and the children.

'Yeah.'

# Chapter 31

*9.00 p.m.*
*Friday Makowa Lodge*

'Nothing.' David had just returned from checking their suite, hoping to find a clue to Gina's whereabouts. He shook his head and walked over to the table where Ellie and Kane were sitting. 'It looks no one's been in there since the room was serviced today.' He picked up Gina's phone from the table. 'Now tell me exactly what happened and how come you've got this?' He pulled out a chair and dropped into it, every angle of his body showing his despair.

'I went to the crèche to see Heather.' Ellie chose her words carefully.

'Who's Heather?' David leaned forward, his eyes fixed on hers. 'Heather Jarragah. She works here,' Ellie said.

'Keep going.'

'And I was surprised to see the kids there so late. The phone was in a drawer in the desk where she was sitting . . . Considering what happened to Bill, I wondered if she knew something.' Ellie frowned; she didn't want to accuse Heather of anything but her behaviour had been strange. 'She said Gina didn't say where she was going. Maybe she just left her phone there by mistake.'

'She was going to the day spa.' David's eyes were bleak. 'Is Heather connected to Bill Jarragah?'

'Yes, his daughter.'

'What do you mean "happened to Bill"?'

'Someone cut his finger off. We had to take him to the

hospital the other night.'

'What?' David's voice was loud and he glanced over at the sleeping children. 'Bloody hell! Cut it off? Is that why his arm was in a sling?'

'Hold on.' Kane stared at David. 'Can you just cut to the chase and tell me what's going on here and why you haven't called the police? And how you know Bill?'

'They're not to be involved.' David's response was terse and he punched his fist into his other hand. 'Fuck. He's is capable of anything. It's got nothing to do with Bill's daughter. That bastard's got Gina.' He dropped his head into his hands. 'He called me just before you did.'

'What bastard?' Kane glanced at Ellie.

'Russell Fairweather.' David lifted his head and his eyes were bleak. 'But he'll have covered his tracks so well, it will be impossible to get him on anything. He told me tonight he had a man killed.'

Recognition of the name chilled her as Ellie's eyes locked with Kane's. Russell Fairweather.

'Whoa.' Kane put his hand up. 'Can we backtrack a little? You still haven't told me your connection with this and why your wife's been abducted?'

Elle rubbed her hand across her forehead. 'You don't know who David is, do you?'

'No? Should I?'

David spoke quietly. 'I'm the Chief Minister for the Territory. I'm being blackmailed by Fairweather. Foolishly, I thought I could handle it and I hid Gina and the kids here . . . but that bastard has connections everywhere. He even has my bloody mobile tapped.'

'Why didn't you get help before this happened, David?' Ellie couldn't understand how someone in such a position could be blackmailed. Surely he had security men or something around him?

'He threatened to harm Andrew and Binny if I did.' He stared at the two children sleeping on the sofa. 'I only had to keep them safe until Monday when there's a committee vote taking place on a drilling licence. That's why I sent Gina and the kids down here.'

Ellie narrowed her eyes as the pieces of the jigsaw began to fall together for her. 'Bill Jarragah is on that committee too, isn't he?'

Kane stared at Ellis. 'You are fucking joking! Do you mean this is connected to the farm and Sordina's murder?'

'Yes, Fairweather mentioned his death when he threatened me tonight. I know he's responsible. I wouldn't put anything past the cold bastard.'

Ellie held his gaze. 'David, you need to know. Panos Sordina was Kane's stepfather.'

'Oh fucking hell.' David's voice shook. 'Too many connections. All to do with this bloody exploration.'

'Fairweather has to be linked to the fracking at the farm.'

'So it's got out then. I'm surprised. Fairweather's even got the media in his bloody pocket. There's been no publicity about the exploration application.' David's voice hardened.

'I didn't read about it in the papers.' Ellie lifted her gaze. 'I saw it myself.'

'Saw what?' Puzzlement crossed David's face.

'The fracking. They're drilling at the back down near

the river.'

'Already? The exploration licence hasn't been approved yet.' Ellie shook her head. 'I saw a huge gash in the land when I flew over last week. The infrastructure is already in place. I went down there for a look and got escorted off the land.'

'Jesus. What's the point?' David dropped his face into his hands again. His shoulders sagged and Ellie put her hand on his arm. 'There must be something we can do.'

Kane leaned forward and his voice was firm. 'If Fairweather wants your vote, she'll be alive.

'Will she?'

Ellie's eyes filled with tears as David dropped his head into his hands.

They sat there quietly and she let everything that had happened run through her mind. Sordina's murder, the fracking, Bill's injury, the break-ins, Gina's disappearance. Maybe she was on the wrong track with Heather.

'Kane?' She took a deep breath as she remembered Henry's cold eyes. 'That guy at the hangar today. I'm sure he has something to do with Gina's kidnapping.'

# Chapter 32

*5.30 am*
*Saturday Makowa Lodge*

'We're missing something.' Ellie put her head down onto the table. 'There's nothing here that incriminates Fairweather.'

While they had waited for morning to arrive, David had stared at his phone but it had remained silent; there was no further contact from Fairweather. Ellie had opened her email, and she and Kane trawled through the files that Emma had sent over until the first rays of light tinged the eastern horizon. Sordina's early connections to the shadowy figure of Russell Fairweather had become increasingly obvious. They Googled both names together and came up with even more connections. In the Darwin social pages. At the races. A game of golf. Early newspaper reports of their association came to an abrupt halt about the time that Ellie's father had died and Sordina had bought the property. The file Ellie's mother had labelled 'P_Sord' was a series of photos of Sordina and Fairweather that were six years old. There was no indication of any association between then after Sordina had been elected to Parliament. Strangely, not one hit on the search engine. And there was nothing to explain why her mother had even included them with all of the articles on fracking.

'It shows us there was a connection between Sordina and Fairweather.' David said.

As they'd pulled up each report, article, parliamentary committee minutes and newspaper article, they were confronted by reports on the dangers of hydraulic fracking; the amount of water alone needed for each drilling operation had astounded Ellie. With the wet season in the Territory dumping metres of rain each year, it was easy to see why Kakadu was such an attractive location for the process. In most areas, water had to be trucked in with tankers; in Kakadu it fell from the sky. Her mother had listed links to hundreds of articles on the carcinogens and toxic chemicals that had to be pumped into the wells. 'The contamination of the ground water would spell the end of Kakadu.' Ellie stared at David as he yawned and put his hand over his mouth. Exhaustion was evident in every line of his face and his eyes were bloodshot. He'd spent the night alternating between sitting at the computer with Kane and Ellie, and resting beside his sleeping children. Twice they'd had to convince him not to go tearing out to search for Gina. He'd gone back to the apartment and collected some clothes and toys for Andrew and Binny.

Ellie tried not to stare at the red scarf he'd brought back with him and now held in his hand. His fingers played with it as he sat beside her.

'Look at this one. Fracking even causes minor earthquakes.' Ellie pointed to the link on the screen.'

Kane's deep voice interrupted her. 'Look, there's no doubt that your mother has done a lot of research into this. She obviously believes there is a connection between Sordina and Fairweather but there's still nothing here to incriminate either of them. We've spent hours and we're no closer to any information about your old place than we were when we started.'

Ellie dropped her head into her hands. 'I know.'

'Could you talk to her? Find out what alerted her to Fairweather in the first place?'

Reluctantly, Ellie lifted her head and looked at him. 'I guess I'm going to have to talk to her about it, aren't I?'

'After we find Gina.' Kane folded his hands on the table and the authoritative tones of his voice filled the room. 'So this is what we are going to do. How many of the staff here do you know and trust, Ellie?'

David went to speak but Kane raised his hand. 'We have to involve others. The park is way too big to try to do it ourselves. You want to find your wife. We need help.'

Ellie thought for a moment. 'You've met most of them. There's Terry and Bill. Jan, Jock, Amanda. Roscoe and his two boys.'

'Are you sure you trust them all?'

'Absolutely.'

'What about Bill?' Kane stared at her.

'I would trust him with my life. He's always been like a second father to me.'

'Okay, this is what we're going to do. David and I will go up to the farm. The house is empty and they, or he or whoever, might have taken Gina there. They've already got their thugs up there guarding the place.' His jaw was set as he fired instructions off. 'Ellie, can you get someone to look after the children this morning?'

She nodded.

'What time do the guys start work at the lodge?'

'They get together for a cuppa and plan the day's work over at the workshop about seven o'clock.'

'I want you to go over there and speak to the group you

can trust. See if they can think of anywhere that Gina could be hidden around here. An old shed, an abandoned farm. Anything. Get them to keep a look out as they travel around.'

David shook his head. 'I'm not sure about this. What if it gets back to Fairweather?'

'Do you have a better plan?'

'No. I guess I'll just have to trust your judgment.' David glanced down at his watch. 'It's almost six-thirty.'

'I'll ask Jan to come and babysit and then I'll make us some coffee.' Ellie turned to the laptop. 'Wait a minute, there's one email I haven't opened.' The message had come in last night but she'd left it as there were no attachments. She clicked on the subject and scrolled down. 'Yes! I asked Em to see if Mum knew the password to Dad's Gmail account and she's sent it to me.'

'Daddy!' David pushed his chair back and went over to the sofa as Binny stirred.

Ellie watched David gather the little girl into his arms and the lump that had been stuck in the back of her throat all night came slamming back. The email was forgotten as she watched David hold his daughter close. Ellie swallowed and caught Kane's gaze, not surprised to see a sheen of tears clouding his eyes.

'Where's Mummy?' Binny asked.

David caught Ellie's eye and the anguish in his expression tore at her. 'She'll be back soon.'

'With our new baby?' Binny climbed down from her father's arms. 'I'm hungwy, Daddy.'

'I've got some breakfast cereal and long-life milk in the cupboard.' Ellie moved the laptop to the benchtop in the kitchen as David carried the little girl over to the table. She pulled out some bowls and put it all on the table for David, and then went back to the computer.

The quiet voices of the children were forgotten as she successfully logged onto her father's email account.

'How sad is this.' She sniffed and wiped her eyes with the back of her hand as Kane gently squeezed her shoulder. 'Emails to Dad. Still being sent five years after he died.

It took a few minutes to scroll back scroll through pages and pages of newsletters and ads covering the last five years. 'Look, there's a few emails from Panos to Dad, just before he –' Ellie took a quick breath and narrowed her eyes as she leaned closer to the computer. 'Oh my God. Read this.'

She turned to Kane and a huge grin crossed his face as he read the email open on the screen in front of him.

'We've got him, David. We've nailed the bastard.'

# Chapter 33

*6.50 am Saturday*
*Makowa Lodge*

Kane kissed Ellie before he crossed to the Jeep where David was waiting. Andrew and Binny had hugged their father as Ellie stood with Jan on the verandah. In the end they had only told Jan that Gina was ill and that David had to go and see her. He waved to the kids from the car.

'We'll see you later, Ellie.' He held up Gina's phone. 'If there's any news, you have this number?' Ellie nodded.

Jan led the children inside and Ellie walked across to the steps after the door closed behind them. 'Be careful.'

'I'll call if we have any news.'

'Me too. After I see the guys, I'll see Heather and I'll let you know what I find out.'

'And Ellie, you be careful too.' Kane held her gaze and she smiled at him.

'I will. Hurry back.'

Ellie watched until the vehicle disappeared around the building. Then she changed into her uniform and said goodbye to Jan and the children.

'I shouldn't be too long,' she promised. Checking that the door was locked behind her, she headed over to the office to check the roster and see where Heather was today. She wasn't going to warn her with another phone call.

Luck was on her side. When Ellie entered the office through the back door, Heather was in the kitchen filling the kettle. She stood waiting until she turned around.

'Bloody hell. Why don't you sneak up on me?' Heather's eyes were red-rimmed and circled with dark shadows. Looked like she hadn't slept either. Ellie closed the back door and flicked the lock over; she didn't want anyone interrupting this conversation. Ellie crossed her arms and leaned her back against the door waiting for Heather to finish. Her friend's hands were shaking and she cursed as she dropped the packet of sugar and it scattered all over the tiled floor.

'Shit. Look what you made me do, Ellie.' Heather reached for the broom.

'Leave the bloody sugar. I want to talk to you.'

'What about?' Her eyes were wary.

'Why were you in such an all-fired hurry to get away last night?' Ellie stared at her and Heather dropped her gaze.

'I can't tell you.'

'Don't be stupid. Of course you can tell me. Do you know where Gina is?'

Heather dropped into a crouch and put her hands over her eyes. 'I can't tell you.'

Ellie kneeled down beside her as Heather began to cry softly.

'It's bigger than we can deal with, Ellie. I should have asked you for help, but it's too late now.'

'Heather, if you know anything at all, you have to tell me. The police aren't involved . . . yet. But this guy has already killed people.' She put her arm round Heather's shoulder. 'For God's sake, if you know anything, tell me. You know you can trust me.'

'I was in the car with Dad when a man rang him and Dad said he wouldn't do it. He told me what the man wanted.

For God's sake, Ellie, Dad was crying when he hung up.' She rubbed at her eyes. 'I've never seen him cry before. They've already cut his finger off.' Heather lifted her face and her eyes were scared. 'When we got home, I took Dad's phone and I rang the man back. He told me they'd kill Dad if he didn't take her. So I took her. Dad doesn't know.'

'Thank God.' Ellie put both hands either side of Heather's shoulders and helped her to her feet. 'Where is she, Heather? You must tell me where Gina is. She's in danger. Her life is in danger.'

'But Dad –'

'Your dad is safe. He's over in the workshop with the other guys.'

'I know, he insisted on coming in with me today, so I couldn't check on Gina on the way to work.'

'On the way to work?' Ellie held Heather's shoulders. 'Please.

Where is she?'

'Not till I know Dad's safe.'

'Look, right now he's with the other guys and he's speaking at that anti-fracking meeting at ten. No one's going to hurt him while he's in front of a crowd.' Ellie shook Heather gently. 'There's safety in numbers and as much as I hate to say it, the rangers always have their Winchester rifles handy.'

'I suppose.' Heather blew her nose and nodded slowly.

'As long as he watches his back, he'll be okay.' Ellie gripped Heather's arm. 'Now for the love of God, will you tell me where she is?

A vast sense of relief flooded Ellie as Heather nodded mutely.

***

Ellie ran all the way to the hangar. She paused to at the gate to catch her breath and called Gina's mobile. No connection. She tried Kane but the call rang twice and then went to voicemail. David and Kane must be driving through a dead zone. The mobile service was patchy all the way from the lodge to Jabiru until you could see the big silver towers behind the town.

She tucked her phone between her shoulder and her chin as she pulled out her keys to unlock the gate to the tarmac. 'Ring me as soon as you get this. You're going the wrong way.'

Ellie lifted the padlock to unlock it and the chain came away in her hand. It slid to the concrete with a loud clang, and she narrowed her eyes. She was sure she'd locked the gate on the way out yesterday afternoon. Pushing the gate shut behind her, she locked the padlock at the end of the chain in case the first group arrived for their ten o'clock flight before she returned.

She hoped she would be back by then. Jock wasn't in the office and it was too early to ask him if she could take the helicopter up; she'd explain it to him when she got back.

Hopefully with Gina as a passenger.

Heather had promised her she was all right. She had food and water and the hut they'd left her in was locked. The river hut was about two kilometres past Bill's house at Black Jungle Springs. It had once been a residence but now the family used it as a fishing shack in the dry season.

Ellie knew the area well; it was on the South Alligator

River scenic flight run. The only thing that worried her was how close the hut was to the water. The place was a crocodile haven. If Gina had somehow managed to escape during the night . . .

She swallowed, pushing the thought away. Surely she would know not to go wandering along the edge of the river.

Please God.

Ellie opened the hangar and took a quick look around. It had been locked up and everything looked okay. Maybe she had left the gate unlocked in her rush to get away from that jerk yesterday. She grabbed her small first aid kit and ran for the helicopter and threw it in onto the passenger seat. A quick pre-flight check was enough; neither machine had been up since she'd refuelled and checked them yesterday. Ellie ran her hands along the skids, checked the rotors and looked over the fuel tanks. Still good; everything in place.

She closed her eyes for a second as an image of Kane doing his three checks pushed into her thoughts. Yeah, she'd probably been too hard on him. She'd apologise later.

# Chapter 34

*7.15 am Saturday*
*Near Black Jungle Springs*

Gina had finally drifted into a light doze just before dawn. The baby had given an almighty kick in the middle of the night and she'd sobbed with relief. The discomfort was welcome because she knew her baby was alive.

She woke with a start as a bird screeched near the window. Sunlight bathed the room and she opened her eyes and looked around. Her head throbbed with a dull ache behind her temples and her mouth was dry again. Her hands were still bound in front of her stomach; she'd given up on trying to pull them apart in the early hours. Now that it was light, she could see the knot and where to pull at it. Pins and needles pierced the skin but the pain was welcome. It spurred her on. She lifted her wrists and used her teeth to work at the soft towelling tie. The baby kicked again as she grunted and strained. Finally the knot loosened and she was able to pull her hands free. She flexed her fingers as the blood rushed painfully into them. When they stopped burning and the numbness had gone, she braced herself and pushed herself slowly to a sitting position. Her back ached from lying straight on the hard bed all night.

She reached for the half-full bottle of water and her hands shook as she unscrewed the cap. The water was cool and sweet and soothed her parched throat. When her headache had eased a little, she rolled over to her knees, supporting the baby with one hand and using the other to brace herself on the wall as she rose to her feet.

The hollow ache began low in her back and Gina took a deep breath. When it spread and gripped her belly like a vice, she leaned against the wall with her eyes closed. A trickle of warm fluid ran down her legs. She took another deep breath as the contraction tightened her belly and the low rumble of an engine reached her.

Gina clutched her stomach as she stood, and crossed the room to the window. A black SUV had pulled up on the road beside the house and a tall man dressed in dark jeans and a long-sleeved white shirt got out of the driver's side.

Thank God. Whoever he was he could get her out of here. She needed to get to a hospital. She ran to the door and lifted her hands to the lock. Her fingers fumbled as she hurried.

'Help! Help me!'

The man turned to her with a smile as she opened the door. She sagged with relief as he walked across from the car, but the relief was short lived. The baby pressed down on her bladder and she fought the building pressure as a shaft of pain speared down her right leg. Another contraction.

He stepped up onto the first step. 'Mrs Johnson?'

'Yes. But, how do you –'

Oh, *Dio*. He knew who she was.

'What a pleasure to meet you.' His eyes were cold as he put his hands together in front of him. Before she could push the door shut and lock it, the deep throb of an approaching helicopter vibrated through the small building. As he turned to look up, she slammed the door and ran.

A line of cupboards with a small sink and stove ran along the back wall of the room she was in. There was an external door at the end of the cupboards and when she reached it, she flicked the lock over and pushed it open. Two narrow concrete steps led down to an open expanse of overgrown grass which edged the thick forest. Gina shivered. She couldn't bring herself to step outside. Her feet were bare and she would be exposed and in full view.

Her speed was limited by the contractions and she could have another one any minute. Her breathing hitched into frightened sobs as she turned from the open door and quickly crossed to the door at the side of the room. It led into a small bedroom, but there was nothing in there and nowhere to hide. She looked from side to side as she hurried back into the larger room. The front door shook as he pushed his weight against it. Gina ran back to the small kitchen. A tall pantry was situated on the other side of the small stove and she pulled the door open. The bottom shelf ran the width of the double door and she crouched down and squeezed herself in. Putting her hand beneath the door, she pulled it shut just as the front door burst open. At the same time, the helicopter roared over the house and the building shook. She bit her lip and held her breath as the next contraction built.

\*\*\*

Ellie banked her bird to the left and looked down to the monsoon forest below her. She'd been in the air for fifteen minutes. The silver sheen of the South Alligator River glistened to the north-west as she swooped over the top of the Gunbumbuk range. She was only a few minutes from her destination.

*Please. Please let Gina be okay.*

As the forest cleared and she approached the wetlands signalling the edge of the river, Ellie glanced down at her watch; Jock would be in the office by now. She flicked the radio switch and called the base.

'Ellie to base. Ellie to base. Come in Jock.'

The reply was instant. 'Ellie, where are you? What are you doing up so early? Did you have a sunrise flight?'

'No. I'll explain when I come back. Jock, I'm sorry but can you please cancel my ten o'clock . . . and get the team at the medical centre briefed. Pregnant woman. We might need a medivac.'

'All right, I'll brief them. What's your destination?'

'Two kilometres south of Black Jungle Springs out on the old Jim Jim Road. Next to the river.' A red light on the dash caught her eye and Ellie craned forward. The low fuel light had come on.

'Bullshit,' Ellie muttered beneath her breath. With a full tank and with only her light weight in the bird, the twenty-gallon tank should have given her at least two hours flying time.

'What's wrong, Ellie?' Jock's voice faded in and out of her earphones as she leaned forward looking for a clearing. She knew she had five minutes of flying time after the light came on.

'I've got a problem here, Jock.' She kept her voice steady as she searched the ground for a flat spot to bring the bird down.

The small settlement of Black Jungle Springs appeared below and she lowered the front of the helicopter as she flew over it. There were too many trees and the flat ground near the river was still covered with water. The wetlands were still drying out after the late wet.

The engine power decreased as the fuel flow lessened and Ellie pushed the collective all the way down to reduce the drag on the rotor blades.

'Shit, shit, shit.'

'Ellie, what is it?' Jock's voice amplified her distress.

'I'm in autorotation, Jock. Mayday, mayday, I'm taking her down.'

Ellie searched desperately for a flat, clear spot below. Trees filled her vision as far as she could see. If the chopper came down there, she'd have no chance. Her heart lodged in her throat. She'd only ever practised an autorotation in the simulator at pilot school and had never done a real controlled crash landing before. The ground inched closer as the engine cut out. Now the whoosh of the air from the spinning rotors was the only sound and she gritted her teeth, fighting to control the bird in the descent without an engine.

The forest stretched all the way to the river. The road wound through scrubby forest and the small fishing hut appeared through a gap in the trees; a dark vehicle was parked at the edge of the fence. She smiled grimly. At least she was coming down close to her destination; someone was looking after her today.

She pulled back on the cyclic and the main rotor blades picked up speed as she scoured the ground below. Levelling off, she pulled up on the collective and prayed. As Ellie brought the chopper in over the river, she noticed the rocks in the grass in the small clearing. She pulled back to slow her forward speed and glanced down to the other side. There was a small patch of pure white sand directly beneath her; holding her breath, she levelled the helicopter.

'Oh, God. Yes.'

Thirty feet to go. Enough to kill you dropping from that height. At least there was no fuel to burn. She overshot the clearing and banked the chopper to come back around to the small sandy patch by the river.

'Come on, baby,' she whispered as the clearing loomed ahead again.

Her control held as the chopper got closer to the ground. 'Almost there.'

She jerked back and the T-bar suddenly whipped from her hand as a sharp crack broke the silence and the helicopter shuddered – she'd clipped a tree. A massive branch whipped across the side of the machine and the canopy split, blocking her vision of the clearing beneath her

Ellie screamed as her bird flipped sideways in one swift movement. The seatbelt held her pinned against the seat as water sprayed in a huge arc around the helicopter. A loud screech of grinding metal mixed with the splash as the passenger side scraped on the rocks on the bottom of the shallow river. Her head ricocheted off the metal panel beside her as the machine came to a sudden stop.

## Kakadu Highway

Kane and David were just a few kilometres south of Jabiru when Kane's phone beeped with an incoming message. He pulled it out of his pocket and listened to his voicemail.

Hitting the brakes, he checked for traffic in the rear-vision mirror before swinging the car around and heading back the way they came.

'That was Ellie. She must have found Gina. She said we're going the wrong way.' He flicked a glance at David, who'd been staring silently out the window for the past half hour as they'd headed north. 'The message was garbled at the end. All I could pick up was black something. Bloody phone service here is shocking.' He pressed the keypad to return the call.

'Is Gina all right?'

Kane shook his head. 'I don't know. That's all she said. I'll call her.'

The call went to voicemail and Kane swore and passed the phone over to David. 'Keep calling till she picks up.' He changed back a gear and floored the accelerator. If they copped a speeding fine, so be it.

David pressed redial until the phone service dropped out again. It was only fifteen minutes until they reached the Yellow Water turn-off which led back to Makowa Lodge.

'Phone service should be okay now,' Kane said.

David lifted the phone to dial again but it rang before he could press. He answered and listened intently, and Kane took his eyes from the road, slowing the car as they approached the lodge.

'Who?' David frowned. 'Ellie? Where is she? Yes, okay, I'll put him on.'

He passed the phone to Kane. 'Someone called Jock for you.'

'Jock?' Kane turned into the lodge and parked in the

front car park. 'Fuck. When? Where?'

Kane focused on his breathing, drawing the air in deep and letting it out slowly as the panic built in his chest. 'No, it's too far to drive. I'll take the other helicopter up.'

David stared at him, waiting for him to finish.

'How long till the National Park helicopter can get there?

Okay, I'll radio in when we're in the air.'

Kane shoved the phone into his pocket and opened the door. He beckoned David to follow him and they ran through the lodge towards the flight centre. 'Ellie took a chopper up and she sent a mayday call about ten minutes ago. Jock said she was out of fuel and in autorotation. And she said there was a pregnant woman needing assistance. I hope to hell they're okay.'

'Thank God.' David hurried along beside Kane ignoring the curious looks of the tourists. 'What's autorotation?'

'It's a controlled crash.' Kane briefly closed his eyes at the thought of what could go wrong. 'But she's a damn fine pilot. She should be right.'

'He didn't say anything else?'

'No. The National Park has got a crew heading out there.

But we're closer. We'll get there first.

They reached the gate next to the hangar. 'Shit, it's padlocked and I don't have my keys with me. No time to get them.' Kane hoisted himself up on the wire fence and climbed to the top, bracing himself for the jarring pain in his hip as he landed on the concrete below. He waited for David to follow.

Kane focused on the R44 sitting on the tarmac in front

of him. He walked around it slowly, checking the skids and the rotor blades before opening the cowl on the fuel tank. His eyes widened when he spotted the piece of hose.

'There's very little fuel left in this tank. That bastard who was here yesterday must have interfered with the helicopters. I'd say the same thing was done to Ellie's.'

Although the delay frustrated him, Kane took his time preparing for the flight. He refuelled the chopper and did another thorough pre-flight check before he was satisfied that the bird was safe to take up. Knowing the helicopter had been tampered with filled him with cold anger and he used that anger to fight the trepidation that threatened.

As he did the final check, the faces of Hawk, and Dirk and Jerry, filled his mind. They were gone and he was damn lucky to be alive. Shutting down the part of his life that he'd once loved wouldn't change anything. Anticipation flooded through him; the desire to be up in the air again.

'Okay, right to go. Climb in.' He shut the door behind David after he'd climbed into the passenger seat.

As he checked the instruments, Kane was surprised at how calm he felt. His hands were steady when he passed over the headphone to David, and he slipped his own on once David was set.

'Can you hear me okay?'

David nodded and Kane lifted the right side of his headset away and opened the right hand door as he started up the engine. Exhilaration rushed through him as the bird lifted into the sky. He was totally focused on getting to Ellie. The first tremor ran through him when he imagined her lying broken in the wreckage. But this time he refused to give in to the fear.

# Chapter 35

*7.20 am Saturday*
*Darwin*

'What do you mean, she's not fucking there?' Russell Fair- weather was sitting in the Cove restaurant of the Sky City hotel in Darwin, waiting for his appointment to join him for a breakfast meeting. A couple looked at him curiously from the next table and he lowered his voice and smiled politely. 'Where is she?' he hissed.

'She got away. The back door's open and there's no sign of her. What do you want me to do?'

'Go and find her, of course. If you lose her, trust me, you will be very, very sorry. Now –'

Before he could finish, a strange sound came through the phone. 'Holy shit. You'll never believe what's just happened.'

'What?'

'Ellie Porter has just crashed her helicopter in the river.' Russell turned away to the window and kept his voice low.

'Go and make sure she's dead and then find the other woman.' Outside at the lagoon pool there was already a crowd lying around on sun lounges and day beds. Indolent tourists; Russell couldn't think of anything worse than lying around with no goal for the day.

'Yes, sir. I'll find her.'

'Do that. I'll call you in an hour.'

\*\*\*

Ellie opened her eyes. The cable from her headset was choking her and she reached up and yanked it off. She was hanging sideways, held in by the seatbelt that was now constricting her breathing. She turned her head slowly and the vertigo eased, but she drew in a breath as she caught sight of the water flowing through the jagged edges of the smashed canopy. The door on her side had popped out in the crash but it was above the water level. If she could get her belt undone, she could clamber up on top of the chopper and stay above the waterline.

Jock knew she'd come down and he knew where she was heading; he'd have help on the way as soon as he could locate a pilot. Ellie focused on the hole in the Perspex canopy, trying to clear her blurred vision and see how far away the riverbank was. This part of the river was a narrow waterway, and only deep in the middle. The sandbanks where the crocodiles basked in the winter sun shifted every wet season. She shivered as she looked out over the water. The riverbank was only about twenty metres away but it might as well have been two hundred. There was no way she'd wade through that.

A movement flashed in her peripheral vision; her heart jumped as she imagined a crocodile slithering at speed out of the water and through the hole in the canopy. She closed her eyes, waiting for the impact.

But when she slowly opened them, it was the face of a man, not a crocodile, that met her.

Mr Henry, her difficult tourist, stood waist deep in the water, peering up at her through the hole in the canopy. She opened her mouth to yell at him to climb up on the skids, out of the water, away from danger, but the words died on her lips when she saw the knife in his hand.

'I suppose you think you were clever, landing like you did. Not so clever now, are you?' His tone was conversational.

'Who are you?' she whispered.

He laughed and the sound was chilling.

'What are you going to do?' Ellie was rigid with fear, her eyes fixed on the knife that was now only inches from her neck.

'Good question. Maybe I'll cut you out of the belt? Or perhaps I'll cut that pretty little throat of yours first?'

Ellie whimpered and tried to shrink back away from him.

He pulled the knife back and shifted to one side as he braced his other hand on the edge of the cockpit. 'You know, you've got the same eyes as your father. He looked at me just like that when I tightened the rope around his neck.'

Ellie shuddered and her chin trembled as his words sank in. Even in her dazed state, her thoughts turned to her mother and her insistence that Dad had been murdered. A heavy weight settled in Ellie's chest. Mum had been right all along, but they hadn't listened.

She lifted her chin, ignoring the shooting pain down her back. 'Why are you doing this?'

'I'm just doing my job, sweetheart.'

He lifted his hand and leaned to the left. The cold steel of the knife touched her throat with a sharp sting, and Ellie lifted her hands and pulled back as far as she could. As he leaned forward again, the water behind him suddenly churned and a massive crocodile broke the surface. The huge jaws clamped down on his legs and the knife dropped, hitting the metal with a clatter as his head slammed against the roof of the cockpit. He disappeared from sight before she could take a breath. The water erupted with red foam as the crocodile rolled, its creamy white underbelly flashing in the sunlight as it flipped over.

One unearthly scream, a last splash and they disappeared below the surface.

He was gone. The water was calm again, just a quiet gurgle as it washed through the broken canopy of the helicopter. The silence was almost obscene, as Ellie imagined what was happening beneath the clear, green water.

A keening sound filled her ears and it was a few seconds before she realised that the noise was coming from her. She had to get out before other crocodiles came. The dominant male had fed, next it would be their turn.

Pushing as hard as she could against the seat, her fingers scrabbled for the catch of the seatbelt but they slipped off before she could release it.

Three times, she pushed herself as far back as she could, and three times the belt jammed. Finally with a grunt Ellie stretched her legs towards the water and arched her back, and the catch released with a loud click. Sobbing, she reached up and pulled herself out through the canopy, using the skids to lever herself to the side of the helicopter that was safely above the water. Her head spun as she stared at the sandbanks in the middle of the river. Four huge crocodiles lay watching her. As she lay on her back on the cold metal, the water churned again.

But this time it was the rotor wash from the other Makowa Lodge helicopter as it headed for the clearing at the edge of the river.

*\*\*\**

David craned forward as the helicopter headed towards the sandy clearing. 'Look, down there!'

'It's Fairweather's man's vehicle. It has to be. There wouldn't be many black Mercedes in this part of the world.' Kane twisted to the left and looked out the other side. The river glinted silver as it snaked around a bend. His pulse sped up when he saw the red Makowa Lodge helicopter on its side in the water.

'Fuck. She's come down in the river.' Adrenaline spiked through him but he focused on taking the chopper lower.

'It's all right.' David pointed. 'Look, Ellie's on top of the chopper. She's okay.'

As the helicopter flew across the water, Ellie lifted her hand and waved to them. The world seemed to go by in slow motion as Kane dipped the bird to the east and brought it down as close to the edge of the river as he could. He shut everything down and gestured for David to wait until it was clear to get out. David tore the headset off and pointed to the building which was set back in a cleared space at the edge of the forest.

'I'm going to find Gina.'

'Wait. We don't know where the guy from the car is. He'll have heard us coming. He's had plenty of time to hide while we landed.'

David ignored him. 'I'm going. Just watch my back.' He picked up a large lump of timber and ran off past the SUV in the direction of the hut.

Kane stepped down from the helicopter and ran towards the water. 'I'm coming,' he called to Ellie.

'No.' Ellie screamed and put her hands over her face. She was sitting up now and even from a distance he could see the blood on her neck and her shirt front.

Kane stopped and looked past the helicopter. An enormous crocodile walked clumsily along the sandbank, its tail moving side to side, and then slid into the water.

His heart was pounding as he took a step back. Ellie dropped her hands from her face. There was blood on her fingers. 'You're bleeding.'

'I'm okay. Go with David. Find Gina.'

'But what happened? Where's the guy from the car?'

Ellie shook her head and all he wanted to do was hold her in his arms. 'He's gone.' She pointed into the water.

'Hang on. I'll come straight back.' Kane walked stealthily towards the front of the house, his eyes scanning the long grass as he moved closer. Stepping onto the front landing, he avoided the gaps in the timber where the floor had rotted away. He was about to try the front door when David's shout reached him.

'Kane, quickly around the back. It's all clear.'

He vaulted over the low railing and ran along the side of the house and up the back steps.

'She's here. Gina's here.' David was standing by the back door, supporting a woman in his arms. She wore a long pink bathrobe. She was bending forward; her long dark hair covering her face. 'The baby's coming.'

'Shit. How long?' Kane was qualified in emergency

care, but he'd never delivered a baby.

David's wife clutched at his arm. 'The contractions are about five minutes apart. There's one building now.' She doubled up with a moan. 'David, I'm scared, it's too early. It's different this time. The pain is worse.'

David stared at Kane, his mouth set. 'How many passengers can you take?'

'Only one.'

\*\*\*

Ellie lay with her eyes closed. She tried to open them, but they wouldn't open. She tried to talk but no words would come out. It must be a dream; she slipped back into the dark and floated painlessly for a few more seconds. Her head ached and when she tried to move, her limbs wouldn't cooperate. The sound of running water surrounded her. Finally, she forced her eyes open and pushed herself up, holding her head until the vertigo passed. She was on the helicopter in the river. There was a tender spot at the back of her head, but her fingers came away clean this time; the bleeding had stopped.

She looked over the side. The downed chopper had settled into the mud and the water was getting higher. The helicopter slipped a little further and she grabbed for the skids as the left side dipped a few centimetres.

Keeping completely still, she examined the water between her and the three large crocodiles on the far bank. The river was flowing swiftly but it wasn't as deep as she'd thought. It was clear, and she could see the stones that formed the causeway only about half a metre below the surface. Maybe she could try to get to the bank. But her legs refused to move.

There was no way she would get in that water and strike out for the shore.

She turned to look at the other bank but the pain the movement caused was unbearable. The scene in front of her wavered as though she was looking at it through water.

Her hands began to tremble. She was in trouble whatever she did. The need to escape, to get away from here, overtook her, but she couldn't move.

\*\*\*

Kane ran the short distance from the hut towards the river. Even though he was moving quickly, his legs felt as though he was running through sand. He gritted his teeth and focused on the present, refusing let his brain take over and put him back in the desert. Ellie needed him; he had to get to her. He looked down at the ground and concentrated on his breathing.

This is Australia and I'm in Kakadu. No sand, just hard red dirt. Gradually, the feeling eased and the solidness of the hard-packed earth beneath his feet calmed him. Strength filled him; he could do it.

Kane ran past the SUV and came to a sudden halt. The vehicle had a large metal hook attached to the bull bar on the front. He ran to the back of the car, flung the door open and spotted the quick access toolbox in the spare wheel compartment.

Please.

He grabbed the snatch strap, ran to the helicopter and threw it in. Back at the edge of the water, he cupped his hands to his mouth. 'Ellie!'

His call disturbed a flock of cockatoos in a tree above the helicopter. They squawked raucously as they lifted off and flew over him to a large dead tree on the other side of the river.

'Grab the rope when I drop it to you.' He pointed to the helicopter and relief flooded through him when she gave him the thumbs up. After securing the strap to the skids, he looked across to the house. There'd been no time to tell David his idea once he spotted the snatch strap, but this wouldn't take long.

Seconds later, the chopper lifted with the rope stretched out beneath the skids as he gained height.

Holding it in a hover was the easy part. Judging the right distance so Ellie could grab the nylon webbing was harder. He shoved the door open and leaned over.

'Shit.' He was too low and about ten metres too far into the river. The snatch strap was in the water.

Using his hands and feet, he manoeuvred the bird until he was directly above her and held it in a hover for the second time. He held his breath as Ellie grabbed for the strap as it swung past her head.

She missed it. The wash from the rotors was ruffling the water and the strap swayed as it caught in the downdraft. Kane held his breath as it swung back towards her.

'Good girl.' On the second pass Ellie grabbed for it and held it. He watched as she wrapped the end of the strap around her waist and looped it over before she raised her arms and held on. She put her head back and nodded as she held the now taut strap with both hands. It was a delicate dance of precision as his feet moved on the foot controls and his hand gripped the cyclic. He did it all by feel, not once taking his eyes off Ellie as she lifted from the roof of the submerged helicopter. Slowly and carefully, the bird responded to his deft movements as Ellie spun slowly above the water.

Seconds later, she was above the ground, well away from the water's edge and as he lowered the bird slowly, she slipped out of the strap onto the bank.

But his relief was short-lived, as she crumpled to the ground.

\*\*\*

Ellie opened her eyes to the sound of running feet. The ground was hard beneath her back and her head ached.

'Ellie. Can you hear me?'

She put her hands to her face and stared up at Kane as he dropped to his knees beside her. Gentle hands ran over her body.

'I'm okay. It's only my head, but it's not too bad.'

'What happened?'

'I clipped a tree on the way down.' Ellie pushed herself up and clung to him. She pushed her face into his neck, and his warmth and the smell of his skin soothed her. Her lips trembled, and she held tightly as she fought for control.

'He killed my father.'

'Shh. It's okay. You're okay.'

'It's not fucking okay.' She pulled her head back and her voice broke as her voice got louder. 'He told me my eyes were like Dad's as he put the noose around his neck.'

Ellie buried her face in his neck again and a sob escaped her lips.

'I'll help you find you what happened. I promise.'

She closed her eyes as Kane lifted her into his arms and began to walk towards the hut. 'But first we have to help David. Gina is in labour.'

The door was open, and he walked inside, putting her down gently on the floor beside a low bed where Gina lay.

David was beside Gina and he reached up and took Ellie's hand. 'You're okay?'

'I'm okay.' She leaned down and spoke to Gina. 'Are you?'

'The pains have eased a bit.' Gina reached out and touched her face. 'How can I ever thank you, Ellie? And Kane, you too.'

Kane frowned down at Ellie. 'You shouldn't be on your feet. I want you to rest while I take Gina to the medical centre in Jabiru. David, make sure she lies down. I know what she's like.'

'What am I like?' A small smile crossed Ellie's face.

'You're invincible,' he said as he leaned in and kissed her.

# Chapter 36

*5.00 pm*
*Sunday Makowa Lodge*

Ellie stood on the verandah outside her apartment, letting the late afternoon sun warm her bare limbs. The only after-effects from the events of yesterday morning were a dull headache and a greater fear of crocodiles. The medical centre had checked her over – luckily she'd needed no stitches – and told Kane to keep an eye on her.

She picked up the small trowel she'd brought out from beneath the kitchen sink. Her black gardening gloves were stiff, and she flexed her fingers, watching as the dried soil fell to the wooden floorboards. Her herb seedlings had been ignored for the past few days and she leaned over the small pots, digging her gloved hand into the seed raising mix.

The soft green shoots had withered and were now stiff and brown.

Ellie wasn't aware she was crying until the first tear plopped with a splat onto the verandah beside the pots. She tipped her head back and closed her eyes and gave way to the tears that rolled down her cheeks as the grief welled into her throat. She cried silently for her father and the sad loneliness of his death. Her tears fell for Kane's mother who had spent her last weeks alone and neglected.

Ellie cried because she knew Kane would leave and she would be alone again; there was no reason for him to stay here now. Her prickly shell would go up and protect her heart again; this time it would be twice as thick.

Maybe it was time for her to consider moving on. As much as she loved Kakadu, all it held were sad memories for her. 'Is your head bothering you?' As usual Kane's movements were silent, and she hadn't heard his door close. He'd insisted on spending last night in her apartment in case she had a concussion and had kept a vigil by the bed as she'd slept. He'd left her only briefly to go and have a shower.

Ellie shook her head and sniffed as her nose began to run with the tears. She wiped her face with the back of her gloved hand. 'My head's fine. It's just been a rough couple of days.' She moved along to make room for Kane as he lowered himself next to her and he leaned back against the railing, his head close to hers.

'It has.' His arm went around her shoulders and she leaned into him, marvelling at the comfort that she drew from his presence. 'But there's some good news. Jock called just as I was getting in the shower. David called the lodge and asked him to get a message to us. They have a new little girl. She didn't make an appearance till lunchtime today.'

Ellie closed her eyes again as his thumb brushed her cheek. 'They're both okay?'

'Jock said Gina and the baby are doing well. They've called her Ellie. Nice name, hey?' Kane's deep voice was soft, and Ellie let it wash over her. She could stay here forever; the afternoon sun warming her skin, Kane's leg pressed against hers. The birdlife on the river creating the usual cacophony of sound as the sun headed for the horizon.

'Beautiful sky tonight.' Kane's breath brushed against her face. 'Are you going to open your eyes and enjoy it with me?' Ellie opened her eyes slowly. Kane's cheek was close to hers. The sky behind him was brilliant orange and the narrow, horizontal clouds above the horizon were tinged with silver. 'Kakadu sunsets are always beautiful.' She looked at him from beneath her lashes. 'Even more so in the other seasons. Banggerreng is my favourite.'

'Banggerreng?'

'Knock 'em down season. One of the six traditional seasons we have up here. It's not the wet and it's not the dry but we can get the most amazing thunderheads.'

'I'll look forward to it.'

Ellie lifted her head and looked at him as hope unfurled in her chest. 'You'll be around then?' She kept her voice casual.

'I will. I've been thinking. There's a lot about this place that I like.' Ellie smiled as he pointed to the sky. 'Sunsets are pretty good.' Kane lifted his arm and put it around her and she leaned into his shoulder as he rested his chin on the top of her head. 'Not hurting you, am I?'

'No, I'm good.'

'And I hear the lodge could do with another pilot.'

Ellie smiled. His healing had begun. 'You'll be working with a pretty cranky female pilot.'

'Not a problem.' Warmth feathered through Ellie's skin as Kane dropped a gentle kiss on her forehead. 'I don't believe that prickly exterior she puts up. She's as soft as butter inside.'

'I'm the senior pilot.' The stubble on his cheek was rough against her face as she grinned.

'I'm the best pilot.' Kane squeezed her arm.

'Maybe. It'll be fun finding out, anyway,' she said bumping him playfully with her shoulder. Knowing that Kane was going to be around for a while lightened her heart. The tears were gone.

'I've got another question for you.'

Ellie moved back a little and looked up at him. Kane's eyes were dark and his expression serious as he held her gaze.

'You love mucking around with this stuff, don't you?' He gestured to the pots along the railing. 'Now that Mum and Panos have gone . . . the farm will be mine. Panos had no family. I've always had a yen to grow something. How would you feel about trying to resurrect a mango plantation?' He rushed on as Ellie felt her mouth drop open. The lightness in her chest was replaced with joy that spread through her entire body as she looked at this man. This man she knew she'd fallen in love with.

'We could knock down the old house, build a new one . . . and the shed. Get rid of all our bad memories. Plant some new trees maybe?' Kane's hand cupped her face. 'Maybe it's too soon but we'll see. One thing I am sure of is I'd really love you to share it with me.'

'Are you sure?' Ellie whispered.

'I've never been surer of anything in my life.

Ellie lifted her head and pressed her lips against his.

'I take it that's a yes.'

# Chapter 37

*One week later*
*Daintree, North Queensland*

When the wound on Ellie's head had healed and her headache was finally gone, Kane travelled to Queensland with her. They'd waited until after his mother's service and driven to the airport the next morning.

Ellie knew her healing could not begin until she spoke to her mother and told her that she'd been right about the farm – about her father's death, and about the men who had wanted to use the place for its resources. The news she had was not the sort of thing she wanted to deliver by email or over the phone. When she'd asked Jock for more time off, he'd understood, knowing the ordeal she'd been through.

'I owe you, Jock.' Ellie hugged him.

'No, I think you've done me a big favour.'

'How's that?' Ellie tipped her head to the side, wincing a little as the plaster caught on her hair.

'I think we finally have another pilot who's going to hang around a while.' Jock grinned at her. 'No ex-wife likely to turn up looking for Kane, is there?'

Ellie smiled back. 'Not that's he's mentioned. I'd better check.'

They landed in Cairns in the early morning and Kane drove to their hotel. Ellie yawned as the beaches flashed past her window. 'Why is it that every flight seems to leave Darwin in the middle of the night?' She looked over at Kane as he drove through the city. His tanned arms held the wheel confidently and the haunted look had left his eyes. His mouth was relaxed but Ellie knew he still had a way to go before he healed.

He had talked more about his flashbacks and the stressful memories that he carried inside him. 'When I think about you on the side of the helicopter in the river . . .' He shook his head slowly. 'I've got another reason to have a bloody flashback.'

Ellie shivered; it would take her a long time to forget the fear that had gripped her while she waited for rescue. She had blocked the memory of the crocodile taking that man. She reached over and put her hand into Kane's, and he squeezed her fingers. The shiver left her as he lifted them to his lips.

Kane was staying at the hotel while she drove to Emma's by herself. 'It'll be better if it's just you, and your mum and sister.' Ellie appreciated his thoughtfulness. She was seeing more and more of the real Kane every day.

Emma and Mum lived in a small cottage on the river in the little village of Daintree, north of Port Douglas. Ellie hadn't called to say she was coming because she knew she would have blurted out what had happened. Her involvement in the rescue of Gina Johnson hadn't made the papers; the only person the journalist had been interested in was the heavily pregnant wife of the Chief Minister.

David had called them on Monday afternoon. Apart from the committee members, they were the first to hear that the vote for the mineral exploration on the edge of Kakadu National Park had been emphatically defeated. David had spent time at police headquarters telling them what had happened. Of course Russell Fairweather had denied any involvement, but allegations about the industrialist were being investigated by an independent corruption body. The email from Panos that Ellie had found in her father's old email account had been filed as evidence.

'Don't let that blackfella talk you out of Russell's deal, Pete.'

Panos had also bragged about the money.

'A million dollars is nothing to Fairweather. We'll all be rich, mate.'

David was resigning from parliament. He'd told Kane and Ellie when they'd visited Gina and little Ellie Rose in the hospital before they headed back to Darwin with the children. He'd been eager to get back for the vote. Bill Jarragah, mortified by Heather's actions, had followed them in his old Land cruiser. David and Gina had elected not to press charges against Heather but the relationship between Ellie and Heather had been tested, and although Heather was contrite and doing her best to preserve their friendship, Ellie knew it would be some time before she'd be able to trust her again.

The small town of Dalrymple flashed past and Ellie shivered as she passed the crocodile warning sign on the river bridge on the northern side of town. A few minutes later she turned off the main road and drove along the river into Daintree.

Ellie parked the car beneath a spreading tree covered in red and orange flowers. A small punt was moored at the old wooden jetty. The boat was attached to a rope that hung across the narrow arm of the river. It was the quickest way to get to Emma's Crooked Cottage unless you took the winding dirt road up through Cooper's Creek. Ellie looked straight ahead and tried not to think of crocodiles as the rope pulled her across the narrow river.

She tied the punt to the post and pushed the gate open. Tears filled her eyes as her beautiful mother rose to her feet from a chair on the front porch and turned towards the front door.

'Emma, come quick.'

The door opened, and a wide grin crossed Emma's face. 'Ellie! What on earth are you doing here? Why didn't you call?'

Ellie reached for her mother and blinked back the tears as the frail shoulders pressed against her arms.

'I have something to tell you, Mum. It's going to be hard for us to deal with. But it will help us move on.'

Ellie smiled at Emma as she held the door open and they went inside.

# Chapter 38

*Gunumeleng - Late October*
*The Porter Farm*

Ellie turned her car off the highway and drove into Kane's farm. She tried not to think of it as the 'old farm' these days. It belonged to him now and although she still had her apartment at Makowa Lodge she'd been spending more and more time here. Kane had tried to convince her to move in, but she wanted to take it slow.

The wet season was not far off and the air was becoming more and more humid. Thunderstorms would build each afternoon and the showers were greening the land. The streams were beginning to run, and the dams filling. Kane had just caught the end of the dormant season. He'd purchased two hundred propagated mango plants and they had planted them in the front paddock. Together they'd dug two hundred holes and mixed fertiliser.

And laughed. And teased each other. And begun to move on from the losses of the past winter.

The machinery in the boundary paddock had been taken away and was being stored in a police compound in Darwin while the investigation into Panos' murder and the inquiry into the illegal drilling were underway. Black Coal Holdings had been registered to Sordina. As far as they could ascertain, there was no evidence to link Russell Fairweather to the company, or to the murders of either Panos or her father. Mick Dawson – Mr Henry as Ellie had known him – was the only connection, and he was dead. Fairweather had publicly expressed regret that one of his staff had been involved in the attempt on Ellie's life. Again there was no concrete evidence to implicate him.

Ellie parked the car, climbed the new steps and pushed open the door of the house. Looking around with pleasure, she dropped the keys onto the kitchen table. In the end they'd decided not to demolish the old house. Too many of the memories were good ones. Kane had had the place gutted and it amazed Ellie how he'd been able to get local contractors to work at short notice. Kane's demeanour had lightened. and he was becoming known and well-liked around the district, as well as at Makowa Lodge where he still worked as the second pilot.

The kitchen, the bathroom and the main bedroom were finished, and the other rooms were lined with drop sheets as the painters prepared to commence work. Mum and Emma and Dru were coming for a visit at Christmas, and as Kane insisted on telling her, there wasn't room in her place at the lodge for all of them. Today, she had news for him. She'd told Jock she'd be giving up her apartment and moving back here.

Kane was taking up the sunset flights this afternoon, so Ellie had offered to cook dinner and had called into the supermarket at Jabiru on her way home.

'Steak and veg, please.' He'd placed his order as she'd left him in the hangar and accompanied it with a long kiss.

'You are such an Aussie bloke.' Ellie smiled against his lips. 'Steak and three veg it is.' It was probably not professional, but there had been no one around to see when he'd lifted her shirt and placed his hands on her bare skin.

Ellie opened the fridge and put the groceries in before she headed to the bathroom for a shower. She heard the front door open as she was drying off.

'You're early. I haven't even started dinner yet.' Knotting the towel above her breasts, she pushed open the bathroom door.

A short, heavyset man in a suit was standing just inside the front door at the end of the long hall that ran down the centre of the house. Kane hadn't mentioned any contractors coming this afternoon. Taking a step backwards, she pulled the towel together tightly. Cold dread washed over her as she recognised him.

'I'm sorry. I wasn't expecting you.' Ellie forced a pleasant smile onto her face. 'Please wait in the kitchen. I'll be with you in a moment.'

Her skin rose in goose bumps when a strange smile crossed his face.

'But Ellie, you must have known I would come for you eventually.'

'Who are you? What do you want?' Her whisper was soft as her heart began a slow heavy beat. Fairweather's photo had been in the papers almost daily since the corruption inquiry had begun. But she wouldn't give him the satisfaction of letting him know she knew exactly who he was.

It wasn't over, like they had thought, but she wasn't going to play his game.

'It seems I made a mistake in underestimating you.' He took one step towards her and Ellie pushed back against the wall. 'The same as I misjudged your father. And I never make mistakes. Do you know how much you've cost me?'

Ellie shook her head. If she could keep him talking, it wouldn't be long until Kane was home. 'Tell me. I have no idea. According to the papers, you have nothing to answer for.'

'Ah. So you do know who I am.'

'I do.' She took a small step to the left and put one hand behind her back, feeling along the wall.

'If your father had been a reasonable man, and not listened to that Bill Jarragah, no-one would have been hurt. They had strange priorities – choosing a piece of land and a muddy river over a million dollars.' He shook his head as she took another step away. 'Take one more step and I'll shoot you from here.' The smile stayed on his face as he reached into the breast pocket of his jacket and pulled out a small handgun. Ellie fought the coldness settling in her chest.

'A Colt .45. Did you know that I love to practise target shooting? Not the sort of pursuit you'd normally expect a man like me would enjoy, you think?'

She stopped. He was mad.

'Over one hundred million dollars, Ellie. That's how much this place was worth to me. And that was just the beginning.' He smiled, but the expression in his eyes was ugly. 'And now? Now I stand to lose everything. I have to front the inquiry next week. How dare they?' He reached up and smoothed his hair with one hand as he levelled the gun at her with the other. 'But there are only two witnesses that concern me. Without you and your army hero around, there will be no one to testify. That other snivelling coward has run off to Italy.'

David Johnson was flying back to Darwin next week, but Ellie wasn't going to share that. Anger burned in her throat. She was face to face with the man who had ordered her father's death. The same man who had ordered her death. Her anger was replaced by a cold calm and she took another tiny step to the left, feeling behind her back for the door to the hall cupboard. Her fingers brushed against the hinge. She needed to take two more steps to reach the cupboard handle.

'Of course I have a watertight alibi this afternoon. No one would doubt the word of the Police Commissioner.' As he glanced down at his watch, Ellie took another step, the wooden boards cool against her bare feet. 'In fact, according to his schedule, we're having a conversation in his office –' Fairweather lifted his head and his slitted eyes were flat and empty '– right this very minute.'

'You have nothing to worry about. We have no evidence. You were too clever for us. We know that.' Ellie let her voice shake. If she could only open the door – there was a shotgun at the bottom of the hall cupboard. The one they used for the rats in the packing shed. Kane had laughed when she said they would need it in the wet season.

Her fingers found the handle; she swung the door open and stepped behind it in one swift movement.

As she bent, a bullet split the panel above her, showering her with particles of chipboard. Fairweather's footsteps pounded on the wooden floorboards of the long hall as she reached to the back of the bottom shelf and grabbed the gun.

'You can't hide from me.' His laugh chilled her blood as she picked up a shell. With shaking hands, she loaded it into the shotgun.

Fairweather laughed again. Ellie kicked the cupboard door back and it crashed against the wall.

She lifted the gun to her shoulder and pulled back the hammer.

\*\*\*

The first shot rang out as Kane got out of the Jeep.

He ran, grabbing the shovel that was leaning against the side of the house as he tore up the steps. A second, louder shot followed, and Kane burst through the door, holding the shovel aloft. A man lay moaning and holding his leg, a small gun on the floor beside him. Kane reached down and picked up the gun, and stepped over the man. Ellie stood at the other end of the hall, wrapped in a white towel spattered with blood; the shotgun at her shoulder pointed at the man on the floor. Her eyes were fixed on the man and her mouth was set in a straight line.

He covered the distance quickly and she lowered the gun and fell into his arms.

'It's over, Kane. It's finally over.'

\*\*\*

Two hours later, Kane and Ellie stood side by side on the verandah, looking out over the new trees in the front paddock. She leaned against him as he held her close with one arm.

*It truly is over.*

They had their lives back. The police had left, and Fairweather had been taken away in an ambulance. His injury was not life-threatening, but Ellie knew that by shooting him, she had saved her own life – and Kane's too.

The greed of one man had led to many deaths, and the

disintegration of more than one family. It was time for the healing to begin.

'Okay?'

Ellie closed her eyes for a moment as Kane turned his head and pressed his lips to her forehead. She nodded and took a deep breath. 'All I could think was that you didn't know that I love you.'

'What would make you think that?' His warm breath puffed against her cheek.

'I never told you.'

'You don't have to, Ellie. I know.'

She pressed her lips against his, and she felt his lips tilt against her mouth. She loved the way he always smiled when he was kissing her.

'Jock spilled the beans about you giving up your apartment.

So I guess that means you're moving in?'

'It does.' Her heart swelled with love for this man.

The sun shot its golden rays into the sky before it dropped below the horizon in one of the most spectacular sunsets of the season. Kane put his arms around her shoulders and her gaze shifted to the north. Towering pillars of white cloud presaged the coming storm, the same clouds her father had loved.

She wondered if he was looking down on her now. If so, she hoped he was smiling.

THE END

The other four books in the Porter Sisters series are available for your reading pleasure in eBook and print.

See book list at the end of the book

**Did you enjoy Book 1 of the Porter Sisters.**

**Here is Chapter One of Book 2 – Emma's story in**

**Daintree… on the next page**

# Chapter 1

*Saturday morning – North Queensland – Daintree Village*

'Hoy!'

Emma Porter pulled the cotton blanket over her head, snuggled deeper into her feather pillow and tried to ignore the voice calling from outside. Cocooned in soft warmth, she slipped back into a doze and tried to pick up the fragments of the dream she'd been immersed in. A sparkling, sapphire-blue swimming pool, a sun lounge, a mango cocktail in her hand and not a patient in sight. A tanned waiter with a beautiful smile offered her a hot towel with a pair of silver tongs. The muscles in his bare chest rippled as he leaned over—

'Hoy! Ya there, Doctor Em?'

With a deep sigh, Emma rolled over and opened her eyes. She'd pulled the blind down low before falling into bed in the early hours of the morning, but a sliver of sunlight still managed to peek through the gap at the edge of the window. Even though her gritty eyes tried to tell her she'd only had a few minutes sleep, the small bedside clock confirmed her fear that it was indeed morning.

*Seven-thirty.* But still way earlier than she'd intended getting up. It was Saturday, and today was her first chance to sleep in after pulling six straight night shifts in emergency. She'd managed to catch a few hours' sleep every morning before she'd headed back into town to her clinic for open surgery each afternoon.

'Doctor Em!'

Her slim hope of staying in bed was shot to pieces with the third call from the kitchen and Bowser's excited yipping. Swinging her legs to the floor, Emma rubbed her eyes and reached for a pair of shorts and T-shirt buried on the bedside chair beneath most of the clothes, scrubs and underwear she had worn this week.

She'd have to get to the washing today. *And* the house cleaning. *And* the shopping. But that would be after she gave her poor neglected animals some attention, and took some time out for herself.

Padding barefoot down the hallway, she rubbed her hands through her tangled hair. The polished timber boards were smooth beneath her feet and the cool breeze coming through the back door carried the muddy smell from the river, but that was preferable to the musty smell pervading the house. The fresh air was welcome; the house had been closed up all week.

Emma pulled her hair back as best she could and dug into her pocket for an elastic band. Last night she'd been too tired to braid it and now the messy tangle would need a good dollop of conditioner in the shower.

'I knew you were home.' A wide welcoming grin of gappy and broken teeth met her when she entered the kitchen. George was an old bushie who'd lived in the village all his life. He'd helped Emma and her mother settle into Crooked Cottage when they'd moved to the Daintree and was almost part of the family—the uncle Emma and her sisters had never had. Now that Mum had moved down to Port Douglas, he looked out for Emma like a grizzled old watch dog.

'You're a pain in the arse. You do know that, don't you, George?'

'And you should lock your door at night. Anyone could stroll in.'

'Don't change the subject.' Emma shook her head and smiled at him. 'I *was* planning to sleep in.'

'But I've got the kettle on for you, luv.' The smile got wider. Beneath his often crusty exterior, George was a larrikin with a heart of gold. 'You look like you could do with a cuppa.'

'Great.' She tried to inject some enthusiasm into her voice. He meant well, and she knew he was lonely, but it was an early visit. She could have done with a sleep in this weekend. 'What are you doing here? I've been on night shift all week.'

'Fed the girls for you.' His eyes crinkled at the edges. Emma softened.

'And I collected the eggs.' George lifted up a bowl full of brown speckled eggs and Emma gave in to a grin.

How could she stay cross with the old coot; he loved keeping an eye out for her and she appreciated it. As usual, his pants were secured with a bit of fencing wire and his khaki work shirt hung open, most of the buttons missing. The old T-shirt underneath proclaimed: *'Leave the Daintree alone.'* A few months back he'd taken great pride in showing Emma and Mum the teeth marks where the German Shepherd police dog had ripped the T-shirt back in '83 when he'd been part of the demonstration against logging in the rainforest. They'd been trying to block the road being developed to Cape Tribulation. Emma hadn't even been born then.

She walked over to the window and leaned over the sink. The stiff sash window creaked as she pushed it up to let more fresh spring air into the musty kitchen. Stretching up to her tiptoes, she leaned forward and glanced down at the riverbank at the bottom of the yard. 'Where's the punt? Didn't swim, did you?'

'Not bloody likely. I've seen what's in that water,' he said with a shiver. 'I came the long way. Have to drive up to Cooper Creek. Got a big day planned. Thought I'd call in and bring you some tomatoes on the way. I came over and checked on Bowser every day, like you asked.'

George lived across the river in the small village of Daintree. Emma's house was on the other side about half a kilometre upriver, and unless you took the vehicular ferry and then the long, winding, back road through Cooper Creek, the only other way to reach her place was by boat—she had a small punt that could be pulled across the water by hand. It was one of the reasons that she'd got Crooked Cottage and the acre of land so cheap. It was only a short walk along the path on the riverbank to the small village. It wasn't really even a village. There were only half a dozen houses and a coffee and craft shop for the tourists that was closed more often than it was open.

'Thanks, you're a gem. What are you up today?'

'A bit of this and a bit of that.' He wouldn't meet her eye. 'Look, I brought you some crickets for your frogs.' A brown paper bag appeared from deep in his back pocket and he handed it to her. I gave the frogs a squirt every day too and switched around their basking bulbs. Can't have them freezing to death while you're out working yourself to the bone.' George crossed to the wooden stand that was tucked into an alcove where the old combustion stove had once stood; her terrarium now filling the space. He ran his hand down the rough timber and turned to her with a wide grin. 'Jeez, the bloke that built this stand for you sure did a good job.'

'You did. And there's no need to suck up. I'm awake now.'

'All the tadpoles hatch okay this time?'

'Yes, this batch has been really successful.' Emma followed him over and reached up and turned the night bulb off, replacing it with the daylight basking bulb from the shelf at the bottom of the stand.

'Do you reckon if I got some tadpoles, that research mob would pay me too?'

Emma laughed and shook her head. 'You know I'm not getting paid. You could volunteer too. A few other locals are logging some breeding cycles.'

George shrugged and a soft grunt escaped his lips. 'Bet those blokes at that rainforest centre get paid.'

Emma slipped in the new bulb and patted his shoulder on her way back to the sink to make the tea. 'Of course they do. They work at the Rainforest Tourist Centre; they're National Parks and Wildlife staff.'

She pulled down two mugs from the cupboard and two tea bags and leaned back against the sink as she covered a yawn with one hand. 'God, it's been a big week. Down one doctor and waiting for the new guy to arrive.'

'Lots of sick people?'

'Yep . . .. and a few accidents too.' There had been a

constant stream of patients at the hospital at night and at her clinic all day. Murphy's Law; it always happened when they were understaffed. She picked up the brown paper bag next to the sink and peeked inside. 'Thanks for these. Oh wow, look at the size of those tomatoes. *Now* I forgive you for waking me up.' The smell of the fat, red fruit wafted through the kitchen.

George smiled at her. 'Ox hearts. Only type worth growing.' His hand disappeared into his other pocket and he pulled out a small bunch of fresh basil. 'Though this would go well with the scrambled eggs and tomatoes you're going to cook us for brekkie.' He rubbed a leaf between his fingers and Emma rolled her eyes as she caught the sharp aroma. How could she stay cross at him?

She touched his shoulder as she crossed to the table and picked up the bowl of fresh eggs. 'So scrambled eggs for two, seeing the girls have performed so well this morning.'

'Sounds good to me. You cook the eggs and put those tea bags back in the cupboard. I'll make us a pot of real tea and we can have a yarn. You can tell me all about your busy week, luv.' George picked up the battered old silver teapot, peered into it and sniffed. 'Phew. The tea leaves have gone mouldy.'

'I've barely been home. It's a wonder there aren't mould flowers hanging from the ceiling.' Emma shivered. The first summer she'd lived in Crooked Cottage, she'd gone away to Brisbane for a month to finish up a course. Mum had gone back to Townsville to stay with a friend; with her mental health being so fragile, Emma hadn't been game to leave her alone. When she'd pushed open the door of the cottage on her return, mould had covered the kitchen cupboards and bench tops. It was one of the downsides of living in the Wet Tropics in the summer—the tourist brochures never showed you *that* side of things.

Emma looked up as Bowser, her little black staffy, came hurtling through the back door, his short tail going nineteen to the dozen as he yapped a welcome in his own unique way.

'Hey, little man, where have you been?'

George shook his head. 'He was out chasing snakes in the side paddock when I walked up the track.'

The small dog ran around her in dizzying circles and Emma bent down to rub his back. 'Haven't seen you much this week, have I, boy?' A cold wet nose pushed onto her hand. 'Have you been good? Did you miss me?'

'He'll end up getting bit one day.' The voice of the old bushie held a smidgeon of worry.

Emma washed her hands and then pulled the fridge open and reached for the butter. 'I wish he'd leave them alone, I'm terrified of the blasted things. Give me spiders any day.'

'Snakes are on the move early this season.' George dumped the sludge of mouldy tea leaves into the sink and gave the pot a scour out. 'You watch out when you get in and out of that boat at night.

'Don't you worry, I've got a big torch and I'm very careful.' Emma wrinkled her nose and busied herself at the stove. 'I don't mind the keelbacks. At least they keep the cane toads down. We've actually had our first snakebite for the season already. Troy brought a tourist into emergency this week.'

George reached up to the shelf above the gas stove for

the tea caddy. '*Hmph*. That city slicker.'

'Who? Troy?'

'Yeah. Don't like him.'

Emma flicked him an irritated glance as she reached for the pan. 'He grew up on a cattle property near Mt Isa. He's about as far from a city slicker as you can get.'

Emma had met Troy Greaves through the Young Professionals social group a few months ago when he'd moved to Dalrymple to manage the Daintree Rainforest Centre. They had a lot of interests in common: he was well-educated, passionate about the environment and shared her interest in preserving the Daintree. He was the one who'd suggested including her frog collection hobby in the breeding research project and they'd hiked into the rainforest together to gather tadpoles from O'Keefe Creek where some of the species were declining.

'You know three frog species have completely disappeared over the last twenty years.'

'What's causing that?' she'd asked and he'd shrugged. 'Global warming is the main theory.'

As they walked to the creek, a colourful swarm of butterflies drifted by. Troy knew each by name: the blue and black Ulysses and the lime green Cairns Bird Wing. . .

As well as being a really interesting guy, he wasn't too bad on the eye. Rugged and outdoorsy, he was very different to the medical students she'd hung with at uni in Sydney.

'Still an outsider who thinks he knows everything about the forest when he's been here five minutes. One of them bloody do gooders. They should stop pandering to bloody tourists and not let them traipse through our rainforest.'

George's gruff voice cut into her thoughts and Emma smothered the smile that tugged at her lips. It had been a long time since she'd daydreamed about a guy.

'He cares about *our* rainforest as much as you do. I think you'd be surprised how much you pair have in common. We all have the same goal.' Emma shook her head. 'And besides, you don't like many people as far as I can see.'

'I'm here with you, aren't I? And I like your mum.'

'That's two.'

George rubbed his fingers on his whiskers. 'When you get to my age, Em, you'll realise there's not many people out there worth liking.

'Oh, George, that's a sad outlook. I meet lots of nice people in my job every day.' Emma smiled at him. 'And with any luck, soon I'll be meeting even more.'

'Yeah. How's that?'

'I've applied for a position with the Outreach Program, setting up some small medical clinics up the Cape.'

'Sounds right up your alley.'

'It will be—if I get it. I've got a pretty good chance I think.'

*Don't tempt fate.* Her dad's superstitious voice flitted through her mind and Emma tapped her knuckles on the wooden counter top. Having a scientific mind and a medical degree didn't mean you let family habits go.

George was standing by the stove and he chuckled as she knocked.

'What?' Emma picked up the eggs. They were still warm from the nest.

'How are you going to fit all that in with the hospital

and your clinic?' He poured the boiling water onto the tea leaves and the smell of brewing tea filled the kitchen.

'I'll sort it out.'

George frowned. 'You could stop all that nature stuff you do.'

'What nature stuff?'

'Working with that rainforest guy, and collecting all those leaves and things you use for your remedies.'

'Maybe.' Emma smiled. She had no intention of putting aside her 'remedies' as George called them. She would reduce her hours at the hospital before she'd cut back on her clinic work. Being involved in the establishment of new medical outposts in the far north would be satisfying. Wilma Randall had already introduced Emma to several of the aboriginal elders and she believed she was well placed to liaise with the isolated communities. 'Anyway, fingers crossed.'

The egg shells made a nice crack when she whacked them on the edge of the stainless steel bowl. The yolks were a deep golden orange.

*'Bright bold orange yolks, healthy, happy hens.'* Emma could almost hear Dru's deep, husky voice. When they'd been growing up, her youngest sister had been the keeper of the hens. As Dru had done with her chickens on their farm in the Territory, Emma had built her chickens a run. She'd fenced off part of the yard and let her ladies roam around to their hearts content. Most afternoons—when she was home—she let them into her small veggie garden to pick off the bugs and eat the broccoli leaves, and she reaped the benefit of orange yolks . . . and memories. She missed her sisters; seeing them

infrequently was the downside of growing up and leading your own lives.

'Here you go.' George's voice intruded on her thoughts and she looked up to see a plate of chopped tomatoes and onions held out in front of her. God love him, he'd even chopped the basil finely and sprinkled it on top.

'Thanks. You want the basil cooked, not sprinkled on top?'

'Course I do. Not meant to be eaten raw.'

Emma smothered a smile. She dropped a knob of butter into the pan, and when it sizzled and turned golden brown, she tipped in the tomatoes, basil and onion. A mouth-watering aroma filled the kitchen and she took a deep breath. 'Beaut tomatoes, thank you.'

'You're welcome.' George pulled out a chair and straddled it, watching Emma as she deftly folded the eggs.

'So what's happening out at Cooper Creek?' She flicked him a glance. 'You're on your way early.'

'Not much.' George dropped his gaze and shifted uncomfortably.

Emma frowned. 'You're not getting yourself into any trouble again, I hope?'

She'd long suspected that George applied his green thumb to more than just his vegetable garden and she knew he'd recently had a caution from the local police, when one of the coppers had come across a small plot of marijuana growing in a clearing deep in the rainforest up near Cooper Creek.

George denied all knowledge and had been most indignant that the cops had even warned him, but Emma knew better. The first time George had taken her for a walk into the ancient rainforest she'd been awed by the sheer beauty of the pristine environment, and she'd turned a blind eye to him watering plants in a small clearing while she ambled along the track beside Roaring Meg Creek.

'Nah. Just going for a wander.'

'Hmm. You know what happened last time.'

'*Pah*. A warning from a copper who looks like he should still be in school. Don't go worrying about me. I can look after myself.'

Emma dished out their scrambled eggs and George followed her as she carried their plates out to the verandah. It was shaded and the mornings were still cool enough to sit outside. The heat of the day would become more intense as the sun climbed higher in the late spring sky. As would the ever-present tropical humidity. Better to be up and get the work done around the place before it got too hot. Then she could spend the afternoon lying around without a list of chores hanging over her.

As they ate, the only sound was the scraping of cutlery over their plates but the silence was comfortable.

'Bugger.' George stood, hitching up his trousers and tightening the wire. He pointed downstream to the punt. 'Looks like you've got company on the way. I don't need another talking to from that wanker. I'm outta here.'

Emma groaned. There was a police car parked at the boat ramp across the river and Constable Craig Anderson was climbing into the punt.

She stood and followed George as he scuttled down the hall to the front door.

'Thanks for breakfast. Do you need anything while I'm up at the creek?'

'If you're going anywhere near Wilma's, I do need some more cocky apple bark.' She frowned at George. 'But don't you go getting it yourself either. Only get it from Wilma.'

Even though he cared about the rainforest, George had no concept of trespassing and considered the Daintree open to him wherever he wanted to wander. Wilma Randall, the local aboriginal healer, lived in the rainforest at the turnoff to Cooper Creek Road. She had come into the clinic to have an infected burn treated last year and had been pleased to see that Emma was using natural therapies and that the infusion of cocky apple bark had quickly healed the wound. Emma had been more concerned about the elderly woman's cardiac health. Their friendship developed and a mutual respect grew but it was a few months before Emma could persuade Wilma to take some tests down in Port Douglas and they had diagnosed a valve problem, as well as her angina. She was supposed to have a stent inserted, but Wilma had refused. So she was on medication as a temporary measure to alleviate her symptoms.

Wilma was happy to share her knowledge of bush medicine with Emma and they had become firm friends. George sometimes accompanied Emma to the rainforest but he always refused to get out of the car when she called into Wilma's house on the way back. Despite all his protesting, he had listened when Emma explained what the plants and barks were used for on the way home.

He stared at her. 'No way. I can't stand the old witch.

Anyway I don't know why you need all that hocus pocus stuff. *You're* a doctor.'

'Yes, and I also practise alternative medicine.'

'Well, she looks like an old witch.'

'Wilma is lovely. Even some of the people in Dalrymple drive out to see her for her bush remedies.'

'She threatened to set her dog on me when I took a shortcut through her land a couple of weeks back.' The creak of the rarely used front door blended with the indignation in his voice as he pulled it open.

'Ah, now we're getting closer to the truth.'

Emma shook her head as she stroked the soft fur behind Bowser's ears. 'I'll ring Wilma and let her know you're doing me a favour.'

'All right. I guess I can pick it up for you. Just this once.'

Emma watched until George disappeared into the scrub at the side of the dirt road, and then whistled to Bowser as she walked back around the side of the house to wait for Craig. She smoothed the dog's shiny coat as she looked across to the river. 'You're a naughty pup. I'm going to have to lock you in if you keep chasing snakes,' she murmured.

The water was flowing slowly this morning, the gentle eddies and whirlpools adding to its silent beauty. A red-tailed black cockatoo screeched as it flew across the water, its giant wings flapping ponderously as it headed for the dead tree in the paddock beside the cottage.

Emma lifted her hands to run her fingers through her hair and then pulled a face and dropped them to her sides. Last thing she cared about was looking good for Craig.

A couple of months ago she'd made a stupid mistake and ended up spending the night with him. Craig had seemed lonely at the Young Professionals dinner at the club and she'd gone back to his place for a coffee. One minute they'd been deep in conversation and before she knew it, he'd pulled her into the bedroom. When she'd woken the next morning, self-recrimination had washed over her in a cold wave. It was the first one night stand she'd ever had and Emma vowed she would never make the same mistake again. She'd opened her eyes to see a wedding ring on the top of the chest of drawers and that had made it ten times worse. She'd shot out of Craig's bed and was out the door while he was still asleep. She'd left a noncommittal note and headed to work at the hospital. And kicked herself the whole way.

Craig had been following her around ever since. In his eyes, it appeared that one night of sleeping together guaranteed the beginning of a relationship. He was in for a shock; Emma didn't date married men. Emma didn't date period.

She'd tried a relationship a long time ago and it had reinforced her need for independence. No man—or his family—was going to call the shots and tell her what to do with her life. Or tell her what was wrong with her viewpoints and philosophies. Or tell her she didn't measure up to some social standard. She was in control of her own life now and it would stay that way. Especially someone like Craig.

No matter how much she tried to get the message to him, he had started to call in at the hospital when she was on shift and the more she saw of him the more he showed his true colours.

*A bully and a liar.*

Happily, being so busy at work with one doctor down over the past couple of weeks meant she'd seen little of him at the hospital. But it looked like he'd finally caught up with her.

Craig was obviously on duty today because he was in his police uniform. She watched as he pulled the rope and propelled the small vessel across the channel, the sun glinting off his blue-black hair. He gave the rope a final yank and the muscles flexed beneath his blue police shirt as the punt sped across the last five metres. She reached out and grabbed the small boat as it nosed into the muddy bank. The punt slewed around and the bottom scraped noisily on the concrete ramp. He jumped out and Emma looped the rope over the steel post and secured the small boat.

'Hi Craig.'

'Emma.' He took her arm and leaned forward to kiss her but she stepped back out of his grip. His eyes narrowed. 'I don't know why you have to live over here when there is perfectly good accommodation in town,'

'I don't like you taking the boat across this river by yourself.'

She didn't bother to tell him that it was none of his business where she lived or how she lived her life. She was tired and didn't want to make his visit any longer than it needed to be.

If only she hadn't already slept with him

'Haven't seen you around for a couple of weeks.'

'I've been busy. I've put in some long days at the clinic and the hospital. We're still one doctor down. How come you're working on a Saturday?'

'Need the money. There was an overtime shift up for grabs and I took it.'

'So what are you doing here? On your break, or is this official business?' She forced a smile.

'I was going to call you, but I had to come down to the village so I thought I might as well come across. Kettle hot?'

'I've only got time for a quick cuppa. I have a busy day ahead.'

'Sounds good.'

Emma turned and strode towards the house and as Craig followed her, she was conscious of her shorts and bare legs.

'Take a seat. I'll be right back.' Emma gestured to the seat George had just vacated.

Discomfort prickled through her when he ignored her and followed her inside. He pulled out a chair at the kitchen table.

'Breakfast?' Craig lifted his head and sniffed appreciatively but his expression darkened as he spotted the two plates and mugs on the sink. 'Overnight company, Emma?'

'An early visitor.'

Emma put the kettle back on and put a teabag into a clean mug, aware of his eyes on her; she felt like pulling her shirt down to cover the backs of her bare thighs. It was way too cosy in this small kitchen. She turned back to the table and waited for the water to boil.

'So why were you going to call me?'

'I wanted to see if you were going to the seventies night at the pub tomorrow night.' Craig's eyes stayed on her at her.

Emma busied herself at the sink as the kettle boiled. 'Yes. I'll be there.'

'Are you dressing up?' he asked. She quickly made the tea and placed the mug on the table before sitting opposite him.

'Yes. I love a good dress up.'

'I'm not. I think it's a stupid idea.' His expression settled into a sneer.

Emma drew a breath and glanced over at the clock on the wall. 'We're a *social* group, Craig. The Young Professionals hold lots of different events to raise money. And getting into the spirit of things is all part of the fun.' His attitude was making her angry and she changed the subject before she lost her cool. 'Wait till you see the get-up of the tug-of-war teams at the Rainbow Day.'

'Whatever.' His tone was dismissive. 'Anyway I thought we'd go together.' He lifted his cup and blew on the hot tea as he continued to stare at her. 'You can get ready at my place and stay the night.'

Emma held up one hand. 'Craig. I'd like to make one thing very clear. When I went home with you I didn't know you were married and there won't be any more "staying the night" at your place.

'I'm not married. We're separated.'

'Look, Craig, even if you're separated, just because I stayed one night at your place doesn't mean we're in a relationship.' She closed her eyes and took a deep breath, biting back the inward groan. 'I'd had a big week, and having a few drinks on an empty stomach wasn't such a good idea.' She could kick herself for the mistake she made that night;

casual sex was way out of character. She softened her words with a weak smile. 'I'm sorry if I gave you the wrong idea I'm not in for the long haul with anyone.'

'But—'

She held one hand up. 'No.'

'I hear you've been out hiking with Troy Greaves.'

This time her voice was cold. 'I don't think what I do in my time off is your concern.'

He shrugged and the cold glint in his eye was replaced by a smile that she felt was forced. His sullen persistence was making her uncomfortable.

'Okay. But you are still going to the pub? I will see you there?' Craig's eyes were wide. They suddenly reminded her of Bowser's when she'd been ignoring him. That hangdog look that said *pat me please*.

Emma forced a conciliatory smile onto her face. 'Yes, I'll see you there. Along with everyone else.'

Craig stood slowly and tucked the chair in, and she walked down to the riverbank with him.

'So I'll see you tomorrow night then,' he repeated. He unlooped the rope from the post and gave the boat a shove. Emma was relieved when he jumped in and pulled the punt away from the bank.

She tried to shake off the bad mood that had settled around her. It had been like Pitt Street Mall in her cottage this morning. The day had to get better.

You can find Daintree, Emma's story here:
http://books2read.com/u/bpD1nJ

# Acknowledgements

Kakadu National Park is one of Australia's special places – World Heritage listed for both its environment and its living Aboriginal culture. In 2013 on the way to the Northern Territory, we crossed the vast outback, travelling through ancient landscapes. Many of these landscapes have been scarred by various types of mining. Visiting Kakadu and experiencing the spirituality of the land made me wonder what would happen if mining occurred in that pristine environment.

The idea for was born.

The development of this story and the wonderful experience of achieving my lifelong dream, of writing a book, being published, and now holding this book in my hand, would not have been possible without the support of many people. I would like to acknowledge them here.

Four years ago my writing journey began unexpectedly. Heartfelt thanks to Lisa Hansen and Tim Francis for reminding me to follow my dreams.

To Haylee Nash for having faith in my story, and the Porter Sisters series.

To the many, many friends I have made in the writing community, and who have supported me on this journey. Friends I have made through local writing groups, particularly Marie Miller, Fiona McArthur and the two 'Js' of Jenn J. McLeod; friends made through the Romance Writers Association of Australia, as well as both author and reader friends made through social media connections. I could fill another book with your names, but you know who you are – both in Australia and internationally.

A few special mentions:

To fellow author, Fiona McArthur, who encouraged me to submit this manuscript, and who was sitting beside me at Dubai Airport when I received the email from Haylee Nash saying she wanted to acquire . The celebratory breakfast of Turkish bread, curry and Moët is a special memory that will stay with me for many years.

Eloisa James, professor of English Literature at Fordham University who also writes best-selling Regency romance novels. Eloisa worked with me in a garden in Tuscany to polish the opening chapters. The friends I made at that writing workshop in Tuscany, who shared their dreams and supported each other as we explored our writing: Cajsa C. Baldini, Sandra Cutting, Bronwyn Jameson, Pamela Light, Fiona McArthur, Katrina Snow, Siobhan Sullivan, Sally Wiesenmayer Teets and Susan Williamson.

My critique partner, Susanne Bellamy; I value your friendship and your feedback.

Chief Flying Instructor, Jenna Ryan at Helibiz Airlie Beach, who took me on a helicopter training flight and explained the technical terms and demonstrated the manoeuvres of flying 'Ellie's' helicopter.

And finally, to my wonderful family:

My husband, Ian, thank you for showing me that love and romance are real and lasting, and for your endless patience as I click away on the laptop in the lounge room, or on the front seat of the four-wheel drive vehicle as we travel and I disappear into my characters' lives. For introducing me to the outback and inspiring me to dream up new stories while we explore the grandeur of this wonderful country in our trusty camper trailer.

To our children, Kate and Dane, their partners, and our grandchildren for loving me, no matter how 'Grandma Daphne' I can be. They know what I mean.

To my gorgeous sister and valued critique partner, Wendy Hamonet, who reads every word I write.

To my dear aunt, Maureen Smith, who has filled the emptiness left by the passing of my parents, and for being so proud of me. Thank you especially for reminding me how happy Mum and Dad would be that I achieved my dream.

And to you, the reader: I hope when you read, that you love it and talk about it, and that maybe you will want to visit this wonderful part of Australia. I hope you enjoy Emma, Dru, Dee, Sandra's and Tarni's stories. Drop me a line at annie@annieseaton.net. I would love to hear from you.

All Annie's books are available in eBook and in print at Annie's store and on Amazon

eBook links:

https://www.annieseaton.net/books.html


Print Store:

All books are available in print at Annie's store

Free postage (Australia)

https://www.annieseaton.net/store.html


Look for Annie's latest series:

THE AUGATHELLA GIRLS

# OTHER BOOKS from ANNIE

*Whitsunday Dawn*
*Undara*
*Osprey Reef*
*East of Alice*

**Porter Sisters Series**

*Kakadu Sunset*
*Daintree*
*Diamond Sky*
*Hidden Valley*
*Larapinta*
*Kakadu Dawn*

**Pentecost Island Series**

*Pippa*
*Eliza*
*Nell*
*Tamsin*
*Evie*
*Cherry*
*Odessa*
*Sienna*
*Tess*
*Isla*

**The Augathella Girls Series**

*Outback Roads*
*Outback Sky*
*Outback Escape*
*Outback Wind*
*Outback Dawn*
*Outback Moonlight*

*Outback Dust*
*Outback Hope*
*An Augathella Surprise*
*An Augathella Baby*
*An Augathella Spring*

**Sunshine Coast Series**
*Waiting for Ana*
*The Trouble with Jack*
*Healing His Heart*
*Sunshine Coast Boxed Set*

**The Richards Brothers Series**
*The Trouble with Paradise*
*Marry in Haste*
*Outback Sunrise*
*Richards Brothers Boxed Set*

**Bondi Beach Love Series**
*Beach House*
*Beach Music*
*Beach Walk*
*Beach Dreams*
*The House on the Hill*

**Second Chance Bay Series**
*Her Outback Playboy*
*Her Outback Protector*
*Her Outback Haven*
*Her Outback Paradise*
*The McDougalls of Second Chance Bay Boxed Set*

**Love Across Time Series**
*Come Back to Me*
*Follow Me*
*Finding Home*
*The Threads that Bind*

*Love Across Time 1-4 Boxed Set*

### Bindarra Creek
*Worth the Wait*
*Full Circle*
*Secrets of River Cottage*
*A Clever Christmas*
*A Place to Belong*

### Four Seasons Short and Sweet
*Ten Days in Paradise*
*Follow the Sun*

### Others
*Deadly Secrets*
*Adventures in Time*
*Silver Valley Witch*
*The Emerald Necklace*
*Christmas with the Boss*
*Her Christmas Star*
*An Aussie Christmas Duo (two Christmas novellas)*

# About the Author

2023: Winner of the long contemporary RUBY award for *Larapinta*

Finalist for the NZ KORU award 2018 and 2020.

Winner ...Best Established Author of the Year 2017 AUSROM

Long listed for the Sisters in Crime Davitt Awards 2016, 2017, 2018, 2019

Finalist in Book of the Year, Long Romance, RWA Ruby Awards 2016 *Kakadu Sunset*

Winner ...Best Established Author of the Year 2015 AUSROM

Winner ...Author of the Year 2014 AUSROM Best Established Author, Ausrom Readers' Choice 2017 Book of the Year

Printed in Dunstable, United Kingdom